Americans at Risk

Americans at Risk

WHY WE ARE NOT PREPARED FOR
MEGADISASTERS
AND WHAT WE CAN DO NOW

Irwin Redlener, M.D.

Alfred A. Knopf New York 2006

This Is a Borzoi Book Published by Alfred A. Knopf

Copyright © 2006 by Irwin Redlener, M.D.

All rights reserved. Published in the United States by Alfred A. Knopf,
a division of Random House, Inc., New York, and in Canada by
Random House of Canada Limited, Toronto.

www.aaknopf.com

Knopf, Borzoi Books, and the colophon are registered trademarks of Random House, Inc.

Library of Congress Cataloging-in-Publication Data
Redlener, Irwin.
Americans at risk : why we are not prepared for megadisasters and what we can do now /
Irwin Redlener.—1st ed.
p. cm.
Includes bibliographical references and index.
ISBN-10: 0-307-26526-9
1. Emergency management—United States. 2. Disaster relief—United States.
3. Terrorism—United States—Prevention. 4. Preparedness—United States.
5. Medical care—United States. I. Title.
HV551.3.R42 2006
363.34'70973—dc22   2006046476

Manufactured in the United States of America

First Edition

To Jason, who lives in all of us who loved him,
to my darling grandchildren, Caleb and Mia, who will live
in this world we're making, to the matriarch, Charlotte, and
to the love of my life, Karen, who makes it all possible.

Contents

Acknowledgments

This book began with a phone call in the fall of 2005, pretty much out of the blue, from Larry Weissman, who had heard me speak on television about the ongoing post-Katrina recovery and relief debacle. I had been talking about the concept of megadisasters and how the country just wasn't capable of responding to a major catastrophic event. Larry thought that concept should be a book—and I agreed. I am very grateful to Larry and his partner, Sascha Alper, for their clear understanding of what needed to happen and for their support from the beginning.

Shelley Wanger, my remarkable editor at Knopf, was incredibly helpful at every step; I cannot possibly overstate the value of her input and guidance—and patience—throughout. Our timeline was ridiculously short and Shelley was available 24/7 from the time we met until the book was completed. Margarethe Laurenzi, my editor/organizer/researcher who worked with me on an almost daily basis, was absolutely invaluable throughout the process. Without Margarethe, this manuscript would not likely have come close to being completed by our most aggressive deadline. And I am also grateful to David Berman, my talented senior policy analyst at the National Center for Disaster Preparedness (NCDP). David coordinated the extensive research needed for this manuscript, constantly checking and rechecking assertions, facts, and sources. General ongoing administrative support was given so generously and cheerfully by Karina Ron, Shay Gines, and Damali Walker. Wil Alvarez and Dr. David Abramson, the brilliant researchers at the NCDP, provided terrific support, and, in David's case, real insight into the terrible long-term consequences of the Gulf disaster.

Paul Bogaards and Erinn Hartman were an integral part of the Knopf team. And I am forever grateful to my friends from Dan Klores Communications for their ever crucial guidance. Sean Cassidy, Ed Tagliaferri, Jo Flattery, and the brilliant Dan Klores truly went all out to help make this happen.

My wife, Karen Redlener, who runs the Children's Health Fund, was an essential reader of this manuscript as it was taking shape. Her insights regularly made a real difference in our perspective and approach to this very difficult topic. She had the distinct advantage of having worked as my partner for more than three decades, and therefore being very practiced in getting her always useful input across in the most effective ways. My son Michael, currently a medical student, gave helpful advice from the beginning, but plenty of moral support and encouragement also came from Neil, Eric, Gloria, Ania, Stephanie, Sheareen, Ruth, Phil, Nicole, John, David, and Judith (a keen editor). Two good friends also gave wise counsel early in the process: Jonathan Alter, senior editor at *Newsweek,* and NBC correspondent Fred Francis both helped me think through the focus of this work. Carol and Bobby Tannenhauser provided both ongoing personal support and very important comments on some of the early drafts. My friend Dr. Michael Kappy, who has long been urging me to write this book, served as a sounding board throughout.

To make the technical portions of the book as accurate and credible as possible, particularly the five detailed hypothetical megadisaster scenarios, I sought advice from experts who each spent time reviewing, suggesting, and conceptualizing these and other relevant parts of the manuscript. The technical experts were Frank Von Hippel, a distinguished professor at Princeton University who is well versed in the consequences of nuclear detonations; Stephen Morse, an esteemed colleague and authority on emerging infections and pandemic influenza; Tom Paulson, a senior science journalist currently at the *Seattle Post-Intelligencer,* who contributed significantly to the earthquake scenario; Dr. Fred Millar, an environmental scientist and expert on chemical spills; and the remarkable Christopher Farrell, director of investigations and research at Judicial Watch. Chris's input was invaluable in the chapter on children as targets of terrorism. Gavin Schmidt at the Goddard Institute of Space Studies helped clarify some of the important climatic issues for the chapter on natural disasters.

I am also grateful for the technical advice offered by former FBI investigator Tarine Fairman, Dr. Andy Garrett, and Beth Fuller. Two brilliant natural disaster experts from Columbia University's Earth Institute were most generous with their time and counsel: Dr. John Mutter and Dr. Art Lerner-Lam. They helped ensure that the science and critical nuances of our earthquake assertions were on target. Nationally renowned disaster preparedness expert Dr. Elin Gursky of the Anser Institute produced some of the key documents we used extensively as resource material. Similarly helpful was material written by Veronique De Rugy, a research fellow at the American Enterprise Institute, and guidance from Dr. Kathleen Tierney, who directs the Natural Hazards Research and Applications Information Center at the University of Colorado. Dr. David Markenson, a nationally renowned disaster response authority, was helpful throughout. And so was Dr. Jeb Weisman, technology and communications guru, who provided sage advice on some of the most highly technical issues and always reminds me that "the technology is easy, it's the human aspect of communications that's the challenge."

A number of people with enormous experience relevant to this book gave very generously of their time and insights, especially former secretary of state General Colin Powell, former FEMA head James Lee Witt, and U.S Surgeon General Richard Carmona. I am grateful to each of them. And I want to thank Bill Lokey, a senior official at FEMA and one of this country's top disaster-response professionals, for his candid insights about the challenges ahead for FEMA.

I want to acknowledge that I gained a good deal of perspective from the first secretary of homeland security, Tom Ridge. I began meeting with Tom before his appointment to the cabinet and while he was director of the Office of Homeland Security in the White House. He impressed me from the beginning as a dedicated, hardworking leader who had the courage to take on the gargantuan task of putting together the new Department of Homeland Security.

In my own work involving the megadisasters of 9/11 and the Katrina catastrophe I have been deeply inspired by people who worked tirelessly and courageously under trying conditions. These men and women, from all walks of life, are the real heart and soul of America in times of duress. Some are political leaders, some are first responders, and some are ordinary people who rise to the challenge, regardless of personal cost or risk. I can't possibly be complete here, but I want to cite a few individuals who have been important role models in disasters.

Rudy Giuliani provided key leadership after 9/11, but there were countless others who were prepared to sacrifice everything to do what had to be done. Firefighters, police officers, emergency medical technicians, construction workers, teams from the Office of Emergency Management, transportation workers, and many others did their jobs with valor and ingenuity. The junior senator from New York, Hillary Rodham Clinton, traveled from one end of the state to the other to speak with her constituents and reassure them personally that their government was on the case. She joined Senator Chuck Schumer, newly elected New York City mayor Michael Bloomberg, and every member of the New York congressional delegation to make sure that the resources to deal with the aftermath would be available as needed.

In addition, a number of dedicated members of Congress on both sides of the aisle deserve recognition and thanks for working so hard to fix some of the serious problems that impair our ability to respond to large-scale disasters. In addition to Senators Clinton and Schumer, who have been on the case nonstop, Senators Susan Collins, Tom Harkin, Joe Lieberman, Jay Rockefeller, and Barak Obama have rallied to the cause. Congressman Peter King has totally immersed himself in the issue and become one of the nation's real experts on homeland security. And North Carolina Senator Richard Burr has taken on his work as chairman of the Subcommittee on Bioterrorism Preparedness and Public Health with great interest and thoughtfulness about the critical issues his subcommittee must address. Senator Burr is a serious player on this issue.

There are several congressional staffers who are providing important leadership and support on the issues. Dr. Robert Kadlec, staff director to Senator Burr, is an extraordinary expert on bioterrorism whom I originally met when he was working at the White House right after 9/11. He has been supportive and helpful to my work on this book from the very beginning. The same is true of Bob's dedicated staff members, Jennifer Bryning, Kathy Hebert, and David Marcozzi. Ann Gavaghan, of Senator Clinton's staff, is another very effective consummate professional who has fully dedicated herself to this terribly difficult work of drafting preparedness and response legislation.

In Louisiana and Mississippi, the dedication and heroism of so many people were not only inspiring, but literally lifesaving. Thousands of emergency responders laid everything on the line to help their fellow citizens. Innumerable police officers and EMTs who themselves had lost everything in the storm stayed on the job helping so many others for weeks and months on end. Even high government officials rolled up their sleeves and worked under extreme duress and at personal risk.

In the immediate aftermath of Hurricane Katrina, I was very moved to receive a call from Mississippi Senator Thad Cochran. Paul Simon, co-founder with me of the Children's Health Fund, and I had met with the senator in the spring of 2005 to tell him about the mobile medical units we were using around the country to provide health care for some of the nation's most medically underserved children. Then after the Katrina disaster, Senator Cochran was among the very first to realize how useful these units might be in providing emergency assistance in the Gulf. Through his influence we reached Mississippi state health director Brian Amy and emergency operations chief James Craig—both incredibly effective public officials who took charge of the public health response to Katrina in their state. They were exceedingly helpful in making sure our units got to where they needed to be.

Three senior health officials in Louisiana, all physicians, have played critical roles in the aftermath of the disaster in New Orleans and the rest of the state: Kevin Stephens, director of the New Orleans Department of Health; Fred Cerise, secretary of the Louisiana Department of Health and Hospitals; and Jimmy Guidry, a state health officer. Not only did they stay on the job nonstop for months, they worked on the front lines during the worst times after the hurricane and flooding of New Orleans.

I have met many extraordinary doctors in my career, but it's fair to say that I have only rarely encountered anyone as dedicated and effective as Erin Brewer, who works with the Louisiana Department of Health. Our first conversation was by telephone just a couple of days after the hurricane. The Children's Health Fund was getting ready to send down the first of our mobile medical units, and I called her to get a sense of the scope of the disaster.

Erin told me what she had seen and I couldn't believe what I was hearing. She had not slept in days. Before she finished her report, she stopped speaking. I heard the anguish in her crying. In a moment she regained her composure and apologized for "being so emotional." She said it had been overwhelming. As a doctor and a human being it was unbearable to her that so many people needed help, and that so few resources were available to meet the urgent demand. From that moment, Erin and I were bonded. She was our local eyes and ears, making sure that our assets—and those of hundreds of others—got to the places where medical help was most needed.

There are many people who support me every day, particularly at the Children's Health Fund. These dedicated professionals

responded as effectively to the Katrina disaster as they did to the
9/11 attacks in New York. Drs. Arturo Brito, Alan Shapiro, Dave
Krol, Mike Duffy, Sue Spalding, Randy Christensen, Isabel Piño,
Pervis Hill, and Paula Madrid, along with so many other physicians, nurses, social workers, and drivers, rose to the occasion of seeing thousands of dazed, injured, and traumatized survivors. Much
of their response was organized by Lynn Seim, CHF senior vice
president and nurse supreme. Our clinical and public health work
in the Gulf after Katrina was dubbed "Operation Assist." We
thought this would be a relatively quick relief effort, but it soon
turned into a long-term commitment providing services to the displaced families of the Gulf. Alison Greene, Operation Assist's director, public health expert Richard Garfield, and Susan Robinson all
were instrumental in these efforts, as was field director Allison
Wynn. They were backed up by the headquarters staff of Carol
Sumkin, Gabrielle Schang, Violet Moss, Roy Grant, and so many
others. On the policy side, Dennis Johnson, my long-time colleague
and executive vice president of the CHF, has been a great source of
insight and encouragement from the beginning.

Many colleagues have deepened my understanding of terrorism
and disasters, including Dr. Tara O'Toole, director of the University of Pittsburgh Medical Center's Center for Biosecurity, and Dr.
Isaac Weisfuse, deputy director of New York City's Department of
Health and Mental Health, to name just two. Judge Joe Bruno,
New York's commissioner of the Office of Emergency Operations,
has been another effective professional who has done a remarkable
job in bringing this department up to a new standard. New York is
also very fortunate to have Commissioner Ray Kelly running the
NYPD. This has clearly become one of the most effective law
enforcement agencies in the world, particularly in its ability to
gather intelligence, interdict terrorism, and prepare its officers for
whatever might occur.

I have been fortunate to have had some very special mentors who
inspired me to write this book. The late Herb Gardner was a dear
friend and a constant source of encouragement about writing in
general. Dr. Jack Geiger, whose comments on the early part of the

manuscript were invaluable, has been a role model as the ultimate public health advocate for me and so many others over the last four decades. Dr. Allan Rosenfield, the highly esteemed dean of Columbia's Mailman School of Public Health, created the opportunity to establish the National Center for Disaster Preparedness and has supported our work in this field since the very beginning. And the late Carl Sagan, who was one of the planet's most articulate advocates for advancing knowledge and exploration as the twin bedrocks of democracy and who taught me so much about what it means to make a difference.

Finally, I want to thank my friend Paul Simon, who seems to be intrigued by my foray into the world of book writing. As cofounder of the CHF, Paul has been there with me since the beginning, simply an amazing friend and supporter of this effort. Paul was one of the first to recognize that the CHF's mobile units were ready-made for work in disaster areas, and he joined me and Karen last September when we greeted the first two units that rolled into Biloxi, Mississippi.

Foreword

The morning of Tuesday, September 11, 2001, was unusually fine. A clear, dark blue sky was beginning to brighten as I jogged west on Twentieth Street toward the Hudson River. Following my departure from the U.S. Senate and Nebraska, my first year in New York City had been much more difficult than I imagined. I was struggling to adjust to the change in physical and social landscape and to the unfamiliar demands of work as president of the New School. And most of all I was waking each morning with the pain of the memory of my role in the killing of civilians in Vietnam in 1969, the details of which I had chosen to discuss publicly.

Approaching the World Trade Center where I made my turn, I could see the reflection of the rising sun in the windows of New Jersey office buildings. All my troubles had been momentarily obliterated by the birth of my third child at a Hackensack, New Jersey, hospital the day before. I was in a hurry to get home and be on my way to join my family. A car was scheduled to pick me up at 8 a.m. The driver was a moonlighting member of the New York City Fire Department.

By the time we reached the hospital, beauty had turned to horror. A plane had crashed into the north tower of the World Trade Center. My wife was watching the scene on television when I entered her room. Within minutes a second plane struck the south tower. An hour later both towers had collapsed, a third plane had struck the Pentagon, and the country was changed forever.

The people of New York City, the United States, and the rest of the world were unified in a way I had never experienced in my life. As we learned the stories of those who died that morning, we shared a grief that pulled the lives of strangers into our own. Christians, Jews, Muslims, Hindus, Buddhists, and atheists died that morning simply because they chose to go to work or to attend a meeting. Citizens of many countries, people of a wide range of political beliefs, men and women who had done nothing wrong. The only thing that seemed to matter was the place of their employment.

A little more than a year later, Senator Tom Daschle asked me to serve on the 9/11 Commission. What I learned during the next nine months surprised me. I learned that the September 11 attack on the World Trade Center was the latest in a series of successful and unsuccessful military operations against the United States that dated back to the early 1990s. I learned that the men who led this effort had declared war on the United States on account of the very thing that made us vulnerable: our openness, our liberalness, our preference to be in a world where people of all religions can live peacefully side by side.

I learned that this enemy was much different than any we had faced before. This enemy did not have measurable and observable military forces. This enemy did not feel remorse about killing civilians. Quite the contrary. That was their objective.

Collateral damage was not a tragedy; it was their purpose. I learned how successful they had been in recruiting from mosques where imams preached hatred of the United States. I learned how they had established a sanctuary inside Afghanistan that was not as remote as we had believed. And I learned that every time we excused the intentions behind the words spoken in radical mosques and schools, every show of restraint on our part, and every moment we had been unwilling to meet force with force, had been seen as a sign of weakness, a signal that we could be attacked without consequence.

This time there were consequences. Most of the world united in a war against the Taliban in Afghanistan where Al-Qaeda had found a safe haven from which to operate. Not only did this war succeed in destroying its sanctuary, but it also began an unprecedented level of cooperation by international law enforcement agencies, accompanied by a recognition that we were far more vulnerable than we had previously imagined.

I also learned we had been woefully unprepared for the September 11 military attack by nineteen men who had found it altogether too easy to enter, hijack, and use four American commercial airliners as weapons. It was the opinion of all five Republican and all five Democratic members of the 9/11 Commission that the government of the United States had done nothing to prepare for a domestic assault in spite of repeated Central Intelligence Agency warnings in the summer of 2001 that the enemy was determined to strike inside our borders. These warnings were ignored. This was not a failure of intelligence. It was a failure to act upon the intelligence that sounded the alarm and called attention to our weakness.

Finally, I learned that in spite of two land wars that continue to this day, hundreds of billions of tax dollars spent, and two massive reorganizations of the federal government, we are much more vulnerable than necessary. The evil and charismatic leader of our most active enemy is still alive and apparently well, threatening not just us but a fledgling nation-state in Afghanistan and a fragile government in Pakistan. The cancer of this threat has metastasized to Iraq, Somalia, and other places whose stability is in doubt.

This is bad news. The even worse news is our lack of preparation to deal with the aftermath of any manmade or natural disaster that could visit our shores. Dr. Irwin Redlener, a respected authority on the subject, has carefully researched five elaborate, hypothetical scenarios on the background, genesis, and consequences of catastrophic events.

Americans at Risk joins other recent and persuasive analysis in making the case that we are not ready for megadisasters—as if we had to be told following the debacle we witnessed in the aftermath of Hurricanes Katrina and Rita. This book also tells us why we were not prepared. Finally, Dr. Redlener offers specific recommendations about what we can do now to get ready for future disasters.

The good news is that we are more or less able to get through the typical major emergencies caused by floods and tornados, moderate earthquakes, and the like. But we totally collapse when the disaster overwhelms local, state, and regional capacity. There are several reasons for this. To begin with, FEMA's functionality has essentially disappeared and federal leadership is a shambles. The result is that our ability to organize a major response initiative is in doubt.

The central challenge Americans face is that we don't know what we mean by the term "prepared" and thus we do not know what to "buy." We presume that spending tens of billions of dollars must make us safer. Dr. Redlener's analysis shows us how wrong we are by detailing a mind-boggling lack of accountability in the system.

We are now paying an extraordinary price for letting some of the nation's basic systems fall into a dangerously dysfunctional state. In particular, Dr. Redlener makes it clear that the most expensive health-care system in the world would be overwhelmed by a major disaster. Just as dire is his analysis of other elements of the infrastructure, such as levees and communications systems.

Throughout this book, Dr. Redlener focuses on the issue of leadership and the smart use of existing resources, including a much more clarified use of the military to help deal with major disasters. He is also unsparing in his critique of nongovernmental organizations like the Red Cross and the general return to complacency that has characterized Americans' attitudes since September 11. He reviews international best practices, recommends specific solutions, and provides examples of preparedness that he considers ideal.

His recommendations include extracting FEMA from the Department of Homeland Security, enacting legislation to create a permanent 9/11 Commission with subpoena authority, fixing our health-care system, and making the surgeon general the public health "czar." He argues that we need to change the congressional oversight process and develop new strategies to engage the public in preparedness. He believes we can and must do all of this without creating disaster paranoia.

In my opinion, Dr. Redlener's diagnosis is accurate and his prescriptions are sound. I hope that our Congress will read *Americans at Risk* and respond with action.

—Bob Kerrey
President of the New School,
June 3, 2006

Introduction

Since September 2001, the United States has seemingly been on a crash course to upgrade the nation's ability to prevent terrorism, strengthen its vital infrastructure, and plan for any future disaster response. By the end of 2006, the expenditures directed toward these endeavors will have exceeded $250 billion, and the majority of these funds will have been diverted from a wide range of unmet health and social programs where they are desperately needed. At the same time, bureaucracies at all levels of government have been greatly expanded, bloated with new responsibilities, yet stunningly unfettered by any appropriate level of accountability to the American people.

For all of this, the nation remains decidedly unprepared. The promised extreme upgrade of our intelligence capacity is, at best, a work in progress. U.S. ports and borders are not secure. Bridges, tunnels, and levees across the country need repair and strengthening. Industries from chemical plants to nuclear power facilities remain vulnerable to accidents and intentional violation. The health-care system, an essential component of effective response to large-scale disasters, is increasingly fragile, apparently unable to mount an effective response to a major, high-consequence catastrophe.

America is failing one of the most important tests of national capability and resolve we have ever faced. This failure will continue to cost lives. Staggering expenses will be incurred to address what well may have been prevented in the first place. Responsible prevention requires prudent investments in the right plan. It takes visionary leadership and the means to carry out an effective and efficient agenda that will make the country stronger, without undermining its fundamental values. Yet these are precisely the qualities that are absent from the governing hierarchies of American society today. To put it as plainly as possible, the current administration and congressional leadership have created and perpetuated a culture of incompetence and vulnerability that needs to be addressed rapidly and methodically.

In many ways, the nation's approach to preventing further terrorism in the United States and improving our capacity to respond to major disasters bears unnerving similarities to the conduct of the war in Iraq. Questionable information, misguided leadership, unclear goals, underinvestment in critical areas, and staggering hubris apply as much to large-scale disaster preparedness as they do to the conduct of the war. For this, the country has already paid a great price, with, unfortunately, more to come.

Americans remain clearly at risk. The threats we face are real and the solutions not always apparent. Sober terror experts talk about deeply embedded "sleeper cells" and coast-to-coast homeland security breaches, made even more troubling in early 2006 with questions about who owns the companies that ultimately secure— or leave open to terror—America's ports. Many medical experts point out the inevitability of such natural disasters as pandemic influenza and our extraordinary lack of preparedness to handle such a crisis. Seismologists remind us that the "big one" could come at any time. And scientists discuss the possibility of "American tsunamis" striking the east or west coasts, much like the megadisaster that killed 250,000 people in Southeast Asia at the end of 2004.

We are clearly on a path of disaster overload. Somebody, somewhere is talking about potential massive failures in the U.S. electrical grid, the consequences of global warming, or the ominous melt-down of a nuclear power plant—either by accident or at the hand of a terrorist.

We hear the experts and, for the most part, we believe them. It's just that we don't quite know what we are supposed to do. Some of the issues seem too arcane to understand, others too big to solve. We expect government to take care of business by strengthening what is fragile or not secure and by responding when called. But mostly we hope against hope that calamity isn't around the corner.

No one has all of the answers for addressing these perceived threats to our safety and stability. But the last thing we want is to live in fear or raise our children in a society where the opportunity to grow, thrive, and enjoy life is undermined by "threat anxiety" or an obsession with the pursuit of absolute security. I believe we can create an environment in which we take prudent steps to reduce risk while still pursuing a life of personal fulfillment and sustaining a realistic sense of hope for the future.

The nation is stumbling through a process of understanding the major threats to the health and well-being of its citizens. We have not yet clarified what we are trying to achieve with respect to being prepared for large-scale, high-consequence disasters. In fact, the absence of a clear definition of what "prepared" actually means makes it almost impossible to establish functional guidelines—or benchmarks—for how to get to a desired state of readiness.

A better state of readiness for major disasters will mean having the courage to accept the threats that are real and the discipline to design and implement strategies that could actually make a differ-ence. This is not a job for any single sector of our society. Getting this right will require a five-way partnership among government, citizens, first responders, nongovernmental organizations, and the private sector, all of which have critical roles to play in disaster pre-vention and response.

Nonetheless, some idiosyncratic realities of our culture and poli-tics pose barriers to making "readiness progress." Getting better prepared for megadisasters, just like making our children smarter, our nation healthier, or the military stronger, requires sometimes costly investments in basic programs that pay off in the future. The return on substantial improvements in our schools, creating an accessible health-care system, or improving military recruitment will mean a smarter, healthier, or stronger nation in the *decades* to come—not next month or next year.

The long-term nature of these investments in social progress is challenging for this nation of hard-core individualists. We are a people who like to live in the moment. We seem innately unable to postpone gratification. Early investment for long-term payoff is anathema to Americans. And if the truth be told, we do not readily embrace the basic concept of prevention. We are often reluctant participants in the programs and recommendations that might improve our health or increase longevity.

September 11 and Hurricane Katrina were each turning points for the nation. Taken together, they define a dramatic transition from theoretical *thinking* about megadisasters to a very real *understanding* of what prevention, mitigation, and effective response can actually mean to people and communities. But were these events a wake-up call—or more like a snooze alarm? They got our attention, but we quickly drifted back to sleep.

In spite of the often-repeated references to these tragedies as "lessons learned," I am skeptical. There may be lessons, but I am not sure what we have learned. In the pages that follow, I hope to provide a sense of our vulnerabilities to naturally occuring events, a degraded infrastructure, and the intentional acts of people determined to kill and demoralize Americans. By understanding these vulnerabilities, and thinking about how enormous tragedies can actually unfold, readers will understand the scope of the problems we face as a nation.

I will conclude this book by describing how much can be accomplished. While we cannot prevent tsunamis, we can develop early warning systems that will save lives. If we cannot stabilize the tectonic plates under San Francisco, we can reinforce its buildings to withstand fairly powerful earthquakes. We can support the Sacramento levees, fix the hundred-year-old water mains in Chicago and every other major American city, and improve nuclear power plant safety in Kentucky and elsewhere. We can even do a great deal to improve border and port security to seriously dampen the possibility of terrorists infiltrating our country with weapons of mass destruction.

Even if the nation's intelligence capability is substantially strengthened and homeland security better assured, these systems will never be perfect. An American city *could* conceivably experience the nightmare of a nuclear detonation. The essential point is that the quality and extent of survival and recovery, even from a nuclear bomb, are affected by the success of our preparedness and mitigation programs.

We face serious threats from many quarters, but they are not fickle vagaries of fate or bad luck. Our future is anything but hopeless, and we are not helpless. We are a nation of 300 million. In spite of wide ideological and political diversity, we have a vast reservoir of talented problem-solvers who share a common desire to examine what puts the nation at risk and determine how best to reduce its vulnerability. We need to start with a long, hard look at what we're doing and where we are. We need new leadership and real inspiration. We need a sense of mission, determination, and investment to make it possible for our children and the generations to come to live lives filled with promise and possibility, facing—and not fearing— the complicated modern world.

Finally, the United States has a great deal of "unfinished business" that has challenged and plagued the nation for many decades—long before we were jolted by 9/11 and horrified by the response to Hurricane Katrina. Intractable poverty in many segments of American society, a deteriorating and ever more costly health-care system, concerns about immigration policy, massive problems in public education in many parts of the country, and struggles to keep up with the new realities of global economic competition are among the many issues that will not conveniently fade away while we focus our attention on terrorism and disaster response. We have to be able to deal with all of these issues simultaneously.

I

After the Storm

1 · Help on Hold, Lives at Stake

Almost a month to the day following the devastating landfall of Hurricane Katrina, I made my third of many trips to the Gulf region of Mississippi. I was there to meet with members of the Operation Assist medical relief team who had been working non-stop to treat the unending flow of displaced and disoriented people who needed medical care. Operation Assist is the collaboration singer-songwriter Paul Simon and I organized between the Children's Health Fund and Columbia University's Mailman School of Public Health to bring emergency relief to people who had survived the storm. On the way from the Biloxi-Gulfport airport, I asked to be driven by some areas that had been particularly hard-hit. I had been to these neighborhoods before but was anxious to see what progress had been made.

We drove down I-90, heading into D'Iberville, a community of some 7,500 citizens, with a Wal-Mart, a Winn-Dixie supermarket, and a couple of dollar stores. The weather was balmy and slightly overcast. It felt like a normal day in a typical small southern town—until we looked out the window. In some neighborhoods, whole blocks had been flattened. Storefronts had been ripped off the buildings and overhead signs were left dangling from one corner of the store or had been blown away entirely. There were about 1,830 homes in D'Iberville before Katrina came crashing through town. In Katrina's wake some 1,250 homes had sustained wind or water damage. Nearly 400 had been destroyed.

In 2000, the median income for residents of D'Iberville was about $34,000 a year, about 20 percent under the national average of about $42,000. People were more or less middle class and mostly white, with fewer than one in five residents African American or Vietnamese. Many families were living at or below the poverty level; few had substantial investments or savings—in other words, little or no financial safety net was readily available. The storm damage, the disruption of the social networks, and vastly diminished public services were taking a toll on the community.

On my first visit, just days after the storm, I was overwhelmed by the extent of the damage, and perplexed and infuriated by so little evidence of any organized governmental response—or even presence. Now, just four weeks later, it seemed that nothing much had changed.

I saw high in the still standing trees of a destroyed middle-class community what seemed to be some toys and children's shredded clothes. Sifting through the wreckage of what had been a home, a family was looking for something to salvage. A few crews of Central American workers were beginning to reconstruct a roof or a house here and there, but in general, time seemed to have stopped altogether.

In a low-income housing project, children surrounded us and clamored for the bottled water and granola bars we had brought. I asked a mother if FEMA (the Federal Emergency Management Agency) or the Red Cross had been there. She said, "Not here. We have to send somebody out every day to find the closest Red Cross center, where we can get water for the community. It's usually a ten- or fifteen-minute drive from here. And we still don't have electricity or fresh water." When I asked if the children were going to school, she said, "Some days."

This visit and every subsequent one to the Gulf reinforced what we have now learned: the emergency response to the hurricane's damage in the Gulf was woefully, painfully insufficient. And as bad as things were in Mississippi, the situation was even worse in neighboring Louisiana, where, even six months after the storm, the news remained disheartening, an endless stream of unanticipated consequences and unresolved problems. Well beyond the acute emergency phase of the initial response, the services and relief efforts seem to be struggling as much as ever in New Orleans and throughout Louisiana. Information is faulty and incomplete. Issues that should have been thought about long before the disaster struck have become intractable barriers to meeting the needs of people who have been through a hellish combination of natural violence and bureaucratic blunders.

Gregory Kutz, the Government Accountability Office auditor who led an investigation into use of federal funds for relief, testified on February 14, 2006, before the Senate Committee on Homeland Security and Governmental Affairs that funds wasted in the Katrina aftermath will certainly amount to millions of dollars, and "it could be tens or hundreds of millions of dollars." And an audit by the Department of Homeland Security (DHS), led by Inspector General Richard L. Skinner and released on April 14, 2006, reaffirmed the chaotic squandering of taxpayer funds. No example better typifies this waste than the FEMA-administered debit card program that gave evacuees cards with $2,000 balances intended to purchase emergency provisions. The debit cards came with no oversight and no guidelines. As a result, the cards were used to purchase frivolous items unrelated to evacuation needs including adult entertainment, gambling, a $450 tattoo, and a diamond engagement ring for $1,100. Moreover, qualification for the cards required very little verification. Consequently, 900,000 of the 2.5 million cards distributed went to people with fake addresses and duplicate or fake Social Security numbers. A total of $24 million worth of cards were given out, with little hope that the total will ever be accounted for.

The basic challenge was finding housing for the estimated 300,000 families whose homes Katrina wrecked. As I write, the hard-hit neighborhoods of New Orleans remain virtually unchanged since the day after the floodwaters retreated. The 300,000 homes destroyed or made uninhabitable represent at least $67 billion in losses. This devastation surpasses the combined damage from the four largest hurricanes in 2004 (Charley, Francis, Ivan, and Jeanne), which ruined 85,000 homes. There are still blocks and blocks of irreversibly damaged houses, their interior walls covered with black mold, and thousands of metric tons of debris and garbage still filling the streets. So much of the mess remains frozen in time that a thriving new business has emerged: entrepreneurs, like the Gray Line bus tour that charges $35 a head, have been taking gawking tourists to see what Mother Nature has wrought and human beings cannot seem to fix.

At the very time when the federal government has begun to cut off funds supporting displaced families being sheltered in hotels throughout—and beyond—Louisiana, thousands of FEMA-purchased mobile homes languish in fields and empty lots in Florida and Arkansas, undelivered and unused. This fact came out in a CNN interview with a FEMA official in Arkansas. The backdrop was the surreal image of a sea of 11,000 empty, brand new white mobile homes.

The reporter asked, "Why aren't these trailers being used to house evacuees in Louisiana? Why are they still here?" The FEMA official replied, "It's hard to find places to put them in Louisiana where the right hookups—like electricity and water—are available." Later in the interview, the FEMA official, referring to New Orleans, offered, "Mobile homes can't be put in floodplains."

The need for temporary housing is still greatest in the neighborhoods that have been evacuated. Workers are needed to clean up and rebuild New Orleans. And employees are needed to restart the businesses struggling to regain their footing. But for workers to return, their families have to have somewhere to live and to go back to school.

Only 2,700 of the 25,000 perfectly adequate trailers used for temporary housing and purchased for more than $850 million had been installed by mid-February, 2006; nearly half of them were sitting in mud in Hope, Arkansas, waiting to be shipped and put to use. Tax dollars are paying for this travesty of a recovery program in a part of the country that Congress is trying hard to forget. There was at least one major military base in Louisiana that might have been a good medium-term housing solution; ironically, it was closed in 1992 through the Base Realignment and Closure (BRAC) process. England Air Force Base in Alexandria, Louisiana, a few hours north of New Orleans, was temporarily used to house about two hundred evacuees. Although a mixed-use property, surely it could have been considered as a location for trailers or other temporary housing. Yet, through February 2006, the government spent $249 million commissioning four cruise ships to provide more than 8,000 cabins for this purpose. The cost of some $5,100 per month per cabin was six times the going rate to rent a two-bedroom apartment. I am still wondering how this makes sense.

The truth is, we weren't prepared to prevent the flooding of New Orleans because we didn't make sure that the levees at the 17th Street Canal and Industrial Canal and along canals extending south from Lake Pontchartrain would stand up to a greater than category 3 hurricane. While the Bush administration's proposed FY 2004 budget included $297 million for civil works projects in the U.S. Army Corps of Engineers' New Orleans district, Congress approved only $40 million, of which $3 million was slated for New Orleans's East Bank Hurricane Levee Project. But the U.S. Army Corps of Engineers project manager, Al Naomi, reported that $11 million was needed. Congress ultimately approved $5.5 million, but because of the project's reduced budget, work on the levee system was halted for the first time in thirty-seven years. To correct this deficit, we should have mounted an organized emergency response, but stunning governmental incompetence and lack of coordination got in the way on many levels. And we are unprepared to recover because everywhere you turn in the Gulf there are overwhelming needs, too few resources, unclear lines of authority and responsibility, and insufficient on-the-ground innovation and leadership.

In late January 2006, Senator Richard Burr of North Carolina asked me to meet with him at his office in the Dirksen Senate Office Building at the Capitol. This meeting was one of a series he had scheduled with experts to explore a range of ideas about what was needed to prepare specifically for a bioterror attack and, more generally, for disaster response. Dr. Robert Kadlec, a former White House expert on bioterrorism and counterintelligence, is staff director of the Senate Subcommittee on Bioterrorism. He had arranged the meeting and told me to be prepared for a frank and open discussion.

The conversation was focused and honest, and the senator listened carefully. One of my main points was how unprepared the U.S. health-care system was to respond to or recover from a major disaster. He responded knowledgeably on the topic and we spoke at length about the chronic fragility of the public health system.

In the senator's office were two other people: Jennifer Bryning, a very capable senior staff member, and Dr. Kathy Hebert. Dr. Hebert had started working in Burr's office as a special policy adviser just a few weeks earlier. Until that time she was in charge of the cardiology clinics at Charity Hospital in New Orleans. The venerable Charity was one of the nation's best-known health-care facilities for the poor. Because more than 25 percent of the New Orleans population was classified as poor, the need for a hospital that took all comers, regardless of income or insurance status, could not have been greater. More than half of the evacuees initially in shelters—some 270,000 people—did not have health insurance; for most of them, Charity Hospital had been their primary place for medical care. Charity took an enormous hit during and after Katrina and the floods that followed. Now the facility is shut down, its fate uncertain.

When the session ended, Kathy Hebert and I walked out to the outer office. As we stood there, in front of the receptionist's desk, Kathy said, "Irwin, thanks for coming. I'm sure this will be helpful. But, I am very worried about my patients." I asked what she meant.

"On August 28th, just before Katrina hit, I had hundreds of patients enrolled in my cardiology clinics at Charity. And my colleagues in other fields were caring for lots of people with cancer, kidney disease, and chronic mental health conditions. Once the storm hit, and Charity went out of commission," she said, "we lost track of heart patients that needed catheterization and other lifesaving procedures. We are now trying to make sure that the kidney patients can get to an alternative dialysis center and that the psych patients can get their medications."

So where are these patients, I asked, knowing that in New Orleans alone, no more than 100,000 of the city's former 480,000 residents had returned. The remainder were scattered in shelters or relocated all over Louisiana and throughout another thirty-five or forty host states.

Kathy responded, "Irwin, I have no idea where my patients are." I asked her what she thought could be happening to her cardiology patients, especially the ones that needed critical medications or procedures.

Dr. Hebert paused, looking at me. Her eyes filled with tears. The receptionist was trying not to look at us, but had been paying rapt attention to this intense conversation. "My patients?" she asked. "They're dying. I am just so afraid that they're showing up in whatever emergency rooms are open, out of meds and out of time."

I tried to come to grips with what this young doctor was actually saying. I know I mumbled something about my willingness to help sort this out—and I did speak with Louisiana health officials. I also asked our Operation Assist medical teams on the ground to keep an eye out for patients who had been at Charity. By March, some of Kathy's patients had shown up in the few medical facilities that were still open for business; others had been evacuated to nearby states and would be there for the long haul. But many were not found.

As I thought about what Kathy's situation really meant, I appreciated anew how badly things were going in the so-called recovery of the Gulf in Katrina's aftermath. At the time, Kathy Hebert could not have known the fates of thousands of evacuees with chronic illnesses who had been rushed from New Orleans and now found themselves in Texas, Florida, Tennessee, and dozens of other states. Like refugees fleeing war zones, these patients were arriving in their "temporary" communities without medical records or the ability to contact their physicians. On the receiving end of this exodus, Dr. Joe Mirro at the renowned St. Jude Children's Research Hospital in Memphis noted, "We received nearly 100 pediatric cancer patients from New Orleans. Our staff tried as best they could to figure out what medications these kids were on, scrambling to look up treatment protocols and find the doctors who had been caring for them before the evacuation. Sometimes we found the information we needed; most of the time we just did the best we could." Four months after Katrina struck on August 29, here were some of the realities:

- The Tulane University School of Medicine in New Orleans laid off 140 of its 540-member physician teaching faculty, including many important subspecialists.

- An emergency room physician at one of the three partially open hospitals had recently warned former residents of the city not to return to New Orleans if they had medical conditions because there weren't enough beds or doctors to care for them.

- Medical leaders were deeply concerned that the vibrant—and vital—training programs for young physicians would collapse because the facilities were damaged and many of the medical school faculty were gone, some laid off, many others simply recruited to other states.

- The military medical facilities, so extraordinary in the immediate aftermath of the disaster, were long gone, pulled back out of the disaster region.

- The one children's hospital was operating at a greatly reduced capacity, and access to medical care, in general, for children was at a fraction of its prestorm capacity in a city where health care for indigent children was barely functional during "normal" times.

Health care in New Orleans was devastated by Katrina. But that was just the beginning.

By early 2006, four months after Hurricanes Katrina and Rita, evidence had begun to emerge of a situation that few could have imagined and virtually no one had predicted. Nearly 80,000 people, mostly poor, who had been evacuated from New Orleans were still languishing in federally subsidized shelters, including trailers, mobile homes, and hotels throughout the United States.

Just outside Baton Rouge, on a treeless tract of flat, depressing land near the airport, is Renaissance Village, the trailer park that FEMA created. The Keta Group, a small business partner of the Baton Rouge–based Shaw Group, won the contract to set up and run Renaissance Village. Both companies are said to be connected to Halliburton, the giant multinational corporation once run by Vice President Dick Cheney.

There they installed 573 travel trailers and a few double-wide mobile homes for administrative offices and surrounded the complex with a 12-foot-high steel fence. Some 1,700 evacuees—the elderly, small families, and homeless singles—are warehoused in Renaissance Village. It is guarded by a private security force, virtually all former military personnel, many said to be fresh from jobs as mercenary soldiers fighting little wars in obscure places. Now, these career fighters are hired by the FEMA contractors to "keep order" and "control access" to the shelters.

On one of my visits to the village, I was told about a sheriff's raid two days before. An unannounced foray of heavily armed Baton Rouge authorities rounded up young African American men who were said to have committed a variety of crimes, from petty theft to felonies to failure to pay child support. Two days before the raid,

FEMA had discontinued providing propane for the trailers—fuel needed for cooking, heating, and hot water. Now village residents were expected to find their own ways to pay for the propane; without jobs or resources, many had resorted to hoarding and stealing what had suddenly become a valuable commodity.

In another unanticipated development in the FEMA trailer saga, by May 2006, it was increasingly clear that many of the trailers were an emerging health hazard: formaldehyde gas, leaching into the interior of the trailers from glues and other construction materials, was present at concentrations twice the level considered safe by the Environmental Protection Agency. Residents were reporting skin ailments, difficulty sleeping, and exacerbated asthma, all attributed to the chemical.

In the village—and in other shelter sites throughout the Gulf region—an environment of fear, despair, and a palpable sense of hopelessness was already becoming a hard reality for the people now in a perpetual state of waiting: waiting for a job, waiting for a permanent home, waiting to get their children back in school, and waiting for health care. In a survey conducted by my team at the National Center on Disaster Preparedness in February 2006, we found that more than one in five school-age children was missing more than ten school days a month—or not enrolled in school at all.

For adults, the village feels like prison. Few of the residents have personal vehicles. There is nothing to do. Most of the trailers do not have television. Boredom and depression have become the twin conditions of life in Renaissance Village.

A chaplain I met told me that he had never seen anything like this. Grown men simply stay in the trailer from morning until night. "And one more thing," he said. "I have spoken to many of the young men who are *begging* for someone to talk to. They're overtly depressed and have no idea what the future holds." He said, "It's just unbearable."

Help of almost any kind is hard to come by. Almost half the children who had regular doctors prior to the storm no longer had access to medical care. And more than 40 percent of the parents and guardians in the shelters reported that their children were experiencing emotional or behavioral difficulties that had not existed before the hurricane and the flood.

Under the leadership of one of our senior researchers at the National Center, Dr. David Abramson, teams of graduate students from Columbia University, as well as Tulane and Louisiana State, spent two weeks going from trailer to trailer interviewing people living under conditions that few students had ever encountered or imagined. After ten hours in the field, the students returned to the base, in a state of emotional shock.

I was visiting with the team, headquartered for the survey on the campus of Louisiana State University in Baton Rouge. I asked one of the Columbia students what it was like. "I couldn't believe it," she replied. "I spoke with a twenty-four-year-old woman who was in one of the trailers with her six-year-old and two-year-old daughters. She said that the older one saw her stepfather die and sat with his body for days before she was discovered. The child was totally traumatized and has tried to actually kill her sister several times." When I asked if they had contacted anyone, the student said, "Yes, of course. And they were told that there is an *eighteen-month waiting list* for a child mental health professional."

Eighteen months to see a child psychiatrist. Back in the real world, even in the mess of a health-care system that many poor people endure, this situation would be considered a true emergency. I would have found a psychiatrist to see this child the same day I heard the story. This was, in fact, more evidence of a societal meltdown in the face of a megadisaster.

Nobody had planned for what now amounts to a domestic refugee crisis. And with no resolution in sight for how well the levees would be reinforced and no sense of when the ravaged communities would be rebuilt, the future was becoming increasingly unsure, and, for many, as frightening as the powerful winds of Katrina so many months before.

While they were waiting, the Katrina evacuees had something else to ponder. The 2006 hurricane season was imminent. But the flimsy, unsecured trailers they were using for shelter were actually designed for weekend fishing trips, not semipermanent housing in a region at high risk for natural disaster. What, exactly, were they supposed to do when the next hurricane warning was issued?

The evacuees would not have taken much comfort from a senior Louisiana disaster response official I spoke with in March 2006. "How are we getting ready for the next disaster?" I asked, thinking it could be just months away. He looked at me and sighed. "We've just begun thinking about it." That, it seemed to me, is the problem.

To be sure, absorbing the monumental failures of government in the response and recovery after Katrina will take some time. Renaissance Village is perhaps symbolic of how badly government takes care of large numbers of traumatized people. On the other hand, it is fair to ask what other options there might be.

I remember the chaplain I spoke with that day in Baton Rouge. We were looking out over the crowded field of white trailers, beyond the security post with its former soldiers in crew cuts and black cargo pants. Our backs were to the high steel fence and I was wondering aloud, "Could we have done better than this? It looks like a military POW camp or a refugee village in the Third World." He half smiled at me. "Of course." He went on: "And it didn't need to be government's job alone. There are scores of churches and community organizations that were willing and able to absorb everybody who's now trapped in here." I said nothing. He continued: "They would have fed and clothed all of these people. They would have helped families get back on their feet and made sure that the kids got the medical care they needed. And they certainly would have made sure that every child got into school."

Maybe so, I thought. But one thing was abundantly clear: this business of responding to a major disaster is not something we know how to do. We don't even know what governmental responsibility should be or what the private sector should handle.

A year from now, another hurricane may have struck, creating more devastation, or perhaps this situation will have improved. Maybe more hospital beds will be available, businesses will slowly reopen, and more people will find a permanent place to settle in what was once their beautiful, cherished, yet admittedly flawed and impoverished New Orleans. The same may be true for some of the other destroyed communities. But we also know that much will not be changed, that finding livelihoods will be extraordinarily difficult for struggling families, and that the health-care system will be years in the rebuilding.

Across the state line, the Mississippi Gulf Coast will also be in some form of devastated limbo for a long time. There were just too many towns reduced to rubble on and near the coast. The failures of planning, response, and rebuilding will leave an indelible impression of abandonment among the former and present residents of the Gulf, and a sense of disbelief among the rest of us.

Some people may say the impact of Katrina was too vast, that no amount of readiness planning could have been enough.

I couldn't disagree more.

II

How Is America Still Vulnerable?

2 · The American Health-Care System: Unready for Prime Time in an Age of Megadisasters

The persistent and worsening health-care crisis in America presents an important complicating factor in managing disasters. Dysfunctions in the system, from the smallest detail to the basic structure and organization of health care, are meaningful in normal times. People bemoan the difficulty of finding a "good doctor." The paperwork is crushing. The waits in medical offices are too long, and in addition to the millions who have no health insurance, millions more live in areas where there are physician shortages and poor access to care in general. For the last decade or so people who do have employer-based medical insurance have been feeling pressure as their companies reduce coverage or increase the cost to employees.

On the public health side, where disease surveillance and large-scale preventive health strategies for whole populations are the main agenda, funding for these vital programs has been inexorably reduced over the past two decades as federal and state budgets become increasingly strapped. To a great extent, though, much changed on September 11, 2001. All of a sudden the public health departments were on the front lines of the "war against terror," developing ways to diagnose anthrax, detect early evidence of bioterrorism, train workers to handle terrorist-deployed chemical and radiological attacks, and more. Money from the federal government began to flow and new strategies were being developed. But even this was disorganized, poorly monitored, and badly prioritized.

The truth is that in mid-2006, the public health system is still not working very well. Any disaster with significant public health implications will be affected by inadequacies in the basic health-care system.

In the aftermath of Hurricane Katrina, for instance, huge numbers of uninsured displaced citizens, many with chronic conditions, became a tremendous burden on health-care delivery systems in Mississippi and Louisiana, which had been severely compromised by the storms. Today, remaining medical providers and facilities are stretched to the limit, literally on the brink of financial ruin.

Now consider what might happen in a major biological crisis, such as the feared avian flu pandemic, a rapidly spreading highly lethal disease that would affect people all over the world. One of the most important keys to controlling the spread of avian flu is early diagnosis and, when possible, treatment. So what happens with the more than 46 million Americans without insurance and the millions more who have insurance but happen to live in communities with long-standing physician shortages? One unfortunate possibility is that these people with reduced access to medical facilities will become the "Typhoid Marys" of the pandemic, carrying and spreading the virus until it's too late to contain. Every hour of delay in making critical diagnoses can make a major difference in identifying and managing a sick patient or limiting the spread of a deadly virus.

In early December 2005, Robert Bazell, the senior science and medical reporter for NBC, asked if I would join some colleagues in briefing a group of NBC journalists about avian flu and the potential for global pandemic. When I entered the conference room at Rockefeller Center, there were sixteen representatives from the news departments of all of the NBC-owned affiliates from around the country. Two other experts were there for the off-the-record briefing. Dr. William Kassler, then of the Centers for Disease Control, described the science and epidemiology of bird flu in particular, the H5N1 virus that is the current concern. Dr. Isaac Weisfuse, an exceptionally capable deputy commissioner of the New York City Department of Health, provided insight into the local preparedness plans. I was there as the "scenario guy," having recently laid out to the New York City Council the stark possibility of a deadly pandemic flu and the havoc it would create in the city.

A reporter asked how long it would take to make a definitive laboratory diagnosis of avian flu from a sample of a patient's blood or secretions. Dr. Weisfuse responded, "The actual processing would take about four hours." Then he added, "But the reagent, the material we actually need to run the test, is still in short supply." I asked what he meant. He replied, "It's about the usual issues—manufacturing bottlenecks and bureaucratic conflicts." In this case, there were ongoing "disagreements" among the Centers for Disease Control, the Food and Drug Administration, and the New York State Department of Health about licensing the reagent. Nowhere along the line had anyone sought to resolve this small but crucial problem in the grinding, complex wheel of public health policies. Without adequate supplies of the reagent in labs across the country, we'll have delays in making definitive diagnoses that may in turn force us to put off key decisions about policies that could slow down a rampaging pandemic.

This example shows that the actual process of "getting prepared" is an arduous ordeal filled with interlocking details, many of which can determine how well prepared we'll be to survive major catastrophes. I don't think many Americans realize how many small details *and* big picture concerns have really not been thought of or addressed. Sadly, we don't have the big picture under control—like how to evacuate the communities surrounding a nuclear power plant in the event of a meltdown or sabotage—nor have we fully considered the small, significant details that we might need to depend upon if disaster strikes, like the availability of the H5N1 virus testing reagent.

Hardly *any* aspect of pandemic preparedness is up to speed. I know this when I go to meetings and hear officials "planning" to develop new protocols, exploring new ways of conducting regional disaster drills, still scratching their heads over the basics. I attended a meeting recently at which New York City hospitals were briefed about state emergency planning. The topic was the supply of mechanical ventilators in New York State and the ability to procure more of these lifesaving breathing machines in the event of a major emergency, in this case, pandemic flu.

A doctor from the state Department of Health said, "I know we're very short on ventilators in the state, we're ordering a backup supply." I asked, "OK, but how many do you think we currently have and how are you determining how many we'll need?"

I already knew the national numbers. In the United States, there are about 105,000 ventilators. On any given day, some 80,000 are in use across the nation. During the typical flu season, this number may rise to about 100,000, leaving only about 5,000 in reserve for the whole country. This situation is pitiful. A moderate-sized metropolitan area would use that many in a few weeks of a major pandemic flu situation. The actual need for the U.S. stockpile could be 750,000, seven times what we have.

The doctor from the Department of Health added, "Well, we're not sure yet what we have in the state right now, but we're trying to find out. And, unfortunately, I am not at liberty to tell you how many we've ordered." I was thinking about this comment as I looked around the room, which was filled with senior representatives from most of New York City's hospitals. Each and every one of them is worried about the possibility of the avian flu's coming to New York and trying to get a handle on what would actually happen—and what they would be called upon to do.

I was wondering: "How can these people plan to care for people in their own hospitals during a major epidemic if they can't get a straight answer from a senior government official?" This meeting took place many months after the country had already absorbed the fact that a biological catastrophe at some point was highly possible. If it actually occurred, having the ability to acquire large numbers of ventilators would most certainly make the difference between life and death for many people.

How pervasive is the lack of preparedness I am describing? If we just take the public health aspects of preparedness—meaning, for instance, how well we are doing in terms of disease surveillance to detect early onset of pandemics or bioterrorism, how capable and available state-of-the-art laboratories are, what the capacity is of our hospitals to respond to a large-scale emergency—we are looking at some truly miserable realities.

More than a dozen major reports from impartial government agencies and highly respected nongovernmental organizations have evaluated the nation's state of public health readiness for major public health disasters. These evaluations, annual "report cards" and assessments of public perceptions about national disaster readiness, began to appear in 2002 and have continued ever since. But whether it is the United States Congressional Research Service, the Government Accountability Office, the nongovernmental Trust for America's Health, or the highly respected Institutes of Medicine, the conclusions are almost universal: America is not prepared to handle the human consequences of a major public health emergency, whether an anthrax attack or the cyclical natural recurrence of a worldwide avian flu pandemic.

A 2004 statement delivered to the House Committee on Government Reform by the director of health care for the United States General Accounting Office said that "no state is fully prepared to respond to a major public health threat" and "gaps remain in disease surveillance systems, laboratory capacity, communications capacity and workforce." And the 2005 preparedness "report card" issued by the prestigious Trust for America's Health was even more damning: it gave the federal government a D+ for post-9/11 public health emergency preparedness, and gave more than half the states a score of 5 or less out of a possible 10 points in major categories of preparedness. The trust uses a wide range of national experts, most of whom are actually working in state health departments, to make the independent assessments of how health departments are doing in a number of key preparedness functions. Shockingly, in many states the situation is actually deteriorating from one year to the next.

There is perhaps no more flagrant example of the extreme fragility of the nation's public health system than the influenza vaccine shortage of 2004. We should have seen this coming. The initial warnings came in the form of a gradually diminishing production capacity, not just for the flu vaccine but for all vaccines in general. The number of manufacturers in the business of supplying all vaccines for the U.S. market dropped from twenty-five in the 1970s to just five in 2004. But of those five, only two actually produced flu vaccine, with the largest manufacturer based offshore. No one seemed to be taking notice or responsibility for monitoring the U.S. vaccine production capacity from a public health perspective. Market forces, questions of profitability, liability issues, and other concerns drove the manufacturers away from the business. Moreover, perhaps most shocking, there was no empowered public health leader (and still is not) who could recognize that limited manufacturing capacity could eventually pose a threat to the public's health.

Then, as we were about to enter the 2004 flu season, the system crashed. One of the two remaining manufacturers of seasonal influenza vaccine, Chiron, was in serious trouble. The processing line of its plant in England where the vaccine was being made was found to be contaminated, and it was immediately shut down by British health authorities. Before the shutdown, Chiron was expected to produce about half the U.S. vaccine supply of 46 million to 48 million doses. There was no way that the sole remaining supplier, Aventis Pasteur, could fill the vacuum. By October, acute shortages of the vaccine were attracting headlines across the U.S., and causing an uproar among physicians, clinics, and patients—especially senior citizens. Older individuals are always most susceptible to the complications of influenza, and the majority of the 35,000 or so annual deaths from influenza are in this demographic group. Senior citizens and their physicians were demanding vaccine—and there was no easy way to gear up production with a single provider as the only source.

I had said repeatedly in the press that this was a public health crisis that simply didn't need to happen, but when I was so quoted on the front page of the *New York Times* in October 2004, I had a surprise fax the next day. Stewart Simonson, then assistant secretary for public health emergency preparedness at the Department of Health and Human Services, wrote to say how "disappointed" he and Secretary Tommy Thompson were to see my comments in the *Times*.

I hardly knew what to think. HHS can solve the problem of vaccine shortages. It was up to that enormous federal agency to sit down with the experts and the manufacturers to hammer out policies, invest in new technologies to increase the efficiency of vaccine production, and put out some helpful communications on the matter to the media and the general public. It was a powerful reminder of government at its worst.

Pandemic Avian Flu Hits New York City

New York is a teeming multicultural American metropolis and a global economic and media hub. Its health-care system, with 80 hospitals and 21,000 acute-care beds, is world class; its physician-training programs produce 17 percent of the nation's doctors and ground-breaking research in virtually every field of medicine. Moreover, the New York City Department of Health is recognized as perhaps the country's most sophisticated public health agency, with capacity and innovation that rival or exceed those of many nations around the world.

The governance of New York is in very good shape. Mayor Bloomberg handily won reelection in 2005; he and his team enjoyed widespread—and well-deserved—bipartisan approval as they entered their second term. The police and fire departments function well and the newly revamped Office of Emergency Management is poised to help oversee any disaster that might befall the city. Yet, for all of its strengths, New York, like the rest of the nation, is simply no match for the biological onslaught currently percolating in Southeast Asia.

The tiny, submicroscopic sequence of proteins known as the H5N1 avian flu virus has been running like wildfire through the bird and poultry populations of Southeast Asia. It has killed more than half of the human beings documented with symptoms attributable to the virus. Nearly all of them contracted the illness from contact with infected birds. This killer bug will be able to create global mayhem once it attains the ability to spread easily from person to person, not just from bird to person.

Two different mechanisms could allow that to happen. First, the virus itself, in its continuing cycles of reproduction and adaptation, will simply change, or mutate, into a form that permits person-to-person transmission. The second, more likely, option is that H5N1 will mesh or blend with another virus, particularly one that already has a great capacity to move among people. A very likely partner for the H5N1 may well be the common form of influenza virus, the type usually responsible for the annual flu season.

When two viruses mesh, their actual genetic material can get shuffled and go through a process scientists call "reassortment." With reassortment, a new form of virus can emerge with characteristics borrowed from each of its two original forms. For example, if a virus that causes relatively mild disease but moves easily from person to person combines with a second more deadly virus that does not transmit well among people, the new form could be the worst of both worlds: contagious and deadly.

That's the fear, a new form of the H5N1 virus that moves rapidly in the human population *and* sustains relatively lethal qualities. Nobody knows when this could happen, but most scientists are convinced that we most certainly will encounter a deadly H5N1 global pandemic at some time in the future.

There's a good deal of "symptom overlap" between what a person would experience getting a case of the typical annual flu and the H5N1 infection. Much of what we know about the human form of avian flu comes from the relatively few cases of individuals who have caught the illness from infected poultry. To put this knowledge into perspective, we can draw lessons from the devastating pandemic of 1918, better known as the Spanish flu, when 40 million people died in one flu season from what researchers now think was a form of avian flu. In some reported cases, people developed symptoms in the morning and were dead by late evening.

If the avian flu does mutate in the most dangerous way, we can expect the disease to take the following course. After one is exposed to an infected person, through direct contact or through contaminated droplets expelled by coughing or sneezing, there will likely be an incubation period of two to four days, perhaps longer. A few of the cases acquired from birds were believed to have had incubation periods lasting two weeks or more. In any case, during incubation, no symptoms will be evident, even though the virus is already reproducing rapidly in your body.

Then symptoms will appear suddenly, generally with high fever and cough as initial complaints. You'll feel achy and tired. Your appetite will be depressed and you may, though it is unlikely, have some upper respiratory symptoms, like sneezing or sore throat. More likely, the cough will rapidly progress to a "deep" sensation in the chest, producing sputum, which, in many cases, will rapidly become blood-tinged or grossly bloody. Atypical for a common flu, some sufferers will get severe abdominal pain and diarrhea. In fact, severe, watery diarrhea may precede any respiratory symptoms by several days. You may be disturbed to see unusual bleeding from the gums or nose.

For many patients who get particularly ill, the H5N1 virus infection can become complicated by a secondary bacterial infection. If this secondary illness is recognized early, antibiotics may be useful. But, more likely, the virus itself will do severe damage, getting deep into the lung tissue, gradually affecting the person's ability to bring oxygen into the bloodstream. Breathing will become increasingly labored, to the point where the lungs fail and an artificial ventilator is needed. This whole process, from first onset of fever and cough, can take anywhere from a few days to almost two weeks. For those who do not survive, the final event will be "multi-organ failure"—in essence, a simultaneous breakdown of the cardiovascular systems, the kidneys, and other vital organs.

Although the World Health Organization and a number of prominent public health scientists have been issuing some warnings about pandemic flu since the mid-1990s, this issue really started to heat up immediately after the U.S. government's dismally failed response to Hurricane Katrina. The government could not be caught short again. We had to have a real pandemic flu plan on the table. When the U.S. Department of Health and Human Services finally released the 396-page *Pandemic Influenza Plan* in the fall of 2005, the document was loaded with detail and many recommendations for states and cities, yet serious questions remain unanswered about which entity of government would pay for which aspects of the plan.

President Bush proposed some $7.1 billion to launch the initiative to combat the bird flu. Of that sum, almost 95 percent was to be dedicated to working on flu vaccine development and the stockpiling of the antiviral medications presumed (so far at least) to work against the more likely forms of avian flu virus. The remaining 5 percent, about $350 million, was meant to beef up local public health systems and local hospital capacities. Based on 5,000 hospitals and more than 5,000 state and local health departments, that translates to an average of about $35,000 per institution. In most instances that sum would only be about half the salary and benefits of a single nurse. Hardly a dent in the funds needed to actually improve hospital capacity to cope with a major public health emergency.

The problem is that until the vaccines are available and until enough antiviral medication can be stockpiled, we need to have a very robust health and medical system that can expand during a crisis to provide enough hospital beds and vital medical services to care for the millions who will need acute care. We are probably looking at a three- to five-year gap before enough vaccine and medication are available, during which time all we'll have is the capacity of our medical system to fall back upon. Yet the federal plan, while giving lip service to this reality, provides neither guidance nor sufficient resources, nor any sense of responsibility for this essential aspect of pandemic preparedness. The government's newly minted plan is, in essence, the mother of all "unfunded mandates."

The truth is we need to do it all. We need the $6.5 billion for the antiviral medication stockpile and to develop and produce the vaccine, but we need to devote at least that much again to hospital and local public health system preparedness. In the absence of enough available vaccines and antiviral medications, it is crucial to bolster the medical system so it can handle a crisis. We're a country with an annual budget of $2.77 trillion a year and a population of 300 million, and we can't seem to appropriate enough resources to make Americans reasonably safe from pandemic flu. This just doesn't make sense.

Leaving aside the planning for the moment, let's imagine a scenario where avian flu hits. Let us assume that we do not have the benefit of another year of preparation, and we have to face a rapidly moving outbreak of the disease.

It's close to 2 a.m. in one of New York's busiest emergency rooms. An aide has just checked a forty-five-year-old man into an examination cubicle, and is holding a clipboard with the initial information sheet, which had been filled out about four hours earlier by the triage nurse. As she helps him into a hospital gown, the aide watches as he experiences a paroxysm of coughing, spitting some blood-laced sputum into the metal pan she has placed on the gurney.

Glancing at the triage form, she sees that the patient had a temperature of 102 degrees and an abnormally rapid respiratory rate. A few lines of medical history record some basic facts: The gentleman is complaining that he is coughing up blood and experiencing severe abdominal pain. A native of Ho Chi Minh City, Vietnam, where he teaches English and French at a secondary school, he is in New York City for the first time to visit relatives who immigrated to the U.S. years before. He arrived at JFK Airport two days earlier, via a connection made through Hong Kong, where he had an eight-hour layover.

Walking back to the nurses' station to find an available doctor, the aide is thinking to herself just how sick that patient looks. Moments later, a twenty-seven-year-old second-year emergency medicine resident enters the exam room, takes one look at the patient, and feels the hair on the back of his neck stand up. Just a few hours earlier, an urgent message had appeared on his Black-Berry—and on the hospital's e-mail messaging system as well. The NYC Department of Health had begun notifying area hospitals that sustained human-to-human transmission of an H5N1 virus had been reported in Vietnam and rural China.

The doctor correctly suspects that he is seeing his first case of avian flu. He grabs an N-95 face mask and gloves, dons a gown, and approaches his new patient. What he does not know is that within a four-hour period, in twelve separate New York City emergency rooms, the same scenario is playing out. People are coming in with similar symptoms of fever and cough.

It is later learned that officials in both Vietnam and China had noted the initial outbreak some twelve days earlier. In spite of great assurances from all nations that they would immediately share information that might indicate the onset of a pandemic, neither country wanted to be the first to do so. Both independently tried to contain the first outbreaks internally and secretly, hoping to avoid the stigma—and economic consequences—that they thought would inevitably follow the beginning of a worldwide biocatastrophe. Sadly, and perhaps predictably, containment efforts have failed miserably.

The health departments of New York City and New York State have an excellent surveillance system in place to identify early the first cases of any unusual syndrome or symptom pattern. And it works. The problem is that by the time the system "sounds the alarm," driven by automated reports of cases from sentinel hospitals, it is already too late to do much containment. The gentleman from Vietnam, now dying in an isolation intensive-care bed, has already infected countless people in Hong Kong, on his two long airplane flights, at JFK Airport in New York, in his sister's family and her neighborhood in Queens, in the subway on the way to the hospital, in the waiting area and throughout the hospital. Any hopes that public health officials had for identifying, treating, and quarantining potential contacts are dashed, rendered totally unfeasible by the sheer number of people and places that a single patient has touched in the past two days. And he isn't the only carrier.

The pandemic has just begun and the carefully thought through "Plan A"—to catch it early before it spreads—is already a nonstarter.

By the next morning, emergency communications plans are up and working in New York, and there is a great deal of work to be done by emergency response personnel, public health officials, and medical workers. Samples of blood and sputum are already being processed to confirm the existence of the H5N1. The city begins to distribute stockpiled Tamiflu, the antiviral medication that people in contact with infected patients must receive daily. But supplies are limited, so great care has to be taken to determine who gets the medication. Since this is a treatment, not a vaccine, no immunity will be conferred upon the doctors and nurses taking the daily pills. As soon as they stop taking the medication, they become immediately susceptible to the flu.

Meanwhile, hospitals begin to implement emergency plans. Elective admissions are immediately canceled and every non-flu patient who could possibly survive without inpatient care is sent home. Isolation rooms and intensive-care units are readied for the onslaught. Within one week, the unimaginable is unfolding as New York and fifteen other U.S. cities see their hospitals filled to capacity with sick, contagious patients.

Three weeks into the pandemic, every isolation bed in the United States is occupied by a flu victim, and every intensive-care unit is filled. New units are being opened on hospital floors not effectively prepared for such sick patients and alternative sites, such as college dormitories and motels, are being fitted out as emergency medical facilities. The approximately 105,000 mechanical ventilators in the United States are all in use. When a patient expires, the machine is cleaned and the next critically ill victim in line gets a few more days of breathing support, hoping that will be enough time to get them through the worst.

Families of the sickest patients get a rude awakening to the realities of disaster triage. Contrary to what most of us are used to in normal times, dying patients are not first in line for anything. With ventilators in very short supply, they are used preferentially for patients deemed potentially salvageable. Tamiflu and Relenza, the two available antiviral medications for treating avian flu patients, are available in only the most limited quantities. Death rates are rising rapidly and disposal or storage of the bodies is becoming a major problem.

To complicate matters, it is discovered that the antiviral medications, like Tamiflu, have virtually no chance of working if given more than 12 hours into the disease. The 48-hour window of opportunity that had been assumed is not accurate. That means that the sickest patients in the hospital are not candidates for the drug, since most had some symptoms for at least one to three days prior to admission. Ideally, the antivirals should have been given to patients as soon as they began developing symptoms. This would have meant distributing the medication to thousands of physicians practicing in offices and clinics around the city. Now supplies are too limited to even consider such an idea.

Citizens are frantic. Before the outbreak, the city had not yet implemented its neighborhood-based public education plan to let people know what to expect if a pandemic were to begin. Once the disaster begins, messages are increasingly distressed and the public is at a high level of anxiety. The Health Department broadcasts reassurances in English, Spanish, and Chinese, but in twelve other key languages there are no messengers or messages that can penetrate many of New York's ethnic communities. Many of the poorest communities in the city confront additional challenges. Hospitals and clinics in those communities were severely overcrowded and stressed before the outbreak. Now they are essentially paralyzed. Hundreds of people every day are dying in their own homes, with emergency medical services often unable to respond; even when they do, no hospital beds are available.

In a particularly odd twist of fate, the long-festering problem of medically uninsured and underserved New Yorkers is making it more difficult to gain control of the pandemic via traditional public health strategies. Officials are exhorting the public to seek care as soon as they show signs of a flu-like syndrome. But for uninsured citizens who were experiencing only low-grade symptoms, like a mild cough or low fever, seeking medical care is not a viable option. Who would pay for the medical evaluation? Since that question was never answered—or even addressed—thousands of uninsured H5N1 carriers roam the city.

By the end of the fourth week, social order is seriously breaking down. Police and emergency management personnel are unable to quell growing unrest that begins in the poorest neighborhoods and spreads as rapidly as the pandemic. Many African American and Hispanic leaders are outraged that their communities are being denied services and are last in line for whatever is available. Low- and middle-income families are clamoring for more assistance since the government has asked for voluntary workplace closures and a sharp reduction in the use of public transportation. These measures may have been appropriate public health strategies in an attempt to reduce spread of the virus, but they are devastating the economy, with serious consequences for both businesses and hundreds of thousands of New Yorkers.

Availability of food and prescription drugs is limited, as well. State and federal officials, in an effort to limit the disease's spread, sharply reduce interstate commerce and travel. These measures and their consequences add to the sense of societal collapse and dread. The situation for New York City is desperate and getting worse by the day. No more mechanical ventilators are even in the pipeline. Supplies and other materials also dry up. Appropriate respiratory masks, IV fluids and tubing, and other essential "disposables" are no more. Causing particular anguish are irresolvable problems with respect to the care of children. The youngest, most vulnerable children are getting sick more rapidly than everyone else, but facilities to care for these patients are by far the most limited. Pediatric intensive-care beds, appropriately trained health professionals, and relevant supplies are all in desperately short supply.

For almost any public health measure ordered by the city, there are unanticipated consequences. When schools and day-care facilities are closed for six weeks—again to reduce the spread of the virus—the city's vital systems virtually shut down. Thousands and thousands of nurses, hospital aides, police officers, and public transportation workers have to stay home to care for their kids. The hospitals are already experiencing a terrible labor shortage. Many employees refuse to come to work because of concerns for their own safety or the well-being of family members. And many people who have the wherewithal actually flee the city altogether.

New Yorkers have some other surprises in store. Although the awful response to the flooding of New Orleans is fresh enough in everyone's minds, citizens have the general sense that when a major emergency occurs, two things will happen: (1) government will "know what to do," and (2) help will arrive from "somewhere else." Neither happens. Government—at all levels—seems increasingly powerless. As for outside help, it's not coming. Every community has its own crisis. Every city and town is struggling to gain control over a virus that is spreading like a global wildfire. And the death toll is simply unimaginable.

For the entire six months of the H5N1 pandemic, which occurs in three separate waves, each with its own peak, the news seems to be getting worse every week. The pandemic is killing many children every day in New York City, across all social and economic strata. No one is spared. The early reports of avian flu, when it was still transmitted only from poultry to humans, showed a significant impact on young people. And the 1918 Spanish flu had an inexplicable mortality peak among healthy young adults between the ages of fifteen and thirty.

As for the people sick or injured for reasons other than the pandemic, they get lost in the shuffle. Every day, in the normal course of life, thousands of people need care for heart attacks, asthma, appendicitis, motor vehicle accidents, accidental poisonings, and for many other reasons. With hospitals shut down, medical staff in short supply, and emergency personnel stressed to the limit, the fatality rates for "regular" medical conditions skyrocket to rates not seen in this country since the days before antibiotics.

By the time H5N1 has its way with New York City, burning itself out over time as the experts predicted it eventually would do, the country and the world are forever changed, humbled by a force of nature that dwarfs any category 5 hurricane and rivals the impact of the worst imaginable war. The final toll for New York City:

Nearly 2,430,000 New Yorkers, or approximately 30 percent, contract a flu syndrome caused by the H5N1 virus. Of these individuals, 194,000 require—or would potentially benefit from—hospitalization. With a barely 2 percent mortality rate among people who contract the virus, just under 50,000 New Yorkers die of the flu. About 13,600 of these victims are children. During the crisis, nearly 280 people, including the 75 children, die every single day in the city from avian flu.

In addition, 15,000 "excess" deaths occur from causes other than H5N1, but are directly related to a breakdown and/or paralysis of the health-care system during the peak pandemic months. In week 2, the governor orders National Guard troops to enforce the "cordon sanitaire" (local area blockade) the mayor has imposed in Brooklyn, after a rampaging H5N1 outbreak is identified in a 12-square-block neighborhood. After intense rioting, and the deaths of 22 upstate Guardsmen and 620 citizens, the troops refuse to remain on duty. The mayor rejects a call for martial law over the objections of the president. This so-called "Brooklyn Massacre" becomes the first of a series of panic-induced riots that eventually claim the lives of more than 1,500 more New Yorkers.

Finally, to make matters even worse, the economy of New York, like that of the nation and the rest of the world, suffers an enormous blow, the effects of which will be felt for years to come. Eventually the city recovers, but the loss of life leaves wounds almost too difficult to bear.

We have assumed here an infection rate of 30 percent and a mortality rate for flu-related deaths alone of just 2 percent, both of which are fairly conservative estimates in disaster planning and preparedness circles. And for every element of the scenario that a legislator or business leader might dismiss as "fear-mongering," an equally plausible element could be added to this frightening situation—workers who don't show up to repair a water main break, leaving parts of the city without water for days, shortages of all kinds, and so on.

This scenario is an altogether plausible vision of what could happen if a major pandemic flu were to occur under current conditions. But much could change that picture, if we develop or implement strategies that can substantially improve the outcome of a global pandemic. In fact, we may find that when the H5N1 does mutate or "reassort" in a way that allows it to be easily transmitted among people, it dramatically loses its punch. It could become so weakened that it behaves like a typical influenza that the world experiences every year.

It is true that the current H5N1, which is now infecting humans only by contact with sick poultry or birds, carries an extraordinarily high mortality rate of more than 50 percent. When a similar virus responsible for the Spanish flu of 1918 crossed the barrier and became a human-to-human strain, the fatality rate was "only" between 1.5 and 3 percent, depending upon the age group. Even at these low fatality rates, the toll was enormous because so many people were infected. So, other than hoping for a lucky break, some chance of "dodging the biological bullet" or wishful thinking that the virus will lose its virulence when it changes its transmissibility characteristics, there are things that can—and should—be done.

That said, here is an "avian flu to-do list" of actions that could dramatically change the scenario as laid out above.

- **The international community must develop reliable working plans to detect and rapidly contain early outbreaks of a potential pandemic.** Though this step alone could theoretically stave off the possibility of a worldwide pandemic, it is not likely that it will happen. Many of the countries most likely to host the initial outbreak are resource-poor—some extremely so. Their capacity to identify, confirm, and contain rapidly is currently very limited. The World Health Organization (WHO) must be the lead organization steering an unprecedented level of cooperation among developing and developed countries. WHO needs to make sure that every country understands what it needs to do and what the internationally accepted standards of early detection, containment, and notification are so that the world can respond effectively. Developing countries will require people, laboratory capacity, and stocks of Tamiflu, much of which will have to come from warehouses in the developed countries. The developed countries have to make a serious commitment to step up to the plate when called. WHO is in the driver's seat: if it does not provide leadership for a collective global health plan and response, no one will.

- **A rapid, innovative technology and accelerated manufacturing process should be developed to permit massive quantities of appropriate vaccines to be available when needed.** The problem is not the lack of a vaccine, but rather producing an adequate supply and then publicly distributing it. New means of producing vaccines and accelerating the manufacturing process are in the works, and it is not unreasonable to anticipate that a new, highly effective system will be in place before the end of the decade.

Once a safe, effective vaccine is widely available, the expected death rates from any pandemic will drop precipitously. The grim scenario depicted for New York would be reduced to a manageable level. The federal government, through the National Institutes of Health, is deeply involved on the scientific side to encourage companies and researchers to develop the new technology. Manufacturers, however, are concerned about investing in vaccine or drug development without liability protection or sufficient confidence in the ability to recoup research investment. While the government has been good so far in stepping up scientifically to promote research, it has to approach the economic and medical-legal challenges with the same fervor. Congress passed the BioShield Act in 2004 to address some of these issues, and a new version is pending in Congress now. But the vaccine companies are clearly skeptical about BioShield, and this is still very much an unsolved problem.

- **The world's capacity to develop and produce antiviral medications should be enhanced.** The fact that we currently have only a single manufacturer of Tamiflu, the major antiviral currently available, is fixable. Roche, a Swiss company, has recently agreed to license the manufacture of Tamiflu to international partners. Even so, more research and innovation will need to be supported to ensure an adequate global supply. This could happen in two to three years, at which point cities like New York could be able to stockpile enough Tamiflu to provide for hospital and other essential workers, first responders, and patients at every phase of the disease.

- **Local health and hospital systems need enough guidance, leadership, and financial support to respond effectively to a new outbreak of infectious disease.** Many hospitals throughout the U.S. have been operating at razor-thin margins for more than a decade. A variety of economic and social pressures, including treating a great number of poor and uninsured citizens for free under charity care obligations, have put these institutions on the edge, making any thought of expanding capacity to accommodate the needs of a major pandemic virtually impossible. If resources could be found to stabilize hospitals' general financial situation, their ability to develop workable plans for expanding their capacity to provide emergency care for infected and sick patients could be vastly improved. The plan would include expanded diagnostic laboratory capacity, as well as much-enhanced outpatient and clinic systems of front-line care. With real upgrades in the non-hospital portions of the system, we'd stand a better chance of keeping mildly and moderately sick people out of the hospital. The ability to save hospital beds for only the sickest patients, while expanding the capacity of non-hospital parts of the health-care system, could save thousands of lives in a real-world pandemic or other large-scale crisis.

- **The general public needs to understand its own critical role in the face of a pandemic: it's not just about what government can do.** There's not much that average citizens can do about the vaccine or antiviral supply (although advocacy with elected officials certainly wouldn't hurt), but they can play a major role in their neighborhoods and communities, where individuals can support one another. The community can organize ways of bringing food and medical supplies to people in homes where residents are ill or incapacitated. Learning what can be done to prevent the spread of disease, including avoiding close proximity with other people, proper use of face masks, and understanding basic principles of hygiene, are important steps. Finally, if hospitals are overwhelmed, patients who would ordinarily require hospitalization will need to be cared for at home. Programs to train citizens in new skills, working with existing home-care providers, and reducing dependency on traditional facilities will be essential.

- **Understanding and addressing key social and community issues before the disaster is essential.** This idea has received scant attention, so far, from public officials, but it could not be more important. All major disasters carry the potential for social discontent or disorder. One of the problems so painfully evident in the events following Hurricane Katrina and the flooding of New Orleans was the degree to which political leaders and other public officials seemed to misunderstand their own local population. For instance, people were told to voluntarily evacuate who had no cars or the money for other means of transportation. In many cities, ethnic diversity requires that the messages and messengers during a crisis should be consistent with the issues and culture specific to the neighborhoods and communities of the city.

- **Ensuring equitable access to the health-care system will make a difference in the overall ability to respond effectively in a pandemic.** There are many reasons to make sure that health care is truly available to every citizen, but in a disaster like pandemic flu, every person who is locked out of the system—for whatever reason—poses a threat to the general population. We have to find a way to fix this problem *before* the next pandemic, because persistent, underlying issues of poverty and lack of access to health care all put us at greater risk as a nation.

If some of these ideas are implemented before H5N1 or one of its lethal cousins becomes a pandemic, the New York pandemic scenario could have a far different outcome. Perhaps we would not yet have enough vaccine to prevent much of the illness, but we would have a good supply of effective antiviral medication and a much more robust health and hospital system. And let's say we had an informed and engaged public and we had taken steps to help ensure that most our essential workers reported for duty.

Here's how the scenario could have played out: Instead of 2.4 million infected, with enough vaccine, we may have only 1.5 million cases of avian flu. With an improved health and hospital system and widespread availability of effective and safe antivirals, we could see the fatality rate fall to no more than 0.5 percent from the 2 percent originally estimated. The total death toll might be no higher than 7,500. That's still a significant number, but far less than the 50,000 or more in the more serious scenario. In addition, we might reasonably suggest that social disorder would be minimal and the number of people dying in riots down to almost zero. And, instead of some 13,000 deaths from non-H5N1 causes, a more robust and effective hospital- and community-based health system could mean that the majority of these people might well survive both H5N1 and the other threats to life during a raging pandemic.

3 · Natural Megadisasters: Not Just Business as Usual

Most Americans know they can expect some seasonal extreme weather: hurricanes, tornados, and floods from melting snow or unusually heavy rains. Though these powerful events can cause significant destruction and loss of life, local emergency officials have become skilled at responding competently and communities can usually rebuild unless, as with Hurricane Katrina, the disaster overwhelms local and regional response capacity. These are the megadisasters for which the nation remains unprepared.

America is particularly vulnerable to natural disasters along its coasts: in the Northeast, where nor'easters can cause major flooding and coastal erosion; in the Southeast, where hurricanes and flooding may utterly destroy highly developed, low-lying coastal communities; and on the West Coast, where volcanoes and tectonic shifts can trigger earthquakes that can cause severe damage in a populated area. And a massive underwater landslide in the Canary Islands could produce a tidal wave powerful enough to cause significant damage to the East Coast.

Even these generally understood natural-disaster vulnerabilities specific to particular regions may have surprising variants. The Northeast, for instance, has subsurface fault lines that some think pose a real risk of serious earthquakes affecting the New York metropolitan area. However, the New York City Office of Emergency Management apparently considers massive flooding of lower Manhattan brought about by a major hurricane to be the most likely potential natural disaster. The consequences of such an event for residents and workers, for transportation and the economy, would be enormous. In making plans to be prepared for such an event, the city needs to consider how to shelter as many as 750,000 New Yorkers who would require evacuation from low-lying areas.

Global warming also plays a part. Recently published reports from climate scientists confirm the steady, although slight, increase of temperatures both on land and at sea. Two important studies published in 2005 suggest new evidence that increasing sea surface temperatures of about half a degree Celsius may, in fact, be contributing to increased severity of tropical storms and hurricanes. This rise in temperature is not only showing up in the Atlantic basin, which affects the U.S. hurricane season, but in basins around the globe. The data powerfully suggest a critical link between such human behavior as the destruction of vital ecosystems and the failure to control carbon emissions from burning of fossil fuels, and global warming. The increased sea surface temperatures in turn lead to increasingly severe climate-related disasters.

Changing behavior and implementing environmentally appropriate policies can diminish or prevent further global warming. We should not see ourselves as passive victims of natural events. Still, whether the climate changes are permanent or not and regardless of their explanation, "megastorms" are likely to be part of our reality for the foreseeable future. And so we need to shore up our capacity to plan for and respond to large-scale catastrophes.

Anatomy of a Natural Disaster: The Unstable Earth

The huge tectonic plates that make up the Earth's crust or surface continually move and shift. Earthquakes occur when these plates collide, spread apart, or grind against each other at the faults along their boundaries. When stresses along those fault lines surpass the strength of the surrounding rock, the fault ruptures, releasing energy in waves that shake and radiate from the source of the quake. The point where an earthquake starts is called the focus, or hypocenter, and it may be located many kilometers deep within the Earth. The epicenter of an earthquake is the point at the surface directly above the focus.

The western U.S. sits along the so-called Ring of Fire, a 25,000-mile band of potential seismic activity that begins on the west coasts of South and Central America and stretches up the west coast of North America through the Aleutian Islands on to Japan, China, the Philippines, Indonesia, and Australasia. More than 75 percent of the world's earthquake activity takes place in this region. Another 15 percent occurs where the Eurasian, Indian, and African plates are colliding, forming a band of seismic activity that stretches from Burma, westward to the Himalayas, to the Caucasus, and the Mediterranean Sea.

The U.S. Geological Survey notes that earthquakes pose a real threat to more than 75 million Americans in thirty-nine states, and that repeats of the 1906 San Francisco earthquake or the 1811–1812 earthquakes in New Madrid, Missouri, could cause as much as $500 billion in damages. Many cities around the country could face significant seismic activity; the agency lists twenty-six such areas, on both coasts and in the middle of the country. John Mutter, associate director of the Earth Institute at Columbia University, points out that communities in the West are better prepared than those in the East for such disasters, where very little of the infrastructure has been built to withstand earthquakes.

The Earth Institute, in cooperation with the World Bank, published a landmark study in 2005, *Global Disaster Hotspots*. Although the United States ranks low on the relative risk charts for multiple hazards, Hurricane Katrina painfully underscored the fact that natural megadisasters still have the potential to cause severe economic and social dislocation here, as in other developed countries.

·   ·   ·

San Francisco just marked the 100th anniversary of the deadly 1906 earthquake, which killed thousands of people and destroyed huge tracts of the urban "built environment." But San Francisco is not the only West Coast city that lives in dread of another major quake. I asked Tom Paulson, a well-respected science reporter for the *Seattle Post-Intelligencer,* to help describe a possible scenario and provide the context for a massive earthquake well north of the Bay Area— the "Big One" coming to greater Seattle, Washington.

Earthquake in Seattle and Puget Sound

The Seattle metropolitan area and the surrounding Puget Sound region seldom have to deal with anything close to a megadisaster, though the Northwest's long stretches of cold, wet weather may test a person's mettle.

Still, as a community that tends to respond to two inches of wet snow with storm warnings on television and widespread school closures, Seattle arguably has a low threshold for declaring crisis. Fortunate in its generally moderate climate and relatively few recurring natural hazards like hurricanes or blizzards, the region's primary plague used to be its economic booms and busts. Even these have diminished. By 2001, when Boeing moved its headquarters to Chicago, the region already had built a more diverse business core around Microsoft, Amazon.com, and Starbucks. Seattle is a largely affluent and progressive city that prides itself on being a model modern municipality. It is an easy, if increasingly expensive, place to live.

The only recent event widely regarded as a serious wake-up call came on the morning of February 28, 2001, just months before Seattle learned that Boeing was moving to Chicago. A magnitude 6.8 earthquake rattled the Puget Sound region, causing nearly $4 billion in damage and one death (from a heart attack). It was dubbed the Nisqually Quake because the epicenter was thirty miles deep beneath the Nisqually River Delta, a sparsely populated area located about thirty-five miles southwest of Seattle and ten miles northeast of the state capital, Olympia. The region was given federal disaster status.

The Nisqually Quake wasn't really much of a disaster, especially when considered in light of the much larger earthquakes expected to strike this region. But it should have sounded an alarm. Instead, it may have instilled in many residents a false sense of confidence—a belief that "the big one" simply will require riding out a bit more shaking and damage. In fact, it could be the difference between riding a bucking bronco and a bucking brontosaurus.

The quake hazard of the Pacific Northwest is complex. In the 1990s, scientists found evidence that shows convincingly that the region is at risk for three kinds of quakes: deep quakes like the Nisqually event; large, upper-plate, or shallow, earthquakes spanning the Puget Sound region; and the more violent subduction-fault quakes such as the one in Sumatra that triggered the 2004 Indian Ocean tsunami.

The Cascadia Subduction Zone is a 700-mile-long offshore fault that stretches from Vancouver Island to Northern California. For many years, experts thought it was slipping without causing earthquakes. But geological studies combined with a review of historical Japanese accounts revealed that the Cascadia Subduction Zone had spawned a "mega-thrust" quake of magnitude 9 and a Pacific Ocean tsunami that hit Japan on January 26, 1700. Further studies indicate that such quakes have taken place every 400 to 600 years, on average.

Since scientists made this discovery, other scholars have interpreted several stories of Native American tribes that describe the 1700 tsunami—in one myth, as a battle between a whale and a thunderbird—telling of massive waves, destroyed villages, and even canoes flung into trees.

Of considerable concern is the shallow Seattle Fault. Now the most studied in the region, it is actually a series of shallow geologic faults that run east-west for some 30 miles from near Bremerton, under Puget Sound, and through downtown Seattle, continuing eastward along Interstate 90 toward the Cascade Mountains.

Though not capable of releasing as much total energy as a Cascadian quake, a large quake on the Seattle Fault could be much more damaging to the city it is named after because the fault is shallower and closer to where the city is built. Bainbridge Island's Restoration Point is a cliff that scientists say was created from a twenty-foot uplift caused by a similar quake 1,100 years ago. West Seattle's Alki Beach has its own thirteen-foot section of uplifted ground from the same quake.

The recurrence rate of earthquakes on the Seattle Fault is unknown. Experts have since discovered at least five other such shallow faults in the Puget Sound region and likewise given them names for the cities they threaten—such as the Tacoma or Olympia fault. By some estimates, the region can expect to experience a major quake on one of these shallow faults about every three hundred years or so. The earthquake by itself is not what poses a hazard. It is the buildings, bridges, natural-gas lines, water systems, health-care systems, and broad socioeconomic interdependency making up modern urban living that present the potential for megadisaster.

For Seattle, a major earthquake is not a question of if, but when. "Geology is inevitable. The problem is how we translate geologic inevitability into the timescale of human decision-making," notes Art Lerner-Lam, one of the Global Hotspots' principal investigators.

Elected officials and emergency management experts like to point to what has been accomplished since the region began to come to grips with its more extensive seismic risk. New construction must meet building codes aimed at protecting inhabitants during a major quake. Project Impact, which was initiated by the federal government in 1998 with a $1 million grant from FEMA but subsequently sustained by the Seattle city government when the Bush administration defunded it, has educated the community about disaster preparedness and helped many homeowners improve the safety of their residences. Scientists, engineers, and emergency managers meet continually to share knowledge. Fault areas are currently monitored, but at nowhere near the levels that would provide adequate information for preparedness.

The threat of a major quake is too overwhelming, too complex, and could come from any direction. For example, in spite of the codes, new buildings are constructed to withstand a shallow fault quake—a California-style quake of violent shaking over a short period. A subduction quake, however, will last much longer and, according to some experts, might cause more damage to the newer high-rise buildings that have been engineered to move with the quake.

The city of Seattle has encouraged increased residential density and multi-unit living spaces like condos, in order to counter urban sprawl. Yet the city has also failed so far to follow through on repeated admonitions from experts to require retrofitting and reinforcement of existing structures and infrastructure that could save lives in a major quake.

The Seattle Fault is just one of the region's seismic hazards, but, because of the population and businesses located near it, it poses the greatest threat to life and property. Understanding what could happen in Seattle during and after a major quake should help illustrate what needs to be done throughout the Northwest to prepare for the region's own version of Katrina.

The autumn sun is shining through broken clouds, and several bundled-up patrons of a small café in Seattle's historic Pioneer Square sip morning coffee outside at the sidewalk tables. It's mid-November, and it's been raining hard for the last few weeks. This "sun break" is a welcome respite that has brought many people outside determined to take in a rare bit of heat and light.

A Seattle man, David Isaacs, and his companion, Judith Goren, who has recently moved from California, notice it first. The ground is shaking. Both have experienced earthquakes before and they leap up, David knocking his metal chair over with a loud clang, to quickly move away from the old brick building.

Suddenly, both are knocked to the ground as the sidewalk beneath them seems to explode, heaving up violently some six feet. Behind them the brick storefront crumbles like the collapsing seaside edge of a glacier, smashing and partially burying the other patrons, who had failed to recognize what was happening. Nobody even has time to scream.

The violent shaking continues, accompanied by the shrieking sound of twisting metal, breaking glass, and the dull thuds of collapsing structures. Everyone outside who survives the initial jolt is on the ground, holding on as if riding an angry whale. Water shoots out of a crack that has opened in the street just as a natural-gas line ignites and a nearby restaurant bursts into flames.

The couple remain splayed out on the heaving sidewalk. Then the quake stops just as suddenly as it had started.

It has lasted less than a minute, but Pioneer Square now looks like a war zone. Piles of brick and building material litter the square beneath gaping holes in buildings. The explosive sounds of physical destruction have largely ceased, replaced by the absurdity of car alarms chirping and wailing. And the fires caused by ruptured gas lines are already visible in every direction, shooting flames forty and fifty feet into the air.

A magnitude 7.3 quake has rearranged Seattle's urban landscape. Streets are an assemblage of cracks, with shattered concrete pieces standing on end next to thrust-up wedges of land. The reverberations have pulled down the exterior walls of many older, multistory masonry buildings to reveal the interiors as if they were giant dollhouses subjected to a toddler's tantrum. Dead and injured residents are everywhere.

Isaacs and Goren, like other survivors, pick themselves up to assess what has happened. A quick glance to the west, toward Puget Sound's Elliott Bay, somehow looks more open, brighter. They quickly realize that one of the city's main thoroughfares, an elevated concrete highway known as the Alaskan Way Viaduct, is gone. Most of those driving south on the lower deck of the viaduct just minutes before have certainly been crushed by the upper deck's collapse. The devastation is stunning.

Over the past decade or so, Seattle and Puget Sound residents have been educated, or at least admonished repeatedly, to prepare themselves for a massive quake. In the mid-1990s, scientists proved to skeptics that the region is at high risk from several previously unrecognized seismic threats. The ground is still, but from Elliott Bay there comes the sound of something like thunder or a freight train. Few had paid much heed to the additional warning that a major earthquake on the Seattle Fault could also produce a localized tsunami perhaps just as destructive—at least within the region—as the 2004 tsunami that hit distant Thailand.

As Isaacs, Goren, and other survivors stand to survey the wreckage of Pioneer Square, perhaps trying to remember what they were told in those workplace disaster drills, a wall of water gushes into the square carrying huge spiky piles of debris, cars, boats, and even a trolley car.

The quake has, as some experts predicted, spawned a fifteen-foot-high tsunami that hits the Seattle waterfront at high tide. Puget Sound is very deep and the heaving seafloor produces a huge pulse of water that comes hurtling to shore at 50 miles per hour. The pedestrians lucky enough to have survived the quake in Pioneer Square are now struggling to avoid its deadly cousin.

Stunned and unable to speak, Isaacs and Goren instinctively run up the hill from First Avenue to Second Avenue. Once on land, a tsunami often slows quickly. Luckily, they only need to gain a few feet of elevation to avoid the turbulent flood of debris that comes sweeping into the square. They watch with others from a fractured perch of broken concrete on the hillside, dazed, not fully able to comprehend what is happening.

Behind them, an office building is in flames and its fire threatens to spread. Below, an angry Puget Sound has surged up on land, bringing more destruction to this already devastated landscape. The water is black and oily, full of garbage and smelling of gasoline.

Watching, the survivors begin trying their cell phones and talking with each other: Where are the police and the firefighters? How can I contact my family or get home? How can we help the injured? What do we do now? The destruction is almost incomprehensible. And this is just one section of the city.

Before this quake, in 2005, experts tried to give the community a comprehensive sense of what kind of damage "the big one" would cause. The Washington Emergency Management Division and the Earthquake Engineering Research Institute in Oakland, California, sponsored an analysis of a major Seattle Fault quake. The experts predicted that such an event would—

- Kill 1,600 and injure 24,000 people.
- Overwhelm the health-care system, leaving most of the injured to care for themselves.
- Destroy 9,700 buildings and render 29,000 other structures totally uninhabitable.
- Close nearly all major highways for weeks or months.
- Cause at least $33 billion in property damage and economic losses.
- Leave 45,000 people homeless and many tens of thousands of others without water, power, or other utilities for weeks or months.

Dire statistics. Yet even these estimates were based on a fairly conservative projection of damage that might he caused by a Seattle Fault earthquake. Organizers of the 2005 project based their scenario on a magnitude 6.7 quake, which, despite the slight numerical difference, is much less severe than the magnitude 7.3 quake that experts knew could hit this region.

Quake magnitude measurements are logarithmic, meaning that a magnitude 7.3 quake is much bigger—something like 20 times greater, in terms of energy release—than one of magnitude 6.7. Why didn't they prepare for the biggest possible event? At the time, officials had said that they didn't want to present the worst-case scenario. They preferred to base their estimates on a "most probable" rather than "worst possible" Seattle Fault event, even though Katrina tells us we have to take the worst possible situation into account.

Privately, several scientists acknowledged that another reason for basing the Seattle Fault exercise on a less severe quake was that few wanted to factor in the additional threat of a tsunami. It would have been just too complicated, too overwhelming to address in the exercise, one of the authors of the report acknowledged. They also left out of the equation the aftershocks and the complications caused by fires. But now the worst-case scenario had come to pass. And, as the world would eventually discover, the death toll was much higher than that estimated in last year's projection.

Above the overwhelmed survivors huddled between fire and water near Pioneer Square, a television news helicopter hovers in the sky. The pilot had been reporting morning rush-hour traffic conditions on Interstate 5, the area's main north-south transportation route, when the quake hit the city.

A former military pilot, he has flown in disastrous situations before. But this is no foreign combat zone. This is the surreal transformation of the city he calls home. At the moment he has no radio communication with his TV station. He has no independent confirmation of what he is seeing or any way to contact officials with information.

When the quake struck, it didn't register at first. Traffic had been stalled on the interstate so there was no sudden halt in the flow as the roads began to heave and sway. The first indication that something was amiss came when many drivers began abandoning their cars.

From up in the air, the pilot first saw cracks appear in the pavement as the columns holding up elevated stretches of the roadway shifted or collapsed. He saw power and telephone lines shaking and snapping and clouds of dust or smoke billowing up from the industrial district to the south. A few of the older masonry buildings below him had collapsed.

Some of the newer high-rise buildings to the north, in the downtown business district, had swayed back and forth during the quake. Constructed to "go with the flow" in such an event, the modern structures appeared to have ridden it out. But the air above the business district had glittered briefly as the buildings' windows shattered and sent fragments of glass raining down on to the streets below.

The pilot hadn't seen the tsunami coming until it was washing some fifty feet into Pioneer Square. Now, however, he can see to the south that the wave was high enough to overrun all of Harbor Island, a low-lying industrial area serving the Port of Seattle. Red and blue cargo containers once stacked high are now strewn about the flats and floating in the Duwamish River amid overturned boats and other debris. One of the huge orange cranes used to move the containers has toppled over onto a ship. The land has turned to Jell-O, the port structures submerged in extensive liquefaction, like quicksand.

Fires are now burning all over the city, some of them growing rapidly. The pilot tries the radio again and listens to some of the hectic emergency communications, but can't raise a response. He decides to continue reporting into his radio what he sees anyway, in case somebody can hear him.

Much of Pioneer Square below him, the pilot reports into the unresponsive radio, appears to be rubble. Some of the reinforced buildings are still partially standing but most of the area's older brick buildings have been destroyed. Dozens of bodies, either dead or injured, are visible from the air in areas further inland. In its retreat, the tsunami appears to have swept other victims into Puget Sound.

The Alaskan Way Viaduct is down for most of its length along the waterfront, the pilot reports. Portions of the seawall have collapsed and many waterfront shops and restaurants have tumbled into the water. He then pulls his helicopter up and around to take a survey of the city as a whole.

As a traffic reporter, the pilot knows how dependent Seattle is on its bridges and a handful of major transportation routes. With Puget Sound to the west, Lake Washington to the east, and the ship canal to the north, access to the city from every direction except south depends entirely on bridges.

As the pilot flies north above downtown Seattle, he sees that even in parts of the city where the buildings withstood the quake there are piles of rubble and dead bodies. He notices a deadly pattern. Parapets, those short decorative walls on the roofs of many older flat-topped office buildings, have crumbled and fallen to the sidewalks below, with pedestrians apparently becoming the unwitting targets of the toppled walls.

Few traffic lights are working and only an occasional police car or fire truck can be seen on the streets, slowly negotiating the debris. It's difficult for the pilot to imagine what they can do. Dazed survivors are starting to fill the streets.

The pilot pulls the helicopter up higher to face northeast. Now he can see the massive bridge supporting a stretch of Interstate 5 hundreds of feet above Lake Union. It appears to be standing, the pilot notes from a distance, but something about it doesn't look quite right.

Below the helicopter now is Harborview Medical Center, the region's only trauma center, which was built in the 1930s. Despite its location on a steep hill on the northern edge of the Seattle fault zone, most of the hospital's newly retrofitted buildings appear largely intact. He decides to make an emergency landing on the hospital helipad to see if he can get more information and provide assistance.

Inside he finds only more chaos. The supervising nurse in the emergency room can't even begin to respond to the calls now coming in from paramedics in the field. The hospital's emergency diesel generators kicked in when the power failed, but many instruments and other life-sustaining medical equipment suffered damage from falling over or being struck by debris.

As the nurses and doctors scramble to stabilize their fragile patients, a ceiling water sprinkler system in one of the supply rooms goes off. Technicians rush in to save as many of the medical supplies as they can, stacking them in a pile on a table in the employee lounge.

Dozens of injured people have already started showing up at the hospital asking for assistance. The ER doctor, recognizing that his staff is already overwhelmed, asks the supervising nurse to hastily begin triaging the walk-ins—making everyone who is not at immediate risk of death sit down and wait.

One mother carrying a small, wailing child with two smashed legs screams at the nurse when told she must wait. She is escorted out of the ER to join the rapidly swelling crowd of people filling the hospital parking lot who must, for now, deal with their own bleeding wounds and broken bones. The hospital staff also quietly agrees on where to put those who are beyond help, establishing a "moribund area" in an out-of-sight location.

The same scene is being played out at many of the other area hospitals that remain at least somewhat functional. Most of the hospitals are tall structures. Since the elevators aren't working, there is no way to evacuate patients. Staff must cope with what they have on each damaged, isolated wing. For those who still have working telephones or data lines, a dedicated computerized system identifying each hospital's functional status provides the basic information that will be needed to coordinate the region's emergency health-care response. Once each hospital gets its house in order, they will coordinate care among institutions by ham radios, if necessary.

Public health officials, well aware that the health-care system cannot possibly look after the tens of thousands of injured, are already in emergency radio discussions with the National Guard to begin establishing field hospitals in Seattle. They have also contacted the National Disaster Medical System, a branch of FEMA, asking for C-141 flights to bring in emergency medical teams and supplies to staff the field hospitals.

Boeing Field, in south Seattle, is too damaged to allow the large cargo planes to land but there are functioning runways ten miles away at SeaTac International Airport. Given the road and bridge damage, transport from SeaTac to downtown Seattle will have to be handled by military helicopters. Navy installations around Puget Sound have also sustained damage.

According to protocol, in the event of a large-scale quake, emergency operations centers located throughout the region have been automatically activated, but officials are unable to reach the centers immediately to begin coordinating the overall response.

The Seattle Fire Department is likewise overwhelmed. Amid the hundreds of reports coming in about fires and hazardous material spills, firefighters are reporting serious damage to some of their stations. Many fire trucks and ambulances cannot move due to widespread road damage and bridges that have either collapsed or are too damaged for safe travel.

Power and water supplies are out all over the city. Substations have been knocked out. Water tanks have fallen or burst. Some of the region's major power and water supply lines carried on those bridges have partially or completely collapsed.

As night falls, many Seattle residents find themselves on their own. Those living in wood frame houses at some distance from the fault zone may still have shelter. But many do not have power or water. The police and the fire departments cannot respond even if residents are still able to call on the telephone for help.

People remain isolated for days. It's still not even clear just how much damage the region has suffered. Aftershocks continue to rattle the city, some of them big enough to again bring down more buildings and kill more people. The cold winter rain returns. Many residents take to burning debris to stave off hypothermia.

Emergency management officials devote most of their efforts to establishing the field hospitals to care for the injured, organizing temporary shelters, and repairing streets for the emergency response vehicles. Slowly, power and water are restored to some areas. After a call from the governor, the president declares the region a federal disaster area and mobilizes high level FEMA and military support to free trapped people, dispose of bodies, and perform other critical functions.

One week into the disaster, officials have a pretty good handle on what has happened to the region. Not only has the quake devastated downtown and south Seattle, the fault has erupted as well in cities to the east such as Bellevue, Mercer Island, and Issaquah, wreaking similar havoc.

What was once an expensive housing development on a steep eastern shoreline of Lake Washington is now simply a huge brown gash. A massive landslide carried the entire hillside, houses, tall fir trees, and all, into the lake.

The Highway 520 bridge that transports Seattle commuters across the lake to their jobs at Microsoft and other Redmond businesses has been severed. The quake generated a tsunami in the lake as well, producing a wave that permanently damaged a few of the bridge's midsections.

Sadly, many of the schools in the region had not yet been retrofitted to meet current earthquake standards. Hundreds of students were killed by collapsing school buildings and many thousands more now have no place to go to school, even if that were feasible.

Two weeks after the quake, many of the region's roads and bridges remain impassable. Somehow, though, a mass migration of Seattle residents is under way, with families picking up and leaving the area for nearby communities that are not fully equipped to handle the stream of newcomers. Military helicopters bring in equipment and supplies. The Port of Seattle is unusable, so most ships cannot unload. Businesses that had been using the "just-in-time" inventory system have had to close, even if they had physically survived the quake.

One month after the quake, some less-damaged bridges in the region have been repaired, allowing traffic to move. But transportation remains sluggish at best and is often simply a massive snarl. It can take eight hours to drive twelve miles. It's clear that this will remain a problem for at least a year, likely costing the region tens or hundreds of billions of dollars in economic losses.

The Seattle waterfront, formerly one of the city's tourist attractions, remains a debris zone. Demolition crews continue to remove the massive fragments from the collapsed elevated highway as the state Department of Ecology deals with a variety of projects to clean up hazardous material.

A year after the quake, Seattle and the region have not fully recovered. The port is still largely not functional. Many businesses have permanently lost accounts and customers because of the disruption.

The buildings in Pioneer Square are mostly gone, either due to the direct hit by the quake or from being torn down later after being judged inhabitable. Surprisingly, few had earthquake insurance and so rebuilding has stalled as property owners seek government assistance. In the end, the great Seattle Quake has killed more than 30,000 people.

David Isaacs and Judith Goren survived the extraordinary catastrophe, witnessing firsthand the destruction of a city and the death and maiming of countless innocent people. They made it to one of the intact hospitals and worked as volunteers for nearly a week after the disaster. Eventually, Judith returned to California. David tried to return to work—he was a lawyer in a busy downtown practice. Within six months, however, he was profoundly depressed. He was diagnosed with post-traumatic stress disorder and unable to work.

This scenario depicting some of the consequences of a major quake on the Seattle Fault may be difficult to fathom, but it is based on the predictions made in several analyses by more than a hundred experts in seismology, geology, tsunami hazards, engineering, emergency management, computer modeling, land-use planning, and other fields. Some may dispute particular details of this fictionalized account. Still, it is just a snapshot—and almost certainly an understatement of the total devastation the region could suffer from a major earthquake.

The fact that the region has not experienced a major quake in its brief settled history tends to deepen complacency. Just as it has taken years for the public and many elected officials to accept some of the basic scientific findings of climate change, so has it been slow for many in the Northwest to accept that the fact that they live on top of one of the planet's largest tectonic time bombs. Officials likewise have been slow to adopt some of the basic measures many experts say are necessary to improve our defense against this threat.

A major quake on the Seattle Fault could well be the worst natural disaster in U.S. history. As scientific evidence of quake risks has rapidly piled up over the past few decades, it is increasingly urgent that the Northwest aggressively pursue ways to minimize risk. There has been some progress in that direction already. In 1998, Seattle's celebrated public-private partnership, Project Impact, began to educate homeowners, landlords, school districts, and businesses on how to make buildings more quake-resistant, and continues today.

Several cities in the area have trained thousands of citizen volunteers to serve as neighborhood-based emergency responders. In Seattle, they're called Seattle Disaster Aid and Response Teams (SDARTs). Their job is to help residents deal with the immediate aftermath of a disaster when the police and fire departments and the health-care system are expected to be overwhelmed. But so far, most of these citizen teams are found in affluent neighborhoods (which, coincidentally, are located in areas less likely to suffer quake damage). And the basic homeowner's quake survival kit that Seattle officials recommend preparing—which includes food and water, as well as tools, sleeping bags, and other gear—can cost hundreds of dollars. Most poor families are unlikely or unable to spend the money.

While the greater Seattle area can celebrate many initiatives aimed at educating and involving private citizens in becoming better prepared, there is perhaps less reason to celebrate what has—or, rather, has not—been done at all levels of government. The federal government has put many millions of dollars into bolstering Seattle's defense against terrorism. The city of Seattle, by the end of 2005, had spent some $85 million on homeland security improvements. While some of this money is "dual purpose" and has gone for emergency equipment and resources that can be used in any disaster, much less money has gone toward protecting against the certain threat of a major quake.

In Seattle alone, thousands of buildings are still constructed of unreinforced masonry or the equally shaky "tilt-up" concrete walls often used in industrial facility construction. After the 2001 Nisqually Quake, many experts called for mandatory seismic retrofitting of these buildings. Others wanted to adopt an approach popular in some parts of California, in which building owners must voluntarily upgrade seismic safety or post a notice letting building users know it is unsafe. Seattle has so far failed to even identify such high-risk buildings.

Seattle is a hilly city surrounded by water, connected by bridges and elevated roadways. Some experts have said at least half of the twenty-eight freeway bridges or elevated structures in the city can be expected to fail in a major quake. The city is already planning to replace the dangerous Alaskan Way Viaduct. Much of the responsibility for upgrading the region's bridges, as well as the major interstate highways, rests with state government. The Department of Transportation's schedule for making the needed improvements to Seattle-area bridges is due to be completed in 2070—a time frame that Craig Weaver, senior seismologist for the U.S. Geological Survey office in Seattle, described as "ridiculous" and a plan for tempting fate.

In 2005, the Department of Natural Resources quietly gutted the geological hazards program, which was charged with creating the "seismic hazard maps" needed by builders, government officials, and others to assist with establishing building codes, identifying critical areas, and developing disaster evacuation or response plans. When the cuts were made public, legislators ordered the agency to resume funding the program. But by then, most of the state's leading experts in seismic hazard work had already taken new jobs. It remains to be seen how long it will take for the program to recover in terms of expertise and capacity.

Getting Ready for "the Big One":
Prescription for America's Earthquake-Prone Regions

Scientists, engineers, emergency management experts, and others have generally agreed upon a set of top priorities. While it's understood that earthquakes cannot be prevented, we can do a great deal to minimize their impact, saving lives and property, facilitating recovery. These recommendations respond to the Seattle scenario, but are applicable anywhere.

- **Establish independent state seismic safety boards or commissions.** State-level boards would recommend policies and programs directly to governors, and coordinate all of the various agencies and programs involved in disaster preparedness. Oregon has such a system and other states, including California, are adopting the same one. Washington State's current approach to quake readiness is uncoordinated; it lacks both the accountability and the authority needed to achieve anything other than haphazard efforts at hazard reduction.

- **Identify and secure the most critical public facilities that will be needed in a disaster.** Hospitals, police, and fire stations are obviously critical in a disaster. But what about sewer treatment facilities, transportation corridors, power delivery systems, schools, or water reservoirs? Because of the current uncoordinated approach to disaster preparedness in many communities, agencies now use different methodologies for identifying and securing critical infrastructure. The U.S. Department of Homeland Security, for example, with its focus on the terrorist threat, may place a much higher value on some facilities than does a state Department of Health. Furthermore, there has not been a comprehensive assessment of the seismic safety of critical facilities in the most earthquake-prone states. Without this first step, it is impossible to develop a comprehensive response strategy to any disaster.

- **Develop state and local legislation requiring mandatory retrofitting of high-risk buildings such as unreinforced masonry and tilt-up structures.** Schools and houses represent a disproportionate number of these buildings. Unreinforced masonry buildings probably represent the greatest threat to life in an earthquake because they are most likely to collapse completely. In 1986, California required local governments to conduct an inventory of all such buildings. Regulations and incentive programs in many California communities have already prompted two-thirds of building owners to voluntarily retrofit such high-risk buildings. In addition to protecting individuals, the program aims to protect businesses from economic losses due to building damage and downtime. After the 2001 Nisqually Quake, the city of Seattle considered following California's example but abandoned it for fear of creating a financial disadvantage for local property and business owners. State legislation coordinated with local government requirements would be necessary to get beyond these obstacles.

- **Protect the critical transportation infrastructure.** Officials need to identify critical chokepoints, designate emergency routes that are robust and redundant, preposition emergency equipment and supplies, and retrofit critically needed bridges and other transportation channels. In Seattle, city and state officials are already moving ahead with plans to replace the Alaskan Way Viaduct. But many of the region's other bridges and elevated roadways remain at risk of collapse or significant damage in a major quake. The Department of Transportation's schedule for upgrading should be accelerated, many experts say. Costs depend on the kinds of replacement materials chosen, but estimates range from $2 billion to $6 billion for the viaduct alone. In the long term, the economic viability of the region for many years to come will be determined by how quickly the transportation system can recover. A quarter of a billion dollars in goods moves through Puget Sound every day. Millions of tons of agricultural products from eastern Washington are transported through the region by water and rail. Seattle could be paralyzed by the collapse of a dozen bridges.

These are the top priorities that need to be implemented if residents in earthquake-prone areas are to improve their odds of surviving and recovering from "the big one." Other recommendations include accelerating the scientific studies needed to better identify and distinguish localized risks (such as was being done by Washington State's geological hazards program); developing financial incentives and other programs that encourage businesses and citizens to reduce their risks; and expanding public education and awareness programs.

If these measures are understood as legitimate investments, the payoff in lives saved and dramatically reduced short- and long-term recovery costs is worth it.

4 • Terrorism:
Still Vulnerable Five Years Later

Our ability to prevent or interdict acts of violence against Americans and American institutions remains limited, even today, because the portals of entry are not secure. If we look at the existing barriers that we have erected to keep out potentially dangerous intruders, there are huge gaps in virtually all of them.

Take the issue of port security. While there has been much talk about securing the ports since 9/11, it still has not been fully addressed. Some 6 million containers pass though U.S. ports each year, and that number is expected to quadruple in the next twenty years. That amounts to 2 billion tons of domestic and import/export cargo annually. Ports are critical to the American economy: 99 percent of American exports leave by ship, and nearly 4 million people work in port-related jobs. And yet only about 5.5 percent of the containers that pass through our ports are being inspected. We are expanding the number of containers that are being screened for radioactivity and nuclear materials, but we are nowhere near an optimal level of screening; we remain vulnerable to individuals bringing these kinds of materials in for the wrong purposes. Proposed bipartisan legislation, the GreenLane Maritime Cargo Security Act, would increase security at more than six hundred ports around the country. Introduced by Senators Susan Collins (R-Maine) and Patty Murray (D-Washington), the bill would direct the Department of Homeland Security to use the fees it collects to prepare a strategic plan for the security of cargo containers as they move through U.S. seaports and from point to point along the transportation chain. DHS would also have to develop protocols for resuming trade activities at ports in the event of a terrorist attack.

Security mainly depends on the integrity and honesty of the shippers who report their cargo contents. And while the systems have grown increasingly sophisticated in assessing which containers merit physical screening, noted expert Stephen Flynn from the Council on Foreign Relations recently called port security "a house of cards" with each U.S. government agency, from the Coast Guard to the Department of Energy to the U.S. Customs and Border Protection agency, "pursuing its signature program with little regard for other initiatives." If a terrorist manages to breach the port security system with a major weapon, international commerce could come to a screeching halt—at least in the short term—with massive repercussions to the world's economy. This concern is what fueled the March 2006 outcry over the Bush administration's proposal to allow Dubai Ports World to take over port security in critical U.S. ports.

To deter terrorists from sending dangerous materials through our ports, it is not necessary to check every single container. The generally accepted threshold for deterrence is the ability to inspect between 20 and 30 percent of all containers. Conversely, at current inspection rates of around 5 percent, the odds of detection favor the terror smuggler. From an administrative or cost perspective, it is not impossible to increase the search ratio. Hong Kong and Singapore, two of the busiest ports in the world, search every container at a price of about $7 per container. Stephen Flynn and Admiral James Loy, former deputy secretary of homeland security and a commandant in the Coast Guard, note that Hutchinson Port Holdings, a Hong Kong–based company, PSA Singapore Terminals, Dubai

Ports World, and Denmark's APM Terminals handle nearly 80 percent of the cargo coming into the United States. Flynn and Loy propose that if collectively these companies agreed to a common security fee of about $20 a container (on par with the security fee airline passengers are levied), the Hong Kong and Singapore 100 percent inspection model could be installed, offering a "powerful deterrent" for terrorists looking to smuggle weapons of mass destruction into the United States via terminal cargo.

As for our borders, securing the 7,500 miles that are important to U.S. safety seems to remain insoluble. Five years after 9/11, our 2,000-mile border with Mexico and 5,500-mile border with Canada remain as porous as sieves. Large stretches of both borders remain unguarded, a fact drug smugglers and extremists know well. With minimal creativity and intelligence, anyone can slip into the country. Along both the Mexican and the Canadian borders, ventilated tunnels pepper the landscape, like prairie dog holes, to transport drugs from one side to the other. Every day, illegal and undocumented individuals come through these borders in droves. We have to assume that some terrorists have entered the country illegally, but for a variety of reasons have simply not yet acted.

Tarine Fairman, a former special agent with the FBI Evidence Response Team and Hazardous Materials Team who interviewed some of the world's most notorious terrorists and is now president and CEO of the National Security and Intelligence Society, echoes this sentiment. Fairman notes that while efforts have been stepped up to prevent Arabic-speaking persons from entering the country illegally, Southeast Asian and African Islamic populations remain insufficiently screened. Moreover, many individuals are entering the country by way of student F-1 and J-1 visas, as structured under the Family Educational Right to Privacy Act, or the Buckley Amendment. Under Buckley, law enforcement, as well as the parents of students, are prohibited from obtaining any information, other than "general directory" information on a student.

Transportation systems, too, remain vulnerable. Part of the problem is that we tend to pay the most attention to the last incident. Since 9/11, much of our attention in the transportation sector has focused on airlines and airports. But relatively little attention has been paid to bus carriers, trucks, trains, and other kinds of transport that are critical to commerce and travel. Trains are particularly important and remain highly vulnerable, as were the commuter trains bombed by terrorists in Madrid in 2003. Is there any reason to believe that Grand Central terminal in New York City is any safer than Atocha terminal in Madrid?

Some of these challenges are more difficult to address than others, but whether it is container inspections or border controls, what's important is that we standardize, institutionalize, and enhance methods of interdicting terrorists and the importation of deadly weapons that are capable of causing massive casualties.

Another area of vulnerability to terrorism has to do with the capacity of our intelligence apparatus, including its real-time ability to deal with communications among terrorist groups. While some colleges have reported that the number of students learning Arabic and other critical languages has doubled or more since 9/11, the FBI demand for able linguists still continues to far outstrip supply. Fairman explains that while FBI recruitment efforts for Arabic and African Ibo linguists have increased, the quotas are not being met. At the end of 2005, the process for hiring linguists was still taking about nine months, down from eighteen months before September 11, 2001, but still slow. "Government agencies are not offering salaries that are commensurate with the ability of these linguists," Fairman says. "Therefore, many [qualified] linguists do not accept government positions and do not recommend these opportunities to their associates." In short, Fairman puts it down to dollars and cents: "The government has not established a salary structure that is acceptable to prospective linguists." As a result, less qualified linguists are taking positions intended for individuals with more experience. Many of the linguists who are hired *speak* Arabic well, but cannot read or write at high levels of fluency.

A follow-up report from the Department of Justice's Office of the Inspector General noted that while the FBI has made some headway, the amount of material the agency has collected has increased considerably, from 1.6 million hours of material in December 2003 to 2.5 million hours as of March 2005. The agency now has a back-log of unreviewed materials amounting to about 27 percent of its Arabic-language files.

Aside from this inability to promptly translate potentially important materials in Arabic, shortages of linguistic experts in other languages is a problem as well. The same report cited above noted that while the number of FBI and contract linguists had increased from 883 in 2001 to 1,338 as of March 2005, the agency has met its own hiring objectives for fewer than half of the fifty-two languages for which it needs translators.

Shortages of expert personnel in critical counterintelligence agencies remain one of the greatest barriers to deterrence of potential acts of terror in the U.S. The CIA has reported increased attrition since 9/11, and more frequent turnovers of veteran officers, with a loss of hundreds of years of accumulated knowledge from the field. Not only are there sustained needs for experts who can effectively ascertain information, interpret data, and "connect the dots," but there is also an ongoing need for people who can thwart potential acts of terror, preventing this kind of disaster altogether.

Without fairly drastic changes in the structure and function of our homeland security systems, as well as the agencies and congressional committees that oversee them, the possibility of making sufficient near-term improvements in the nation's ability to prevent terrorism is remote. All the more reason why it is essential to make sure that we've done everything possible to plan for effective responses to the man-made disasters that we cannot reasonably expect to prevent indefinitely.

Going Nuclear: The Ultimate Terror Nightmare

During their 2004 campaign debates, President George W. Bush and Senator John F. Kerry were asked to name the greatest terror threat facing the United States. While they agreed on little else, they had the same answer: use of a nuclear weapon. Since the dropping of the atomic bombs at the end of World War II, through the build-up of nuclear weapons by the superpowers during the Cold War, and to the expansion of the "nuclear club" of nations possessing or thought to possess these weapons, the possibility that a rogue state or terrorist group could purchase or construct a nuclear device has actually increased.

In the 1980s, the Soviet Union had some 30,000 nuclear weapons. When the country was dissolved, the weapons themselves, as well as the scientific and industrial knowledge to produce nuclear weapons and energy, remained in newly independent (and underdeveloped) states such as Belarus, Kazakhstan, and Ukraine. Many of these weapons have now been identified and transported to Russia, but certainly not all. Furthermore, the expertise required to build weapons is now dispersed across the globe, as is some portion of the 2,000 tons of weapons-grade nuclear material (enough for about 100,000 nuclear weapons) that has been produced over the past sixty years. Despite the bilateral treaty with Russia that removed all nuclear weapons from Ukraine by 1996, Ukrainian scientists were accused of providing suitcase-sized weapons to Al-Qaeda in 1998.

Similar problems have grown out of other former Soviet re-publics as well. In 1992, U.S. officials raised concerns that "two or three tactical nuclear weapons are unaccounted for" in Kazakhstan. What was not known was if it was a question of missing weapons or bookkeeping irregularities. One concern, according to a *New York Times* report, was that the weapons may have been transported to Iran.

The bottom line is that unaccounted-for "loose nukes" and the ease with which a trained scientist can now construct a nuclear device from scratch—provided enriched uranium or plutonium can be obtained—creates an ongoing threat of large-scale terrorism.

This is hardly a case of hype and spin. A successfully deto-nated nuclear device, aside from enormous explosive power and enough heat to start raging fires far from the explosion site, has the ability to produce huge quantities of radiation, which is sometimes immediately lethal and other times the cause of serious longer-term health problems such as cancer.

Many factors determine the lethality of atomic weapons, including the power of the device, the topography and characteristics of the target area, and where a bomb is detonated (on, below, or above the surface). A small, fairly crude weapon, less powerful than the atomic bombs dropped over Hiroshima and Nagasaki in 1945, could kill 150,000 to 200,000 people if exploded in midtown Manhattan during the day, with an equal number expected to sustain major injuries. Buildings would be destroyed in the immediate 600-square-block (5-square-mile) vicinity of the explosion and others would burst into flames in a ferocious firestorm. Every manner of emergency response system would be immediately incapacitated; communications and electronic systems would be put out of commission and medical facilities essentially destroyed. Long-term radioactive contamination would make large portions of the city uninhabitable for decades, and the impact on the U.S. and world economies would defy prediction.

A terror or rogue organization would not have to acquire a nuclear weapon that was already constructed and ready for deployment. In fact, it would be extremely difficult to move such a weapon into and around the United States. More likely, a terrorist would acquire parts and pieces from a global "parts bin," bring them in as components, and assemble them secretly here. Once assembled, a very powerful nuclear device could be easily moved, potentially in a panel truck, to a critical location in any major city. Eventually, as the nation develops more effective and efficient ways of detecting the transport of nuclear materials, that process will become more challenging. At the moment, however, the technology and the protocols for effective detection are not sufficiently developed.

The process of detonating a device is not particularly complicated, especially if the perpetrator were willing to sacrifice his or her life. The atomic attacks on Japan at the end of World War II were much more complicated. On August 6, 1945, the *Enola Gay*, an American B-29 bomber, dropped the atomic bomb called "Little

Boy" over the Japanese city of Hiroshima. It was timed to explode some 1,600 feet over center city. The gun-type bomb was nearly ten feet long and weighed more than four tons. Three days later, a similar bomb, this one called "Fat Man," was detonated over Nagasaki. This device was an implosion bomb, about the same length, but wider and weighed nearly five tons. While the exact numbers are still not known, it is generally believed that about 150,000 people died in each of the target cities.

The idea that any rogue organization could build, move, or deploy a four- or five-ton weapon is unlikely. But new technologies have greatly simplified and, in some important ways, miniaturized the process. In a scenario that I will summarize here, but that is also painstakingly detailed in a document called "National Planning Scenarios," the U.S. Department of Homeland Security lays out how a modern-day terrorist organization might acquire a supply of "highly enriched uranium" (HEU) from a facility in another country. With it, a small crew of properly trained technicians could gather in a "terror-friendly" country and assemble the electronics, hardware, and propellants needed to create a usable nuclear explosive device. It would be almost as powerful as the bombs used more than sixty years ago in Japan, yet small enough to fit in a delivery van.

Once assembled and checked out in the host country, the device would be disassembled and organized as eight separate packages for relatively easy transport into the U.S. Trained sleeper-cell agents would then reassemble the bomb in a well-hidden location near the target city. Because the chemical materials needed for the bomb's propellant would be detectable at certain U.S. ports of entry, all evidence of these substances would be cleaned off the components prior to transport.

The only slightly radioactive—but potentially detectable—HEU would be transported to the final assembly location in a specially made two-inch-thick lead canister, making its contents virtually nondetectable by typical radiation monitors.

The DHS document correctly points out that HEU supplies are

highly regulated and monitored (although the system is hardly perfect). However, the missing HEU is not likely to be noticed or reported to the world community before the material and other bomb components make it safely within U.S. borders.

That is how it could happen.

As I write this, I am uncomfortable passing on information about how a genuine nuclear weapon of mass destruction could end up in the hands of terrorists poised to do the nation great harm from within our own borders. The reality is that the U.S. government has already published even more extensive scenarios on publicly accessible Internet sites. As Carey Sublette points out on her website, www.nuclearweaponarchive.org:

> The United States government conducted a controlled experiment called the *Nth Country Experiment* to see how much effort was actually required to develop a viable fission weapon design starting from nothing. In this experiment, which ended on 10 April 1967, three newly graduated physics students were given the task of developing a detailed weapon design using only public domain information. The project reached a successful conclusion, that is, they did develop a viable design (detailed in the classified report UCRL-50248) after expending only three man-years of effort over two and a half calendar years. In the years since, much more information has entered the public domain so that the level of effort required has obviously dropped further.

In fact, the students designed a Nagasaki-type bomb because they thought a Hiroshima-type bomb would be too easy.

It's a bright and busy spring afternoon in a major U.S. city. Working people are returning to their offices from lunch and meetings, parents and child-care providers are waiting outside school yards to pick up students, delivery people are loading and unloading goods in and out of trucks. The day is entirely ordinary.

Without warning, a massive, blinding flash of light and an over-

powering surge of heat and debris emanate from a midtown blast site.

At the site of detonation, a ten-kiloton nuclear device blasts a crater about 120 feet across and up to 20 feet deep. An immediate flash of overwhelming light and heat has already blinded people staring at the blast from as far away as ten miles. Everything goes dark. (Depending on whether the bomb detonates aboveground or at ground level, the fallout can contain dirt and debris, as well as droplets of water, within the mushroomlike cloud that almost immediately follows the blast. Although all estimates of deaths, injuries, destruction of structures, and radiation contamination are subject to many particular circumstances—time of day, wind speed and direction, construction characteristics of buildings, and more—some general sense of the impact, based on more or less average conditions, is worth thinking about.)

Virtually every building within a half-mile radius is destroyed or damaged beyond recognition. Occupants of these buildings and individuals outdoors are dead. Massive burn casualties occur within a 2.5-mile radius, and severe blast injuries, including those incurred from flying debris, are seen as far as two miles away. Within the 2.5-mile radius, thermal energy from the nuclear blast has created a horrific blazing inferno, creating treacherous conditions for people who survive the initial blast and radiation effects.

Up to nine miles downwind from the blast site, as many as 50 percent of exposed people will die of acute radiation poisoning. Even at fourteen miles, at least half of the unprotected citizens will likely be radiation casualties.

In Chicago, for example, the "prompt effects" of such a blast would be responsible for as many as 300,000 deaths and severe injuries. (Fewer victims would be seen in less densely populated cities.) People will have been killed or badly injured by some combination of explosive force, burns, and acute exposure to lethal levels of radiation. If such a scenario were to unfold during the workday, casualties and injuries will be far greater, because of commuters, visitors, and others who travel in from surrounding communities and increase the population of a city during daytime hours.

In Washington, D.C., for instance, the Oak Ridge National Laboratory Geographic Information Science and Technology Group suggests that the nighttime population of less than 575,000 expands to more than 1,000,000 people during the day. Disaster-response planners must have this kind of information in order to fine-tune resource and logistic planning following a major event.

It is difficult to overstate the extraordinary immediate consequences of a nuclear detonation, or the physical and psychological toll it would take on American society. The immediacy and the sheer power of these weapons would seem to defy description—except that eyewitnesses have recorded every unbearable detail of what actually happened in Hiroshima and Nagasaki in 1945. This vast and searing literature is sobering on every level.

Long-Term Impact

In addition to an apocalyptic human toll, the economic and political consequences of nuclear terror would be almost incalculable. The U.S. would suffer an enormous psychological wounding, unlike anything ever before experienced. Many studies after previous major disasters, especially terror-related ones, have documented the psychological toll taken by these high-consequence events. The 1995 bombing of the Alfred P. Murrah Federal Building in Oklahoma City represented the first major terrorist attack on American soil. In addition to the hundreds killed and injured, many Americans far from Oklahoma City were traumatized by the attack. The Oklahoma City bombing provided the first set of major empirical studies examining how the American public responds to terrorism that targets civilians within the nation's borders.

These studies showed that individuals who were either close to the incident or had increased exposure to information about the bombing experienced increased levels of post-traumatic stress disorder (PTSD). September 11, 2001, provided a new opportunity to consider the impact of domestic terrorism on the U.S. populace. Studies of those both directly and indirectly exposed to the attack documented varying degrees of PTSD and changes in behavior, including the challenging finding that "there is no psychological Ground Zero." In other words, psychological trauma is pervasive beyond the physical location of the attack.

Survival Strategies That Can Make a Difference

Few Americans have thought much about a nuclear calamity, and since the days of the Cold War "duck and cover" instructions for schoolchildren, little has been done to encourage U.S. citizens to consider what they might do in the event of nuclear terrorism. Many people harbor fatalistic thoughts about any possibility of surviving a nuclear explosion. Those within the lethal inner rings of destruction would not survive. But for those on the periphery and in the gray zones in between survival is possible. Many lives could be saved if citizens were informed about what to do, and if there were competent governmental and nongovernmental agencies, like the American Red Cross, involved. Each of these "response partners" would have a vital role to play and the better these roles are understood, coordinated, and practiced, the better the potential outcome.

The following strategies could significantly improve the chances of survival.

- **Rapid, Safe Evacuation.** Maximum survival after a nuclear attack depends upon rapid, safe evacuation from the contaminated areas. Since search and rescue teams cannot enter the hot zone to find survivors, people who survive the initial blast of fire and radiation must know to move as far away as possible from the blast site. No form of public or private transportation is likely to be operating in the immediate aftermath of a nuclear blast.

Individuals should move quickly on foot, away from the blast zone and perpendicular to (or at a right angle from) the direction of the plume.

- **Quick, Effective Self-Decontamination.** Individuals who survive the initial blast must decontaminate themselves of radiation as rapidly as possible. This could involve just holding one's breath, taking off and discarding clothing, and rinsing off, even with a simple hose in an evacuation center. If planning is effective and the response protocols are beginning to function, decontamination showers will be set up by response agencies and surviving health-care facilities at appropriate distances from the blast site.

- **Timely Medical Care.** Many survivors will need urgent medical care, including potentially thousands of people with combination injuries: trauma, burns, and radiation poisoning. The treatment of these victims will be very complicated because the original blast will have destroyed or disabled many components of the hospital and first-responder systems. In addition, if injured individuals are also contaminated with radioactive materials, they will pose a substantial risk to the medical personnel caring for them. Even lifesaving surgery may require extreme precautions and significantly more time in order to protect the surgeon, nurses, and other medical support personnel—assuming that sufficient personnel have survived the attack or are willing and able to come from surrounding communities. Again, if planning is effective, remaining health-care facilities (such as hospitals and clinics) will be ready to implement emergency protocols and use alternate sites to provide some degree of critical medical care.

- **Adapting Disaster Triage Principles in the Medical Response.** Triage will be critical in the aftermath of a nuclear detonation. Medical personnel who have served in extreme battlefield conditions, understand the concept of saving the most salvageable first. Busy urban emergency rooms under normal circumstances will take the sickest, most critically injured patients first, utilizing whatever resources are necessary and available. On the battle-field—and in the aftermath of nuclear devastation—resources and time are extraordinarily limited. Ensuring the survival of the most people will require focusing on patients likely to make it—and abandoning those who need excessive resources and, even if treated, have little chance of surviving.

- **Early Response to Psychological Impacts.** Planners cannot neglect the psychological ramifications of a nuclear attack. Not only will citizens of the affected area experience cataclysmic acute and long-term psychological trauma, but so will emergency responders. Planning to deal with these concerns is critical. Researchers who have studied the aftermath of atomic attacks in Japan and other major disasters have long estimated that "one-third of the survivors will be in a marked state of anxiety" characterized by extreme states of fear, anxiety, and confusion. Of particular concern are some specific psychological consequences of large-scale catastrophes: diminished problem-solving capacity, impaired judgment, and even hallucinations. These symptoms can occur in both survivors and responders. Ways of recognizing and treating them are essential to ensure appropriate and lifesaving behaviors in the aftermath of nuclear terror.

- **Power and Communications Backup.** Many of these vital systems will be disabled by the "electromagnetic pulse (EMP)"—the enormous energy discharge from a nuclear explosion. Systems will be disabled in one of three ways: (1) equipment close to the blast site will be physically destroyed; (2) equipment that is far enough away from the blast but is turned on or is on "standby/hibernate" mode may have its circuitry destroyed by the EMP; and (3) systems that are completely off or in a "safe" standby mode may survive the blast but be temporarily disabled. Agencies with critical functions need to field-test their equipment to make sure it is "EMP survivable" and also to establish safe rooms—known as Faraday cages—with wire mesh enclosures that absorb the electromagnetic waves and serve as a shield against radiation. Faraday cages are used, for example, to protect satellite communication equipment from solar flares in space. NASA and the Department of Defense have important information to share with state and local governments about precautions that protect sensitive equipment.

Unfortunately, whatever happens from a geopolitical perspective among the current and emerging superpowers, the threat of nuclear terrorism will remain a part of our future. In addition to the personal strategies noted above, government also has essential responsibilities to help citizens deal with the aftermath of a nuclear detonation.

- **Create Recovery Zones Around Potential Urban Nuclear Terror Targets.** Since we know that the key to optimizing survival after a nuclear blast is rapid evacuation, adequate resources must be provided at likely safe areas ringing the target cities. Advance positioning of supplies, equipment, decontamination units, mobile hospital beds and the like could help ensure survival for people able to leave the affected areas. Importantly, many of these supplies could also be used in the event of pandemic, natural megadisaster, or industrial catastrophe.

- **Mount a National Campaign to Educate Citizens.** Such a campaign must emphasize that survival is possible following a nuclear detonation. Incredibly, some of the information currently available to the public is potentially dangerous and simplistic. The Department of Homeland Security's educational website, www.ready.gov, for example, includes an instruction graphic showing a man walking around a corner to protect himself from a nuclear blast. While Ready.gov offers some practical recommendations like establishing emergency contacts and stocking provisions and appropriate supplies like battery-operated radios, the campaign itself is barely promoted to the public and lacks integration with other education efforts by local and state offices of emergency management. Rand researchers have pointed out that the government's advice could actually greatly increase the risk of injury and death to people in a nuclear detonation zone.

- **Provide First Responders with More Training on the Critical Aspects of Nuclear Attack Response.** All first responders, police, firefighters, and emergency medical services, need to be fully educated regarding the particular issues relevant to rescue, relief, and survival following a nuclear blast.

5 · The Built Environment:
A Crumbling Infrastructure and
High-Consequence Industrial Accidents
Waiting to Happen

Of all the reports that have been written about our state of readiness to face megadisaster, the news from the American Society of Civil Engineers (ASCE) is particularly unsettling: Major U.S. infrastructure systems are increasingly and dramatically failing to meet basic standards of safety, and we are not paying enough attention or doing what's needed to shore them up. The great network of roads, bridges, tunnels, dams, levees, and water mains that represents our built environment in the United States supports most of the crucial functions of our society, from clean water and sewage treatment to transportation and agriculture. By controlling the elements, including the waterways, we are able to develop communities at or below sea level and to enjoy the benefits of coastal living. We fine-tune the infrastructure, moving water resources from places of plenty to regions of scarcity and channeling electricity to virtually every corner of the United States.

Part of the problem with America's infrastructure relates to age and expected longevity. The bridges that were part of the national interstate highway system, for example, begun in 1956, were not built with reinforced materials. The 2005 ASCE Report Card is stunning. Not a single aspect of America's infrastructure received better than a mediocre grade, and the overall rating was poor, a D. This assessment took place over four years and slipped from the D+ given in 2001 and 2003. Conditions remained the same for bridges, dams, and solid waste and worsened for roads, drinking water, waste water, public transit, hazardous waste, navigable waterways, and energy. New categories added were parks and recreation, rail, and security.

The New Orleans levees are but one example of a national infrastructure in crisis. Not only were they in extreme disrepair, but the federally supported levees first erected in 1966 were not built properly in the first place. Even with emergency repairs completed just prior to the 2006 hurricane season, New Orleans may be subject to reflooding from moderate-size storms.

California's capital, Sacramento, like New Orleans, has a significant portion of low-lying real estate. More than 1,500 miles of federal and state-controlled levees protect the Sacramento–San Joaquin Delta, much of which is below sea level. This vast region comprises nearly 750,000 acres of rich farmland and provides drinking water for 22 million Californians. The delta itself is home to some 2 million residents, many of whom live in Sacramento and its sprawling suburbs. While local responders and officials have experience in dealing with moderate flooding, no one has experience dealing with the severity of flooding that could occur should the current levee and dam systems fail.

Farmers and settlers built some of the levees along the Sacramento and the American rivers 150 years ago. Most of them do not meet current engineering standards. Folsom Dam, built in 1950 to the north of Sacramento, cannot handle the increasing water flows from the Sierra Nevadas. Many of the rich farmlands of Northern California are protected from seawater by equally fragile levees—so fragile, in fact, that two of them gave way with unusually persistent rains in early April 2006.

Just a month before, Michael Chertoff, beleaguered secretary of homeland security, took an aerial tour of this vulnerable central California region with Governor Arnold Schwarzenegger. Although there are no known eyewitness accounts, one can imagine their conversation. The governor probably pointed out the two dozen or so critically eroded sites along the levees that, from the air, look like an irregular geometric pattern of nineteenth-century fences on the rolling agricultural landscape. The secretary, still reeling from blistering congressional and public criticism of his handling of the Katrina debacle, must have taken this all in, aware that in September 2004 Schwarzenegger requested $90 million in federal assistance to repair levees. While the urgent repairs were expected to cost at least $100 million, most of which is the federal government's responsibility to provide, the U.S. Senate approved only $41 million. Both men must have been well aware of the "investment mathematics" of the situation: investing $100 million now could save literally countless lives and communities later, not to mention billions of dollars.

Scientists at Columbia's Earth Institute say the Sacramento delta system is highly vulnerable to multiple hazards, including earthquakes and flooding from a major storm. A breach of the levees would wreak havoc on the low-lying Northern California farmlands and on the supply of water to the Bay Area. Northern California is New Orleans plus: the spectrum of threats require preparedness policies that treat the area holistically, not just in a single-hazard context. The question is whether we will take these warnings more seriously than we heeded the decade or more of urgent messages about the levees protecting New Orleans.

Many large American cities have hundred-year-old water mains that are at or nearing the end of their lifespans. New York's system covers 2,000 square miles, and there are more than 4,000 miles of mains in Chicago. New York's City Tunnel no. 3 is the largest water transport construction project in the city's history; the new tunnel will span 60 miles and will not be completed until 2020. Perhaps New York's or Chicago's networks of water pipes are not cause for worry about a true megadisaster, unless three or four of them blow at a critical time, say during a health crisis or a major chemical spill.

We operate under a strange and false sense of security that critical elements of the nation's infrastructure have been in existence forever and will do their job safely long into the future. This is just not the case. It is true that much of what concerns the engineers can be repaired and stabilized, but it won't be a cheap fix. According to the American Society of Civil Engineers, fixing America's infrastructure would cost a staggering *$1.6 trillion over the next five years,* or about $320 billion a year. The annual U.S. budget was estimated at $2.77 trillion for 2006, so fixing the infrastructure should not be dismissed out of hand because of cost. Not only is repairing America's infrastructure crucial, but the 5 million engineering, construction, and service jobs created and sustained by this long endeavor would boost the economy.

The built environment also includes the vast industrial complex. Here, too, we are vulnerable. Chemical manufacturing and transport, nuclear energy production, and hydroelectric power production are traditional American industries that may be much more accident-prone or vulnerable to attack than many would care to contemplate. Many of the existing safeguards and response systems are not secure—and we depend on them at our peril.

In his illuminating book *Inviting Disaster: Lessons from the Edge of Technology,* James Chiles shows with one chilling example after another that the increasing complexity of our technological world requires a greater, not lesser degree of vigilance than in the past. Transparency and systemic accountability are key to increasing our ability to circumvent disaster. Chiles writes:

It's human nature to let things slide. Delayed maintenance is part of our trial-and-error, stretch-it-out style. We also look to cases where people shaved away at the margin of safety by shutting off safety devices or letting them break without replacement. Typically, each person assumed that enough slack remained to avoid causing a safety problem. And so it goes, people "working together" to crash a system.

Chiles argues that we need to create high-reliability organizations, where employees are empowered and trained to address problems. He calls on organizations and corporations to create operating practices that make safety a priority, build in deep redundancy so that inevitable errors or malfunctions are caught in time, foster decision-making at all levels, keep workers sharp with practice and emergency drilling, and place a premium on learning lessons from trial and error.

The chemical industry, for example, would do well to heed Chiles's advice. According to the Environmental Protection Agency, there are 123 large chemical facilities around the country where a worst-case scenario of accidental or deliberate release of chemicals could expose more than a million people in the surrounding areas to a toxic gas cloud. There are another 700 or so facilities that could each potentially threaten at least 100,000 people living nearby and, finally, some 3,000 facilities where at least 10,000 people could be harmed in the event of a serious breakdown.

And it's not just safety and structural issues that are of concern. Significant security lapses also make some of these potentially dangerous facilities even more vulnerable. In May 2005, a particularly troubling news story reported that a major New Jersey chemical plant just outside of Manhattan was virtually unguarded despite the extraordinary threat it would pose if attacked. It is just one of several such plants along the border between New Jersey and New York. A *New York Times* article outlined the scenario:

It is the deadliest target in a swath of industrial northern New Jersey that terrorism experts call the most dangerous two miles in America: a chemical plant that processes chlorine gas, so close to Manhattan that the Empire State Building seems to rise up behind its storage tanks. According to federal Environmental Protection Agency records, the plant poses a potentially lethal threat to 12 million people who live within a 14-mile radius. Yet on a recent Friday afternoon, it remained loosely guarded and accessible. Dozens of trucks and cars drove by within 100 feet of the tanks. A reporter and photographer drove back and forth for five minutes, snapping photos with a camera the size of a large sidearm, then left without being approached. That chemical plant is just one of dozens of vulnerable sites between Newark Liberty International Airport and Port Elizabeth, which extends two miles to the east. A Congressional study in 2000 by a former Coast Guard commander deemed it the nation's most enticing environment for terrorists, providing a convenient way to cripple the economy by disrupting major portions of the country's rail lines, oil storage tanks and refineries, pipelines, air traffic, communications networks and highway system.

Serious concerns about the lack of security at chemical plants are not new. A 2003 General Accounting Office report on the vulnerability of the chemical industry points out that while many of the manufacturers have taken responsible steps to safeguard critical plants, to date "no one has comprehensively assessed the security of chemical facilities." In fact, the GAO called on the Department of Homeland Security, which is now the lead governmental agency responsible for preventing attacks on these critical businesses, to develop a comprehensive security assessment of chemical facilities. The GAO revisited this matter, issuing a January 2006 report that urges Congress to give DHS the authority to require the chemical industry to address plant security and calls on DHS to complete its chemical sector–specific plan in a timely, although undefined, manner. The report also urged that DHS work with EPA to study the security benefits to plants of using safer technologies, something that DHS has expressed reservations about doing.

Congress has taken this matter up every year since 2001. Of the three bills that were awaiting action in the 109th Congress in 2006, the most extensive bill is S. 2145, the Chemical Facility

Anti-Terrorism Act, introduced by a bipartisan group of senators led by Senator Susan Collins (R-Maine). If enacted, the bill will charge the Department of Homeland Security with reviewing and approving vulnerability assessments, site security plans, and emergency response plans of chemical plants and other facilities that store large quantities of hazardous chemicals. While the non-profit research and advocacy group OMB Watch has criticized the bill for failing to require "that companies consider and report on potential use of safer technologies to reduce the consequences of a major attack or accident," the bill takes security of chemical facilities in the right direction, bringing it under closer federal scrutiny. This legislation is critical, but more regulatory oversight will be equally important if the law is to have its desired impact. The other two proposals in the House call for somewhat less stringent guidelines.

Inexplicably, DHS Secretary Chertoff supports legislation that allows the chemical industry to police itself. He also advocates a third-party evaluation system—rather than have DHS take on the regulatory authority—and supports a provision in which third-party evaluators would prevent states from passing their own stricter, more tightly enforced rules. Governor Jon Corzine of New Jersey, who as U.S. senator pushed without success for more stringent regulation of chemical industry safety standards, signed new state laws in 2006 to toughen plant security and inspections. The legislation that Chertoff supports, however, plays to the chemical lobby and would diminish the effectiveness of New Jersey's new requirements. Dan Katz, chief counsel to New Jersey Senator Frank Lautenberg, called Chertoff's proposal evidence of an "Enron mentality: trust the industry and put the public at risk."

The nuclear industry is another area of concern. In 1955, when the first nuclear plant came on line in Idaho, it was touted as "safe and clean." Nuclear energy may be clean, but we haven't begun to figure out how to safely store, move, or dispose of its radioactive by-products. In its 2004 report *U.S. Nuclear Power Plants in the 21st Century,* the industry watchdog Union for Concerned Scientists makes clear we are depending far too much on the owners of plants themselves in carrying out risk assessments and security testing of the nation's 104 working nuclear power plants and 37 other reactors currently licensed. We do not know if the companies are conducting appropriate tests. And what is the Nuclear Regulatory Commission (NRC) prepared to do about it if they don't?

Safeguards are insufficient, security is often extraordinarily lax, and evacuation plans in the event of a major nuclear meltdown at many of the plants are sketchy. At the Indian Point Nuclear Plant, owned by Entergy Corporation, thirty-five miles up the Hudson River from midtown Manhattan, the NRC modestly increased security precautions following 9/11. But critics point out that the plant remains vulnerable to air attacks and ground assaults.

In 2004, the Union for Concerned Scientists called for enhanced emergency and evacuation procedures that "provide some protection from the fallout from an attack at Indian Point to those New York area residents who currently have none." The group also demanded an upgrade in security "to a level commensurate with the threat it poses to the region." Without such increases, as many as 44,000 people could die in the immediate aftermath of a nuclear disaster, and nearly 500,000 could perish from subsequent disaster-related cancers. Millions could be forced to relocate. The environmental watch group Riverkeeper recently urged the NRC and FEMA to "address the glaring deficiencies in a plan needed to evacuate over 300,000 residents living within Indian Point's 10-mile peak fatality zone. While the surrounding counties have diligently tried to improve the plans, they cannot reduce the population density nor can they change the roadways and infrastructure. In the event of an emergency at Indian Point, we're all sitting ducks," said Riverkeeper's Lisa Rainwater van Suntum.

Persistent calls for action have gone unheeded. In January 2006, four U.S. congressmen joined a bipartisan group of New York officials to ask FEMA to refuse recertification of the disaster response and evacuation plans for the Indian Point Nuclear Plant. The plant owners are required by law to register their plans on a regular basis.

Certification had already been rejected by Westchester, Rockland, and Orange counties, as well as by New York State's Emergency Management Office. Much like their outcries about chemical plant safety, local officials are calling for the federal government to take appropriate action—and to enforce its own rules.

Many observers and experts have questioned the testing and accountability procedures designed and deployed by the manufacturers themselves, with minimal oversight by the NRC. The age of the nuclear facilities and the amount of spent fuel being stored on their premises make them more dangerous. Spent fuel is a particular problem, because it is stored in areas that are an easier target for sabotage. While safety advocates point out that no new regulations are required to safeguard the pools of spent fuel, the NRC needs a stronger legislative push to enforce safety standards.

From industry's perspective, regulations and additional safety precautions cost money and eat into profits. Industries always resist any imposition of new "guidelines" by government. Executives won't publicly proclaim that they're against safety; they just don't want to be overburdened by unnecessary regulations and unfunded mandates.

Many regulatory industry processes were not particularly effective to begin with, and lobbyists have been fairly successful in watering down regulations in many industries. One recent example was the EPA's move in October 2005 to relax the reporting requirements of chemical producers under the Toxics Release Inventory, increasing the level of emissions allowed before they have to be reported from 500 to 5,000 pounds. Clearly, this represents a giant step backward in protecting the interests and safety of the public.

If the safeguards built into the systems are, in general, not reliable and dependable enough, the response plans for coping with an emergency are even worse. The chemical and the nuclear industries are prime culprits here. While the NRC and FEMA are both required to review nuclear power plant emergency plans annually and federal licensing is contingent on them, these plans are totally inadequate.

Prevention—or Tragedy

In early 2006 several mining accidents took place in the U.S. and Canada. Two in West Virginia claimed a total of fourteen lives. The miners could not escape the collapse of a deep shaft and died of asphyxiation; there was no safe room as a backup retreat and the oxygen tanks they carried on their backs provided just six hours of oxygen. In fact, the sole survivor of the Sago, WV, mine accident confirmed that at least four of the oxygen tanks never functioned at all. Just a few weeks later, in an Esterhazy, Saskatchewan, potash mine owned by the U.S.-based Mosaic Company, a major fire trapped seventy-two miners. The Canadian miners retreated to refuge rooms required by provincial law that seal off toxic gases and have enough food, water, and oxygen available for at least three days. These fortunate workers sat tight and, twenty hours later, rescuers extinguished the fire and got to the men. They *all* survived.

While there are differences in the ways potash and coal are mined, the positive outcome in Esterhazy was the result, in part, of a thirty-year history of cooperation between employers, unions, regulators, and workers to establish and maintain stricter safety precautions. Companies in Canada have invested in equipment and underground refuges that save lives. In Saskatchewan, a joint safety committee is required to check the rescue stations monthly to ensure they are properly stocked. Employees conduct two drills a year to practice retreating to these safe havens, and companies send employees to annual competitions in the province to demonstrate their skill in mine rescue and to learn from others. In Carlsbad, New Mexico, the Mosaic Company is installing refuge stations in another potash mine, although no regulation requires them.

A Chemical Release in a Tornado-Risk Zone

In a widespread disaster, there may well be an immediate shortage of, and serious shortcomings in, emergency response resources. You, your family, and your neighbors may well be the real first responders—so, although government should be expected to provide some resources, don't depend on it to be there as soon as the emergency unfolds. This simple reality represents a critical message for citizens: Individual and family preparedness and action are crucial to survival.

Think about a typical Midwest community, located on a main transcontinental rail line and known to be in a tornado-risk zone. Assume that the local response systems are thought to be in generally good shape: there are average numbers of personnel in law enforcement, fire, and emergency medical systems, involving the typical small-town mixture of professionals and volunteers. The community has a typical volunteer infrastructure, including a Red Cross chapter. Because of outstanding and energetic leadership from a local emergency planner, the radio and communications systems of the various official agencies work well and are "interoperable," meaning that fire, police, and emergency medical services can communicate relatively easily with one another on shared wavelengths and have practiced this in local field exercises. The local community hospital, a sixty-bed general medical facility, has a professional staff and a competent emergency department, although, because there is no major chemical facility nearby, the hospital has developed no special expertise or training in chemical disasters.

The community has done sporadic drills to test resources for the most anticipated local disasters, including tornados. A number of relevant personnel have received special training in all-hazard response. Assume as well that local newspapers have run periodic stories on citizen preparedness for disasters.

One might reasonably assume that this hypothetical community was "ready." In the most predictable cases, that assumption would be correct. If tornados hit a residential neighborhood or the local river overflows after a torrential downpour, appropriate government and volunteer responders are out in force immediately, rescuing people, restoring power, minimizing further property damage, and doing whatever else might be necessary.

Assuming a disaster in which the most severe damage occurs in a relatively limited geographic area, citizens rightly expect that trained rescue professionals would be on the scene in short order. In fact, paramedics from several local agencies might be providing lifesaving emergency medical care at the site, quickly transporting critically injured people to the local hospital, or perhaps arranging for air evacuation of more severe cases to a regional medical center for advanced treatment. Finally, if the local response people, equipment, and facilities could not handle the situation, help would rapidly be on the way from surrounding communities that have mutual aid pacts. Versions of this local scenario are played out hundreds of times a year around the United States. For these emergencies the system usually works.

But, in fact, we cannot depend on it to work. The likelihood of all of the key elements being in place, even for a relatively small disaster, is not at all guaranteed. Historical and recent disaster experience and reports from official investigative agencies, such as the national Chemical Safety and Hazard Investigation Board, suggest that communities are often not well prepared for larger events. We have learned painfully that the governments we assume are protecting us may not be taking care of some of the most significant disaster vulnerabilities, for instance retrofitting schools and public buildings in earthquake zones.

Consider the following hypothetical scenario.

It's a Thursday evening in mid-May, the ground has cooled after the heat of the day, and the overcast skies over Republic, Missouri, a city of 15,000 about eight miles due southwest of Springfield, are looking somewhat ominous. The temperature is a comfortable 70 degrees; the wind, as usual in the evening, is a steady two to three miles per hour from the west.

Welcoming the evening breeze, shift workers are heading home from a small meatpacking plant, the cornerstone of the local economy. Many of them are new residents of Republic, Hispanic workers, some illegal, many with limited English capabilities, but hardworking and socially conservative churchgoers. Their children are in local schools learning English and the families are gradually establishing themselves as full-fledged members of the community.

Thunderstorms in the area had been predicted since early that morning, but with little warning, several residents notice what appears to be a twister coming in from the east. They call 911, the local emergency hotline. Operators confirm the sightings and report that the emergency response agencies have already been contacted. In a matter of a few minutes, tornado warning alarms sound in Republic and in nearby communities.

While many residents are taking the usual precautions, the tornado suddenly turns northward. Directly in its path is an active freight route for the Burlington Northern Santa Fe Railway. As it roars through, the twister severely damages the Abbey Road railroad overpass on the east side of town. This bridge had been cited for "issues" by state Department of Transportation inspectors several times over the past decade; the citations noted specifically that support buttresses were rusted and metal cracks were visible in key stress points. Worried county officials had nonetheless repeatedly deferred repairs, mostly because of local and state budget constraints.

Only minutes later, barreling down the tracks from Springfield toward the Abbey Road bridge is a freight train pulling dozens of cars of mixed freight, including lumber and grain, and six fully loaded chemical cars containing liquefied, pressurized chlorine. The train crew, unaware of the damaged bridge, is unable to brake in time; the leading cars of the train crash off the damaged overpass in a jumble of crushing steel. The bridge abutments and massive steel railcar frames tear jagged holes in the steel railcar jackets, rupturing four of the six ninety-ton chlorine tank cars, which were traveling up near the front of the consist.

The chlorine blasts out of the damaged tank cars, in an aerosol and gas mixture, with gradually diminishing force over several minutes, then it slumps toward the ground. From each ruptured car an acrid, visible greenish yellow poison gas cloud expands rapidly to 500 times the size of the tank car. The toxic clouds merge and move out rapidly over crowded neighborhoods on the east side of Republic and beyond, into the countryside. Now a heavier-than-air, cold chemical cloud hugs the ground, enlarging slightly and diluting only gradually under overcast skies. It envelopes homes and medium-sized trees; it settles down into low-lying areas, pushed by the persistent steady wind over the generally flat terrain in its path.

The first local volunteer fire department crews arriving on the scene see the rapid release of the massive gas cloud. They immediately move to keep cars and pedestrians out of the hazard zone and begin hasty ad hoc evacuations of nearby neighborhoods. First responders attempt to make contact with the train crew, but cannot establish a link. The fire commanders hurriedly call the radio and TV stations and give their best guess as to the direction of the cloud, urging them to advise residents in a wide quadrant on the east to flee without delay. Unfortunately, the town sirens are programmed to signal only tornado warnings.

Neighbors enjoying their suppers in the "near zone," the blocks closest to the wreck, become engulfed quickly by the choking gas cloud. Scores die, some trapped while trying to shelter in their houses, others in futile efforts to run or drive away through the cloud smothering their neighborhoods. As in other toxic cloud disasters, luck plays a key role: some nearest the release who think to quickly climb onto their high roofs survive, though barely. Others manage to cover their faces with wet towels. Still others who try to escape through nearby low-lying areas get trapped by the cloud and perish.

Firefighters and police, who have some limited breathing gear in their vehicles, decide to race in their cars well around and ahead of the leading edge of the cloud, which the steady wind is propelling eastward with quiet menace, and alert those residents farther downwind who stand a fair chance of getting out before the cloud arrives. Scores of exposed victims who have somehow stumbled out or driven through the cloud to safety also need to be transported immediately to nearby hospitals, all but one of which are luckily outside the path of the cloud.

With virtually all police, fire, and EMS personnel struggling to deal with what is becoming a major catastrophic event, another problem is now apparent: a neighborhood of local homes and a nearby trailer park have been completely ravaged by the tornado. Hundreds of injured are in the rubble, not knowing that the existing emergency response system is being completely consumed by the chemical disaster across town. By now many police officers and volunteer firefighters have already perished in brave but risky rescue attempts; more have survived, but are overcome and seriously debilitated by the chlorine fumes. The responders' supply of bottled air for breathing gear is quickly being exhausted, and the crucial imperative is to keep all potential victims moving away from the path of the cloud to safety.

In the immediate vicinity of the train wreck, the scene is utter chaos. Emergency calls for assistance have already gone out to neighboring jurisdictions, as well as to the state. Emergency response crews, ambulances, hazardous materials (haz-mat) teams, and many volunteers and family members are rushing to Republic. Many of the professionals are not fully trained in the new Incident Command System that is meant to coordinate the many various arriving teams and individuals. Confusion reigns as to who is in control, and information is incomplete about what capabilities and backup supplies, such as spare breathing gear, are available in nearby towns. Meanwhile, local residents and travelers have moved toward the accident scene, hoping to offer assistance. Stunned by what they see—prostrate victims, the rubble of the crashed train, and scores of people coughing and gasping—they turn and begin to run or drive speedily from the scene.

About three miles east of Republic, in the smaller town of Battlefield, a number of houses on West Third Street had also been hit by the tornado. The Jones family, recently transferred to Springfield from their home state of New Hampshire, owns one of these houses. Harry and Susan Jones know little about tornados, have never thought much about disaster planning, and know nothing about the tanker rupture. Their house, partially damaged by the immediate effects of the tornado, is also in harm's way as the chlorine gas cloud drifts steadily toward them.

Power is out, so their television and radio are not working. They went into the storm cellar in time (everybody has a storm cellar), but when they come out, Susan trips on some rubble near the front porch and lacerates her foot badly on a shard of glass. Harry attempts to call 911, but gets only busy signals. But that isn't his only problem. He's not sure what to do about his children, ages eight and ten, currently at two different friends' homes for playdates and dinner.

Harry Jones hears sirens in the distance, seemingly from all directions; he doesn't know what they mean. A police cruiser suddenly appears, moving rapidly through the neighborhood, and the officer urgently commands on his loudspeaker: "Please evacuate this community immediately. A potentially deadly chemical has been released into the air nearby, and it could be here in moments. You are in danger. Leave immediately." Harry thinks about running to the next block to try to flag down the officer to get help for his wife who is still bleeding heavily and feeling light-headed. While he's trying to figure out what to do with her, the cruiser moves on.

He thinks of his children, but has no idea what to do next. His car is unscathed, though he vaguely recalls that it is almost out of gas. He wraps Susan's lacerated foot in a towel and sits her in the front seat. He decides to head for the hospital. He notices how pale his wife looks, not aware of the fact that she would be much better off reclining in the back seat. He tries to absorb the scene he's driving by, of damaged houses and dazed neighbors out in the streets. And he's now desperately worried about the safety of his two children. He wonders if there is someone to call for help.

Jones turns his car onto State Highway FF and heads north toward St. John's Regional Medical Center in Springfield—and directly into the path of the deadly still-spreading cloud of chlorine. Of course, he is not the only one heading in precisely the wrong direction. Hundreds of other Battlefield citizens know nothing about the chlorine cloud, having not yet heard any official news or local advisories. Those in the path of the cloud as it spreads and only gradually dissipates encounter a strong, pungent smell and experience a vague sense of irritation on the skin and in the mouth and nasal membranes, accompanied by a dry, hacking cough. Children become irritable and restless. The irritation in the nose and mouth descends gradually into the lungs, making breathing difficult and painful. Coughing becomes paroxysmal and violent, with the sufferer anxious from growing symptoms of "burning in the chest" and shortness of breath.

Individuals exposed to the gas need immediate medical attention. Without appropriate care, many of the gas victims will not survive. Others will be left with chronic loss of pulmonary function, some perhaps with persistent skin and eye conditions.

But what about the Jackson family? Peter and Cheryl Jackson live in Battlefield only two blocks away from the Joneses and their property also suffered significant damage when the twister touched down not far away. They went into the cellar in time and tuned in the emergency frequency of their battery-powered radio. They learned immediately about the general extent of the tornado and heard the alarming news about the looming chemical cloud disaster, as well as the official order to evacuate. They listened intently to specific instructions for their neighborhood: Do not head west— you'll run into the toxic plume from Republic. The announcer exhorted all Battlefield residents to leave fast and head east or south.

The Jacksons race through the kitchen and living room, stopping at the hall closet to pick up a small case that contains copies of important personal and financial papers. The car is in the breezeway, which has collapsed on the vehicle, denting the hood and the roof, but not affecting operability. In the trunk is a "go pack" designed for all-hazard emergency evacuation purposes. Bottled water, some dried food, a crank- and battery-operated radio and flashlights, spare clothes, a survival blanket, a backup supply of their prescription medications, and a copy of their own family "emergency plan" are all there. The fuel tank is three-quarters full.

The Jacksons' older child, Mary, is away at college, but their fourteen-year-old son, Adam, is playing in an evening basketball game at the middle school. The school is located due southwest of their house, not beyond the danger zone of the current eastward movement of the toxic gas cloud, though not affected by the earlier tornado. Still, there is no way to safely get there, and no guarantee that the school would allow relatives to pick up students.

In accordance with their family emergency plan, Peter Jackson's brother, Bill, who lives one town away, has been designated as backup responder for their son. Peter tries to call his brother by cell phone. Local telephone landlines are down and his brother's cell phone isn't responding. By previous plan they have agreed to use an out-of-state relative as a central information hub. He leaves word there for his brother to pick up Adam at the middle school. As soon as Bill learns of the Republic emergencies and is able to locate a working phone, he, too, calls their out-of-state emergency contact number and learns he needs to try to pick up Adam at the school. After an initial period during which the school is battened down and not releasing students to relatives, he does so, bringing the boy back to his own house.

Meanwhile the Jacksons are in the car headed east from Battlefield toward an official evacuation destination. Three blocks from their house, Jackson stops the car when he sees one of their neighbors walking dazedly in the middle of the street. It is an elderly gentleman who is bleeding from a head injury, pale and disoriented. Cheryl Jackson, having taken two Red Cross courses in emergency care and CPR, applies pressure to the wound. She helps the man to their car where she makes sure he is able to lie down in the back seat. She keeps pressure on the wound, after ascertaining that his breathing and circulation are stable, as her husband races to the evacuation center, where, the radio had said, emergency medical care would be available.

The mild five-mile-an-hour spring breeze shifts north, sending the cloud of chlorine northward toward Springfield. Residents there, having heard from TV or radio or by word of mouth of the emergency in Republic, have more adequate warning than those nearest the gas cloud. Except for those persons who do not receive any information or the very hard-to-evacuate, most flee hurriedly and manage to escape, some without their pets, some without knowing whether children, relatives, or friends are safe.

A few thousand Springfield residents are exposed to low levels of the poison gas. Along with the families of those more seriously exposed, dead, or injured in Republic, these people will later join in class-action lawsuits against the railroad, the chemical company shipper, and the state contractor responsible for bridge evaluation and maintenance. Frightened citizens and mayors in cities along the rail route will demand advance notification of future hazardous shipments; sober agencies and politicians will hold hearings on bridge safety and local emergency preparedness planning; environmental activists in town meetings will demand that poison gas chemicals be phased out in favor of alternatives that won't cause disasters if they leak a spill.

The Jackson family's chances of surviving are reasonably good. The Jones family, on the other hand, will likely be counted among the victims of a "double disaster," suffering the consequences of being unprepared for either the tornado or the subsequent chemical accident. Individual survival in this scenario has little to do with official response and much to do with individuals and families learning to care for themselves during and in the immediate aftermath of a significant disaster. In the Republic emergencies, as in so many other cases of significant disasters, official capabilities were inadequate, uncoordinated, and overwhelmed by the scale of the events.

The Republic government's years of ongoing preparedness efforts proved crucial. Thousands of survivors were able to make use of basic response services at many stages of the disaster: the alerting sirens, some ad hoc monitoring of cloud direction and police cruiser warnings to evacuate, radio-provided information on the event and on where help was available, the medical care available there, outreach to the public on how to prepare a "go pack." All are basic governmental responsibilities, but for their successful utilization they depend crucially on individual and family preparedness.

This multihazard megadisaster—a tornado combined with a chemical accident—or some version of it is possible in many parts of the country. The combination of factors contributing to the catastrophe may well be different, but the chances of its happening are good.

While we cannot control the natural forces that produce tornados and other damaging storms, there are a number of initiatives that could better protect this country from chemical and other industrial accidents. In the hierarchy of chemical risk management, the first and most important and effective way to reduce chemical disaster risks is to press vigorously for use of safer substitute chemicals and inherently safer technologies at all stages of facility design, production, use, storage, and transportation. The Department of Homeland Security has been loath to require that companies pursue safer technologies, but it must be done.

Key Proposals

1. **Adopt best practices for active government oversight and regulation of chemical safety.** In addition to the proposed federal legislation discussed earlier, numerous examples of relatively effective systems exist at various levels of government. One of the best state-level accident prevention programs is the Toxic Catastrophe

Prevention Act program, operated by the New Jersey State Department of Environmental Protection. One salient result of the program's operation—which includes a fee system for on-site storage of dangerous chemicals, state inspection and enforcement, and worst-case-scenario analysis—is that fifteen years ago 575 New Jersey chemical facilities reported on-site storage of chlorine gas but this year there are only 26—a clear demonstration that safer alternatives are available.

Another excellent local accident prevention program is the Industrial Safety Ordinance program operated by the Health Services Department in Contra Costa County, California. It requires managers of regulated facilities to consider the potential for inherently safer technologies that would reduce disaster risks and to explain why the safest technologies have in some cases not been adopted.

Critical to adopting best practices is the need for an ongoing government accountability and preparedness evaluation program that includes strategic planning and objective measurement of specific, desired disaster risk reductions.

2. Increase public understanding of the dangers of industrial accidents by improving the mechanisms for educating the public. In the absence of vigorous government agencies, a legislature will sometimes enact right-to-know laws that, instead of rule-based regulation, rely on mandating that the most dangerous facilities simply provide key risk and safety information to the public, workers, and the press. A workable chemical disaster right-to-know law puts the burden on chemical handlers and transporters to provide information on the risks of their chemical to workers and the public, and to train both in appropriate safety and security measures. The hope is that newly informed citizens will then press for significant disaster risk reductions.

Congress enacted, with mixed results, two major federal right-to-know laws after the Bhopal, India, toxic gas disaster in 1984 that killed 6,000 people overnight and injured more than 100,000. The Union Carbide Company had not shared its own risk documents saying that such a disaster was possible with the local Indian authorities. Both of the new U.S. laws enshrine truth-telling as the basic democratic principle of U.S. chemical disaster risk reduction and emergency response: first, calculate and show the worst-case scenarios, so the public can decide how seriously to consider a problem, how many resources to spend to eliminate or mitigate the risk, and what appropriate emergency response to take. With these laws, it has become officially un-American to leave the public at high risk and in blissful ignorance. But the great majority of industry managers and local officials are still mainly concerned "not to alarm the public," and thus undercut the impact of the laws.

Media and universities also have important roles to play in informing the public about disaster risks and about the state of preparedness capabilities.

3. **Reroute hazardous materials away from sensitive locations.** It would make sense to transport hazardous materials away from densely populated areas, populations, and sensitive environmental resources. Equally important is the enforcement of stricter regulations governing the storage of railcars carrying hazardous material. Railcar storage of these chemicals in urban areas needs particular attention. A federal Department of Transportation regulation (HM-223) transferred responsibility as of June 1, 2005, to local and state officials for regulating the safety and security of large sectors of haz-mat railcar storage. Many officials do not know about this transfer of authority. A recent Baltimore city railcar storage ordinance has some suggestive language, but other localities need to experiment with new regulations that improve their oversight of haz-mat railcar storage and security.

4. **Focus emergency response planning on specific operational goals.** The U.S. Army and the U.S. Government Accountability Office employ this strategy effectively and it should guide our

planning. Instead of asking communities how many emergency preparedness plans they have languishing on a shelf, we should turn our attention and action plans to what a city or county is capable of doing during a disaster.

Communities can do the following:

- Prevent the most horrendous consequences from potential chemical releases, for instance, by use of zoning to keep dangerous facilities away from residential areas and by sensible rerouting of hazardous chemical cargoes.
- Detect serious chemical releases in a timely way.
- Alert the whole public, especially sensitive or hard-to-evacuate populations, about the scope and nature of the event, any time of day or night.
- Evacuate populations.
- Shelter in place (stay where you are) when possible and appropriate.
- Provide appropriate medical care.

Drills and exercises with the many players that make up a municipality's first-response team, as well as citizens and nongovernmental organizations, are critical to assess the extent of a locality's reliable, functioning capabilities, to identify gaps, and to take concrete steps to fill those gaps.

6 · Special Populations, Special Needs, and Soft Targets: Why I'm Worried About the Vulnerability of America's Children

Nobody said the process of preparing the nation to cope effectively with major disasters would be easy, especially since we have never actually defined what "prepared" means. We want to do enough to make the country more secure and ready to respond to disasters that are in the realm of possibility, but this is an expensive, multifaceted challenge filled with uncertainty, lack of definition, and an infinite variety of specific risks. Limited only by imagination and resources, disaster planners face the persistent problem of becoming over-whelmed—and it's easy to see why. However, as I have already emphasized, the purpose of disaster planning is to find that "sweet spot" where we set goals reflecting a *prudent level of readiness* that neither drains the treasury, nor fosters an obsession with disaster risk. Still, the planning process needs to be based on concepts that reflect real issues likely to arise in major disasters.

For instance, it remains poorly understood by most disaster planners that not all populations can be managed in the same way during a major disaster. A typical healthy adult exposed to a toxic gas may well be aware of how to respond, is capable of fleeing, is treatable with well-known doses of an antidote or antibiotic, and can be decontaminated (showered clean) using standard equipment. The same is not true for an infirm elderly person who is dependent on continuing care, suffers from a chronic medical condition, and cannot leave a danger zone unassisted. That person will not be able to evacuate and if he or she is taking medications, the antidote or antibiotic needed during or following an acute exposure event may require a very different dose. The "usual dose" could be deadly in interaction with another medication or because the antibiotic may linger in the system, causing unwanted side effects. First responders, including emergency personnel, need guidance in administering correct doses and managing older people who have been exposed to a noxious agent.

Caring for individuals with a variety of disabilities also presents special challenges to disaster planners and responders. Not having thought through these "special situations" in the aftermath of Katrina created a significant complicating effect on the evacuation and recovery effort and cost lives. Approximately 23 percent of residents in the city had disabilities, more than the national average of 19.2 percent. These individuals, and the people assisting them, faced extra challenges in getting out of harm's way.

For people with hearing disabilities, emergency television broadcast information should be captioned. If evacuation maps or shelter locations are shown on television, the information should also be read out loud so that the visually impaired are not excluded. Then, too, emergency shelters should be equipped to provide services for individuals with disabilities. In a survey conducted after Hurricane Katrina by the National Organization for People with Disabilities, less than 30 percent of the shelters had access to American Sign Language interpreters and 60 percent did not have TVs with open captioning capabilities. Emergency plans need to accurately reflect the real needs of a community.

Children Are Not Just Little Adults

Children represent another special population for disaster response planning. The U.S. health and public health communities have dedicated some attention to preparing for, responding to, and treating children in the event of a terrorist attack. However, most of the literature addressing the issue of children and terrorism considers children as collateral victims rather than intended targets. In fact, the majority of this literature focuses on mental health and behavioral consequences of terrorism on children, with very little on pediatric mass casualties or exposure to nonconventional weapons such as bioweapons, radiation, and chemical attacks.

If children are not recognized as a special population and planned for accordingly, they can be at grave and disproportionately higher risk in major disasters. Many factors influence the degree to which children are in more danger than adults. Children are more vulnerable in environments that have been sprayed with aerosolized chemical weapons that tend to settle to the ground. Why? The closer to the surface, the more concentrated the toxin. A small child, who is shorter than an adult, and whose nose and mouth are closer to the surface, will breathe in a higher concentration of poison. More than that, the breathing rate of children is more rapid than that of adults and their skin more permeable, causing their bodies to absorb toxic agents more readily.

Most medications used for adults need to be modified—at least in terms of dose—for safe use in children. Children exposed to dangerous chemicals or radioactive materials will need, just as adults, to be decontaminated in special showers. However, the younger the child, the greater the need to carefully adjust treatment protocols. Small infants exposed to cold water in the decontamination unit, for instance, can go into shock. Parents or rescue workers need to have access to equipment that can ensure temperature control so that children can be treated safely. Additionally, the units need to be larger than standard equipment because young children need assistance and comforting from a parent or caregiver.

Most disaster and emergency planning does not take into account the very difficult questions that arise when children are separated from their parents. Guardianship and permission issues remain largely unanswered, creating potential liability and legal complications that can present moral challenges when life-and-death decisions must be made. Very tough decisions may have to be made about the triage of very sick children. Who gets care and who does not when personnel, equipment, and supplies are extremely limited? Who decides when to shut down life support in borderline situations, with or without the permission of parents? Planners need to think about these concerns *before* the crisis.

Many other considerations require advance planning. Children exposed to anthrax would need different doses and perhaps different antibiotics than adults. When an effective vaccine against avian flu materializes, it may not be effective or safe for children. If it is safe and effective, the quantity needed to produce an immune response will likely be far less for children than adults. Caring for children who have been severely injured requires special skills, training, and experience. Even a well-trained office pediatrician can be intimidated by a very sick or severely injured young child; so can a surgeon who is trained only in adult care. That is why we cannot count on adult-focused medical staff to respond to and/or properly care for the children who need care most.

The generic "one size fits all" approach to disaster response preparedness can mean that many populations, like the disability and aging populations and children, never receive the special attention they need. Getting the health-care and disaster response systems to focus on these issues, particularly those related to children's interests, has been a very difficult—and largely unsuccessful—effort.

A Telltale Briefing

On September 25, 2001, precisely two weeks following the 9/11 terrorist attacks on New York City's World Trade Center, I attended a special briefing on the fifteenth floor of the GM building on the west side of Manhattan. We gathered at the offices of the Greater New York Hospital Association (GNYHA), a trade organization founded in 1904 to represent more than 220 hospitals, nursing homes, and other health-care facilities in the New York metropolitan area. Dealing with large-scale disasters had not really been high on the agenda of the GNYHA, but its vice president, an attorney and natural leader named Susan Waltman, had stepped forward on the day of the attack and was almost single-handedly mobilizing the organization. She made sure the GNYHA was adequately represented at the city's Emergency Operations Center and helped develop a level of coordination among the hospitals that was virtually unprecedented. Most of us recognized Waltman as one of New York's unsung heroes during the terrible days following 9/11.

The audience for the several-hour briefing consisted of representatives from almost all of GNYHA's member institutions, including a number of medical personnel who had camped out at and near Ground Zero after the attack. Federal, state, and local officials briefed the group on the status at Ground Zero, and shared insights on the meaning of the attack, what we could expect next, and the general level of preparedness for further attacks. Needless to say, the general mood was serious and focused. When the formal presentations were done, Susan Waltman called for questions from the audience. After listening intently to a good deal of relevant back-and-forth, I finally raised my hand.

I had one question: "We've been listening for quite a while to these informative remarks, but, as a pediatrician, I must say that I heard not one mention of children in any of the discussions. Although the towers were office buildings, with virtually no children inside when the planes struck, several schools were in the vicinity and could have easily been in harm's way." As it was, many schoolchildren had witnessed the attacks; some of them were watching, horrified—and traumatized—as victims jumped or fell from the high floors in the moments before the collapse of first one tower, then the next.

I continued: "What I would like to know is what plans are in the works to make sure that the needs of children would be accounted for in the protocols for managing mass disaster situations, especially if the next attacks utilize chemical, biological, or radiological weapons."

There was a pause in the low-level buzz in the room. The government officials looked at Susan Waltman. They looked at each other, shaking their heads. The federal official responded: "Actually, nothing really has been done in terms of planning for the children's needs under those circumstances." I was only half-surprised.

I thought about this a great deal and decided that the situation was unacceptable. Children could well be in harm's way from terrorist acts, natural disasters, or large-scale industrial accidents. Could it be that they were simply not on the radar screen? I had to find out. My first call was to an old friend, the revered pediatrician Lou Cooper, then president-elect of the American Academy of Pediatrics (AAP). I asked him if the academy could set up a task force so that children would not be left out of disaster planning. He said he was thinking the same thing and would make some calls. In a matter of a few days, we saw some action. The AAP established the Task Force on Terrorism, which eventually led a national effort to make sure pediatricians and the relevant disaster response planning agencies had an expert resource on children and terrorism.

The next day I called the new junior senator from New York, Hillary Rodham Clinton. I had worked with her in 1993, during the first year of President Bill Clinton's first term, on the noble but ultimately unsuccessful attempt to reform the country's health-care system. We had stayed in touch since then. I explained my concerns regarding children and disaster readiness, and she got it immediately. Just days later, she was at a hearing with federal officials on emergency readiness and asked them about the issue of children in the planning process. They confirmed what I had told her and she called back to tell me that she was determined to do something about it. That was an understatement. Senator Clinton wrote legislation requiring that the needs of children be included in all planning efforts regarding terrorist attacks. The language she wrote was eventually included in the first Public Health Security and Bioterrorism Preparedness and Response Act of 2002, which was signed into law in June of that year.

New York Times columnist Bob Herbert got wind of what was going on and wrote a powerful piece about the need to make sure children weren't forgotten in the essential work of preparing the nation for this new era. The *Today Show* picked up the story, and a few weeks later, Senator Clinton and I were able to voice our concerns about the lack of focus on children on any level, including how schools might best prepare for any potential disaster.

By late 2005, some of these areas had been addressed—but only in a few states such as California, Connecticut, New Jersey, and New York, and with little accountability or understanding of what strategies are most effective. For instance, under the Safe Schools programs and other campus security initiatives, a number of U.S. Department of Education grants have been awarded specifically for school preparedness efforts related to terrorism. However, the net result of these collective funding efforts is not clear, as a Department of Homeland Security official described in February 2005 to the Associated Press: "[It is] difficult to give a nationwide assessment of schools' disaster preparedness."

The Department of Education's Emergency Response Crisis Management Discretionary Grant Program is one of the key national programs helping schools prepare to deal with terrorism. However, the grants awarded decreased from 2003 to 2004 not only in total amount (from approximately $40 million to $29 million) but also in average award (from approximately $295,000 to $262,000) and the total number of grants given (from 135 to 109). There are 15,000 public school districts in the United States. With some 250 grants given to the 15,000 districts, less than 2 percent of districts have received funding.

The disconnect between spending and accountability is further compounded by what studies of school preparedness have described as an overall deficiency in monies provided. A 2004 report by the America Prepared Campaign on the state of terrorism preparedness in the twenty largest school districts in the United States found seven "Needing Improvement" (Broward County [FL], Clark County [NV], Dallas, Duval County [FL], New York, Philadelphia, and San Diego districts) and two "Failing" (Chicago and Detroit districts). Of the remaining eleven districts, only two—Fairfax County (VA) and Montgomery County (MD)—scored "Best." In essence, the current status of emergency planning in U.S. schools is extremely variable with relatively few having developed and implemented adequate plans to ensure the safety of its students. The conclusion of the report was simple: "Money was almost always a problem."

Keeping Children Safe

Five years after 9/11, planning for the possibility that children may be mass victims of a terrorist attack remains minimal. The federal bioterrorism preparedness legislation mandated that a pediatric advisory committee be established to provide the Bush administration with specific advice about the needs of children in disaster planning. A group of experts was convened, but it met only once, in Washington on May 21, 2003. With staff assistance, the group prepared and presented to Tommy Thompson, then the secretary of health and human services, a comprehensive report with concrete recommendations. Neither the secretary nor his office ever responded with actions or follow-up on any level. At the urging of Dr. Sally Phillips of the federal Agency for Healthcare Research and Policy, a real hero in pediatric advocacy, the expert panel reconvened in 2005 and pressed to have its advice more widely heard. A stalwart group of dedicated pediatricians will not let this go; they have been producing reports, holding consensus conferences, and pushing hard, with little to show in terms of influencing the process to ensure that the needs of children have been properly understood and addressed.

American Children as Targets of Terror

One would like to think that certain truths or values would be universally understood as rules of engagement, formally declared or otherwise. Noncombatant civilians in a war zone should be off-limits as deliberate targets of aggression. The sanctity of children's well-being should be unquestioned, regardless of the issues at stake in the larger conflict. Sadly, history shows that this understanding is neither universally shared nor uniformly valued.

Intentional attacks against civilian populations have long been employed to undermine morale and secure political objectives. The military historian Caleb Carr, writing in *The Lessons of Terror,* says, "For in truth, the purposeful targeting of civilians is nothing new in warfare—in fact it is, as said, as old as warfare itself—and the world has been more than willing to accord the status of 'soldiers' to some of its most vicious practitioners." And in their distressing book *Innocent Targets,* Michael and Chris Dorn chronicle in some detail the deliberate use of violence against children to demoralize an enemy or seek political gain. When children are targets of terror, the emotional stakes are virtually off the charts. Long-standing policies of "no negotiating with terrorists" often collapse under intense public pressure to save children at high risk.

In January 2005 I wrote an op-ed in the *San Francisco Chronicle* reviewing the reasons I remain worried about the possibility of deliberate targeting of children. These were among the principal incidents and findings that made me increasingly concerned:

- An Al-Qaeda attack on the American school in Singapore was thwarted at the last moment by U.S. and Singaporean counterintelligence teams. Three thousand students were in the school at the time.

- The Al-Qaeda terror groups that attacked a nightclub in Bali in 2002 were found to be planning to strike U.S. and other western children attending international schools in Indonesia.

- One of the most vicious and deadly attacks against children ever conceived was planned and implemented by Chechen rebels, with significant Al-Qaeda backing. On September 1, 2004, the first day of school in the Russian city of Beslan, Chechen terrorists seized Beslan School no. 1, taking 1,220 hostages, including children, parents, teachers, and staff. Fifty-three hours later, 334 persons were dead, 186 of them schoolchildren. The impact on the city and all of Russia was cataclysmic. Far-reaching effects on the psychology of the Russian-Chechen conflict helped reinforce the terrifying notion that targeting children potentially influences public attitude and, too often, governmental policies.

- In the fall of 2004, coalition forces in Baghdad captured a foreign insurgent who had in his residence a computer disk containing extensive descriptions and maps of U.S. schools in California, Florida, Georgia, Michigan, New Jersey, and Oregon.

Schools are typically "soft targets" and are difficult to secure without seriously undermining a preferred state of comfort and freedom in the building and on the campus, in general. Creating a "lockdown" atmosphere results in an armed camp environment, diametrically opposed to what most students, parents, and schools would find acceptable. Unfortunately, there is significant reason to believe that American children may be explicit targets of terrorist organizations wishing to take retribution for policies and actions of the

U.S. government alleged to have cost the lives of millions of innocent Muslim and Arab children.

An Al-Qaeda computer recovered after the U.S. invasion of Afghanistan contained an unfinished theological justification entitled "The Truth About the New Crusade: A Ruling on the Killing of Women and Children of the Non-Believers." It argued that "the sanctity of women, children, and the elderly is not absolute" and concluded that "in killing Americans who are ordinarily off limits, Muslims should not exceed four million noncombatants, or render more than ten million of them homeless." In essence, Al-Qaeda's rationale and killing quotas seek a reciprocal effect equal to U.S. bombing and embargo campaigns against Iraq and Afghanistan. The Al-Qaeda position could not be more clear:

> We have not reached parity with [America]. We have the right to kill four million Americans, *two million of them children,* and to exile twice as many and wound and cripple hundreds of thousands."(Emphasis added)
>
> **Suleiman Abu Ghaith**
> Senior adviser to bin Laden and Al-Qaeda spokesman, November 2001

I fear that an attack on American children is not outside the realm of possibility. What follows is one hypothetical scenario of how it could happen, drawn entirely from unclassified print sources. Christopher Farrell, director of investigations and research for Judicial Watch and a former military intelligence officer with expertise in counterintelligence and human intelligence, helped structure the premise and unfolding of this story.

Tucson, Arizona, lies approximately sixty miles from the U.S.–Mexico border, a barrier that is largely unsecured, with rough terrain, little or no fencing, and sporadic U.S. Border Patrol (USBP) coverage. The USBP estimates that they apprehend only one-third of all persons illegally crossing into the United States. Sophisticated criminal smuggling operations (of both drugs and

humans) consistently enable over 1.5 million persons to cross into the United States, via southeastern Arizona alone, every year. The smugglers, known as *bajadores*, use three main trafficking corridors into Tucson: Altar Valley, Cochise County, and passes through the Chiricahua Mountains. Each corridor has its strengths and weaknesses for terrorists seeking clandestine entry into the country.

For individuals who seek to travel quickly while losing themselves in the high volume of smuggled drugs and humans, the Altar Valley corridor southwest of Tucson and the San Pedro River, which cuts through the center of Cochise County southeast of Tucson, are preferable. The Chiricahua Mountains corridor, which is still further east of Tucson, enables travelers to pass with a less likelihood of detection by Border Patrol agents, but the very rough terrain is physically quite challenging. It is a fact that in June 2004, agents from the Willcox, Arizona, Border Patrol station reported apprehending seventy-seven males of "Middle Eastern descent" in two separate incidents trekking through the Chiricahua Mountains. Many were released on their own recognizance pending immigration hearings.

The objective is to cross the border undetected and move north on foot, across sparsely populated high desert terrain, toward Interstate 10, the major east–west route in southern Arizona. A quick vehicle pickup of the illegal crossers at a prearranged point along a deserted county or state road signals the end of the toughest phase of the journey. Normally, in little more than one hour they would be in Tucson.

For a variety of reasons, Tucson has become home to numerous radical Islamists dating back to the early 1980s, when their efforts centered on raising money for the Afghan mujahideen fighting the Soviets. Tucson's ties to radical Islamists shifted and radicalized over the years. People with a Tucson connection named in the 9/11 Commission's report include the following:

- Hani Hanjour, who piloted American Airlines Flight 77 into the Pentagon, was a student at the University of Arizona.

- Wadi el Hage, bin Laden's personal assistant, is currently serving a life sentence for the 1998 East African embassy bombings. El Hage is tied to the murder of Dr. Rashad Khalifa, imam of the Islamic Center of Tucson.
- Wa'el Jelaidan, who co-founded Al-Qaeda with bin Laden, was president of the Islamic Center of Tucson in the mid-1980s.

At least thirteen other Al-Qaeda figures also have ties to Arizona, mostly in the Tucson, Phoenix, Mesa, and Scottsdale areas.

Armed with this knowledge, a team of forty to sixty terrorists enter the United States, using all three corridors over six to eight months, paying the smugglers' "coyote" guides to facilitate clandestine access to the U.S. To reduce the chances of detection, the terrorists enter the country in small cells of three to seven persons. Some of the group need "identity laundering" before leaving Mexico. For that, they seek readily available assistance in the "tri-border" region between the cities of Foz do Iguazú, Brazil; Ciudad del Este, Paraguay; and Puerto Iguazu, Argentina. This is a notorious destination for persons seeking new identities and easy visa entry to Mexico. Entry to Mexico is easily facilitated with high-quality false documentation or bribes to border and customs officials, particularly in Paraguay. The tri-border area is also home to more than a hundred aircraft landing strips, none of which are regulated by any authority, facilitating clandestine travel for terrorists and criminals avoiding security forces and watch lists.

The plan is to attack two schools in the Tucson area using several suicide fighters, heavily armed and determined to wreak havoc on the city and the nation.

The terrorists concoct a three-tier organization. The shooters and bombers constitute the first tier. The second tier consists of persons committed to providing logistic, administrative, and transportation support to the first tier. Second-tier supporters are not willing or able to actually carry out acts of terrorism, but they are willing to drive someone to a train station, allow a stranger to spend a couple of nights in a spare room, or pick up supplies from a hardware store.

The third tier comprises individuals who sympathize with the terrorists. Members of the third tier contribute financially on any given Friday evening at their mosque to a vague solicitation to "support our brothers fighting the infidels." They may not know precisely where their contribution is going, but they support the general outcome, however it manifests itself. They will not take the active steps of the second-tier supporter. They will not be able to remember anything or anyone when the police conduct a neighborhood canvassing operation in the hours and days immediately following an attack.

The terrorist team assembles in the United States over a period of several months. Early arrivals establish contact with the well-developed, discreet second tier of supporters in Tucson. These supporters have arranged for safe-house accommodations and are facilitating transportation and other logistics. Other supporters of the mission have been busy "fronting" financial transactions to avoid law enforcement detection. They are also instrumental in procuring firearms, ammunition, and explosives. Part of the support network includes so-called home-grown terrorists—American Islamists or converts to radical Islam. These individuals have been invaluable in the long-term planning and are now deeply involved in mission implementation.

The terrorists, still operating in cells, have familiarized themselves with the local area and their targets. Over the past two weeks they have finalized their reconnaissance, planning, logistics, transportation routes, and contingencies. They rehearse many of the preliminary steps of the attack itself and identify potential problems and complications. Arizona offers the terrorists plenty of remote, isolated areas for weapons training.

For operational security reasons, cells will not assemble into strike teams until the point of attack when the suicide sieges commence. Only a very few of the high-level leaders have full knowledge of the overall plan and each of the team members.

Female terrorists in their late twenties and early thirties scout out the schools. Dressed in western clothing and driving minivans, they show up with toddlers in tow, claiming to be new to the area, and interested in the school for their children. They gain largely unrestricted access to school buildings, playgrounds, sports fields, gymnasiums, assembly halls, auditoriums, parking lots, and bus yards, and all kinds of information from helpful school staff. Eventually they know more than enough to provide the terrorist cells with information to effectively plan and carry out an assault on the schools.

The terrorists schedule the attack when they are absolutely ready. They plan a suicide mission, with no need for hostage-taking, kidnapping, or escape routes. Their ultimate objective is terror—and its psychological and political fallout.

On a perfectly ordinary Thursday in late October, the terrorists move in on two large elementary schools: a large public elementary school with just over nine hundred students in kindergarten through grade 6 and a Catholic parochial school of more than four hundred students in pre-kindergarten through grade 8. The targeted schools are identified and reconnoitered with maps and satellite imagery available on the Internet, and from vehicles on the street. Their locations on main thoroughfares off the interstate enable the terrorists to obtain quick access, surprising and shocking the buildings' inhabitants. The terrorists enter school property using minivans that call no attention to themselves in the parking lots and give them plenty of room for their weapons, ammunition, explosives, and other supplies.

The raids take place almost simultaneously. The terrorist teams communicate easily between each other, using commonly available walkie-talkie-type, "push-to-talk" cell phones. As backup, the teams have commercially available frequency-hopping radios with basic digital encryption, although little communication is expected because the attacks are suicide missions.

At both schools, the terrorists employ simple, devastating tactics: they approach the schools quickly, fire their weapons, use physical force, and shouting loudly, destroy property violently as they subdue and rapidly impose control over school staff, parents, and students in and around the buildings. Their tactics work: school officials and everyone else are totally surprised and unable to act.

Following the lessons of the Beslan siege, within minutes the terrorists secure the schools' exits with explosives, occupy key positions, construct barricades, and position lookouts armed with heavy machine guns, rocket-propelled grenades (RPGs), and regular grenades. Several of the attackers don suicide explosive vests. Some of the explosive charges are wired with "dead man switches," which are rigged to detonate if the terrorist manning that position releases pressure on the electronic contact for any reason. Such switches are designed to thwart sneak attacks, snipers, incapacitating gas, rescue assaults, or other techniques aimed at disarming or "neutralizing" the terrorists. As the drama unfolds, five of these devices are passively tripped during failed assaults on the facilities by heavily armed SWAT teams from Tucson Police Department and the FBI, instantly killing the terrorist wearing the vest.

Meanwhile, other terrorists divide the students and staff into five separate groups in each school. Terrorists treat the initial pockets of resistance or aggression among the captives with indiscriminate executions. They dispose of bodies out the school windows, where television crews capture the scene with their long-range lenses.

To magnify the shock of the attack and complicate emergency services response, the terrorists launch two simultaneous suicide bomber attacks as the elementary schools are seized. One female suicide bomber detonates her bomb in the only trauma center in southern Arizona, at the University of Arizona's University Medical Center. Specifically and deliberately, she chooses the pediatric emergency room as her target. At almost the same moment the second female suicide bomber enters the downtown lobby of Tucson Police Department headquarters and detonates her bomb. The two bombings have a devastating effect on the immediate ability to respond to and coordinate law enforcement and lifesaving care. The explosions in the medical center and police headquarters kill scores of officers and medical personnel.

Within minutes of the attacks on the schools, hundreds of 911 calls from nearby residents or parents who have heard gunfire and explosions flood the emergency switchboards in Tucson. The explosions at police headquarters and the medical center have thrown all response systems into chaos. All available police and medical units in the county are dispatched to the four scenes, but extraordinary confusion reigns. State and federal officials are called immediately. The governor calls the president, who in turn convenes relevant cabinet officers, military leaders, and intelligence agency heads in the White House situation room.

The governor authorizes mobilization of relevant state agencies, including the Arizona National Guard, although the guard response is seriously diminished by its ongoing responsibilities in Iraq and Afghanistan. Every relevant federal agency races to the scene including FBI, the Bureau of Alcohol, Tobacco, Firearms, and Explosives, counterintelligence officials, and Department of Defense assets.

With major destruction at the University Medical Center still being assessed, the governor calls his counterparts in surrounding states and medical units start to flood in from every part of the state and beyond. The governor's state emergency director requests military assistance, including mobile field hospitals to be established in the perimeter areas of both schools.

Meanwhile, top law enforcement officials try to establish contact with the terrorists. But the attackers appear to be in no hurry to issue demands or negotiate. After all, their primary mission, already accomplished, is to secure each school and maximize television coverage. Supporting that second objective, during the first twenty minutes after they establish total order and discipline, the terrorists force hostages to call friends, family, television and radio stations, newspapers, and politicians. Once these calls are made, all cell phones are collected. Several of the hostages who attempt to withhold cell phones are executed.

Police and their negotiation teams continue frantic attempts to make contact with the terrorists at both schools. Negotiation protocols called for playing out all hostage sieges as long as possible, thinking that time is generally on the side of the police. The terrorists know these practices and have designed their attack to exploit them. Each terrorist aspires to be a *shaheed,* or martyr.

Terrorists at the Catholic school request that representatives from major television networks approach the school, along with a pool camera crew, guaranteeing safe passage in return for having their demands communicated. With police consent, the media eagerly agree. The terrorists make two demands known to an international audience, in real time: (1) the immediate withdrawal of all U.S. and coalition forces from Afghanistan and Iraq, and (2) the immediate repatriation of all "detainees" held in America's "global war on terror," including those held at the U.S. Naval Base at Guantánamo and the CIA "black sites," reportedly in Poland and Romania.

The terrorists announce on live broadcast that failure to comply with the demands will result in hostages' being executed at regular intervals; no further discussions, negotiations, or offers will be entertained. Nobody knows how to deal with the demands or the announced consequences of failing to meet them.

Conditions inside the schools deteriorate rapidly. As during the Beslan siege, basic sanitation, food, and water become critical for the hostages, most of whom are in a state of shock. Adults and children have witnessed and been subject to brutal acts of physical violence, including beatings, gunshot wounds, and trauma following the explosions. Some bodies of dead adults and children have been dumped from windows while others lie where they were executed, in the same rooms as the hostages. Terrorists moving through both schools use children as human shields near windows and doorways.

Outside the schools, police work furiously to establish cordons, evacuate nearby residential areas, and control media access to the schools and the surrounding areas. Still reeling from the attack on police headquarters, these efforts are disorganized. As members of each new agency arrive from surrounding jurisdictions or higher levels of government, the situation deteriorates further. Overall responsibility for directing response and rescue efforts is unclear. No one seems to be fully in charge. Exacerbating the coordination chaos is an enormous presence of politically influential forces, including the governor, the mayor of Tucson, the superintendent of schools, the acting chief of police, regional heads of the FBI, the Diocese of Tucson, and a slew of other federal agencies. The U.S. attorney general, in Washington, acts as chief liaison with the president of the United States.

As was the case on 9/11 and following the flooding of New Orleans and the hurricanes of 2005, radio communications among different first-responder groups are not interoperable. Tests done on a new system earlier that year revealed an inherent problem with all radios being on the same frequency. In the middle of a major disaster drill, the single frequency had been overloaded and dysfunctional, thereby disabling communications among all first responders.

None of the plans devised for dealing with catastrophic events in southern Arizona had included school officials. On the medical side, some level of planning had also occurred, but it was even more sporadic in terms of managing a substantial regional disaster. The possibility that a major medical facility might be attacked had not been considered. What was more problematic for this particular event was the virtual absence of pediatric experts in the planning protocols or exercises. Large-scale trauma to children was never imagined.

The siege and seizure of the schools and hostages lasts twenty-eight excruciating hours. What prompts the simultaneous storming and rescue of the two schools are the televised executions of schoolchildren at twenty-minute intervals. Commandos rush through the corridors, breaking down doors into hostage rooms. All terrorists attempt to detonate explosive vests and other prepositioned bombs before being killed. For a variety of reasons, nearly 50 percent of the explosives fail to detonate.

A veritable army of medical rescue teams follow the commandos, arriving to transport injured children and teachers to the U.S. Army mobile field hospitals established earlier. All told, more than four hundred schoolchildren, teachers, school officials, first responders, police officers, and military personnel have perished.

More than two hundred children and adults have been injured, many critically. Many lives have been saved, both at the scene and in the field hospitals. A report released sixty days after the siege reveals that the lack of pediatric-trained trauma surgeons and sufficient pediatric equipment may have contributed to the loss of more than seventy-five lives of seriously injured younger victims.

Protecting Children

The very concept of children's being deliberately targeted is profoundly abhorrent. My experience is that even professionals who deal with terrorism response and preparedness have difficulty absorbing the possibility of a Beslan-style attack in the United States. Still, it is extremely important that we consider measures that prevent such events, terrible as they are to contemplate. And in addition to terrorism, as I noted earlier, children are uniquely vulnerable to other kinds of megadisaster scenarios, including large-scale industrial accidents that release, for instance, toxic chlorine clouds. Keeping children safe always starts with prevention strategies, so it's worth thinking about the Tucson scenario—and other kinds of large-scale disasters—from that perspective.

Preventing Terrorism: The Preferred Strategy

The United States continues to struggle with persistent problems in the staffing, coordination, and accountability of its intelligence and counterintelligence programs, and while it is tempting to think that we're "doing well" because there have been no significant attacks on

U.S. soil since 9/11, that would be a dangerous assumption. Al-Qaeda is notoriously patient, having waited eight years between the 1993 and 2001 attacks on the World Trade Center. Terror organizations actually remain very active around the world. According to the National Counterterrorism Center, in 2005 alone approximately 11,000 attacks occurred, killing more than 14,000 individuals. This was up from about 3,000 in 2004, with part of the substantial increase attributed to terror attacks in Iraq.

In March 2006, a scathing report to the Department of Defense by one of the nation's most respected retired generals blasted the continuing coordination problems among the key agencies. Proliferating bureaucracy, duplication of effort, and poor communication among military and nonmilitary counterintelligence agencies were significantly impeding their ability to move quickly against suspected terrorists. The *New York Times* quoted the study's author, retired four-star general Wayne A. Downing Jr.:

The interagency [counterintelligence] system has become so lethargic and dysfunctional that it materially inhibits the ability to apply the vast power of the U.S. government on problems. You see this inability to synchronize in our operations in Iraq and in Afghanistan, across our foreign policy and in our response to Katrina.

All of this makes me concerned about the general capacity of the U.S. intelligence apparatus to effectively seek and act upon potential evidence of terrorist "interest" in American children as targets. Even after expressing my concerns about the possibilities to local and federal law enforcement officials, I do not have the sense that this issue is on the radar of any agency.

One might also question our ability to prevent attacks involving cross-border access. In the Tucson scenario, illegal entry was altogether too easy for determined terrorists. The United States urgently needs to upgrade its immigration policies to make safe, legal entry into the country a matter of national policy. Porous, unregulated borders—north and south—leave U.S. citizens including children vulnerable to infiltration of terrorist operatives wishing to kill and demoralize Americans. The Secure Border Initiative recently proposed by the Department of Homeland Security would increase funding to hire 250 new criminal investigators to target human smuggling organizations and other criminal activity. It's a start, but hardly enough, given the sheer extent of the borders and the massive scale of illegal entry into the country.

Preventing Mass Casualties of Children from Other Disasters

Aside from a terrorist attack, there is concern, for example, about the reinforcement of schools and day-care facilities in earthquake-prone communities. In California, the Division of the State Architect reviews school designs for seismic stability. Noting the 100th anniversary of the 1906 San Francisco earthquake, a *USA Today* article pointed out that a state architect survey done in 2002 found that some 7,500 schools built before 1978 could be severely damaged by a strong earthquake. "School districts have no money to retrofit, and only one in 10 has even asked for the survey results. Private schools, attended by a third of San Francisco children, weren't surveyed," it reported. And according to a September 2005 report by the *San Francisco Chronicle,* the division does not reveal which schools do not meet current standards—and the report is not public.

In terms of industrial safety and the protection of children, the paradigm is straightforward: strong regulation and enforcement of safety and emergency-response protocols save lives. For example, if we aim to ensure that children are not harmed by a major meltdown in the local nuclear power plant, then safety and security measures must be as tough as possible. Similarly, freight trains carrying highly toxic chemicals should be rerouted far from populated areas and schools. Accidental derailment—or sabotage—near a school could kill large numbers of children. It is reassuring to know that determined advocacy *can* work. Fred Millar, an environmental activist and recognized expert in rail transport of dangerous chemicals, was instrumental in persuading the Washington, D.C., City Council to pass the Terrorism Prevention in Hazardous Materials Transportation Act of 2005, requiring rail lines to route dangerous shipments around the city, not through it.

When Prevention Fails

When prevention fails, we need to be ready to minimize casualties among children during, and after, both intentional and nonintentional disasters. As suggested earlier, preventing pediatric casualties starts with disaster planning that takes the needs of children into account in all medical response guidelines, including child-specific medications, doses, and general treatment protocols. It also entails making sure that appropriately trained pediatric medical and surgical experts are available to provide necessary interventions.

In the case of a terrorist attack against a school, like the Tucson scenario, there are a number of specific strategies that can reduce the potential loss of life. The after-action analysis suggests several factors that resulted in excessive loss of life—all of which could have been addressed by good planning, practice drills, and clear understanding of optimal protocols during the actual event. Here are some examples:

- For a response to be effective, there can be only one person in charge of overall incident management. That person must be invested with complete legal, strategic, and tactical authority for responding to the terrorist threat. Without this clarity, government bureaucracies and agencies with competing agendas have real difficulty making decisions, establishing priorities, and collaborating. A single commander or director with authority, capability, and courage needs to be identified from among participating agencies. This level of oversight and authority did not materialize in the Tucson terror scenario, with dire consequences.

- Synchronization of police, fire, emergency medical, and pediatric specialists and school administrators is particularly important, and it can be accomplished only by joint planning sessions and frequent drills. Disaster practice drills simulating school attacks can be tabletop "war-gaming" sessions, or practical, on-the-ground exercises that employ actual equipment, vehicles, and personnel. Whatever form these practice sessions take, school officials must actively participate on every level, and not just school security staff. Consideration of the special needs of children in mass casualty events was not part of disaster planning in the hypothetical Tucson scenario, and this omission led to much of the chaos and at least some loss of life following the storming of the schools.

- Adequately performed drills may reveal issues that can become major problems in an actual disaster. The availability of pediatric trauma specialists is a significant challenge in most communities. Identifying this concern well before an actual event would have at least stimulated thinking about innovative solutions, like cross-training programs to upgrade pediatric skills among adult-focused trauma health-care professionals. Similarly, at least in the Tucson scenario, a tabletop exercise postulating the destruction of the main pediatric emergency facility could have resulted in planning to accommodate a children's mass casualty event in adult medical facilities.

- Other general concerns affected the outcome in the Tucson scenario and are also important lessons for actual disaster response. For example, there is still an urgent need for uniform radio equipment and emergency services wavelengths for all law enforcement, fire and emergency services across the country.

These deficiencies plagued rescue efforts on 9/11, and not enough has been done to rectify the situation.

• Any school siege involving hostages will immediately become the lead story on every television, radio, and Internet news venue in the country and around the world. Media coverage complicates matters for law enforcement and security forces in such incidents. Authorities must thus work closely with editors and news directors long before an actual incident to discuss ground rules and critical on-scene coverage decisions—which may mean a large cordon must be imposed, keeping reporters and cameras well away from the site.

III

Why We're Not Prepared:
Four Barriers to Optimal Readiness

7 · Barrier 1
Goals and Accountability—
or Random Acts of Preparedness?

Assume for the moment that the United States has spent approximately $200 billion on homeland security and disaster preparedness since September 2001. Understand that this figure does not include money generated by state and local governments for disaster readiness programs, nor does it count funds raised and spent by nongovernmental organizations like the American Red Cross on postdisaster relief operations.

The money spent by the federal government on preparedness comes from congressional appropriations designed to prevent terrorism, strengthen the resiliency of our systems, and respond to disasters when prevention is not possible. All of this makes sense and is well within the realm of government's obligation to protect citizens and safeguard the homeland.

But how does the federal government make decisions about what to spend, and for what specific programs? This question is much more difficult to answer than most people imagine. Congressional and executive branch staff with expertise in germane areas research and propose programs, experts testify before committees and panels, and special interests appeal to decision-makers from their own particular perspectives. The presumption is that the funds allocated for these purposes will make the country safer, and better prepared to respond to disasters.

That would be ideal. But it is simply not working. Money is being spent with little regard for overall security objectives and there is no way of judging whether the investments are making us more secure or not. It might be helpful to consider an everyday situation that is analogous to what is happening with our preparedness dollars.

Imagine that you are interested in buying a new music system for your home. You head over to the local electronics store and tell the salesperson you'd like a music system and ask how much it would cost. He'd say, "Well, that depends. To my right we have clock radios for as little as $29.95; to my left are high-end component audio systems that can range as high as $15,000. And right behind me are options everywhere in between. What do you need or want?"

At that point, you have to decide how important the quality of the music is to you and know how much room you want to take up with the new system. You need to know your budget and your spending priorities. You might have $5,000 in the bank, but a list of other things you need to buy and bills to pay. Meanwhile the salesperson is waiting to help you with your selection. A smart move might be to thank him, go home, and think about what you want and how much you want to spend.

A somewhat less wise response would be to simply wander around the store picking up random pieces of equipment. Top-of-the-line speakers, a piece of cable, a turntable (even though you have no records), an old eight-track tape player, a flat-screen video monitor, and an advanced digital CD recorder all end up in your shopping cart. Your tab is $5,875. When you get home, you realize that you overspent your entire budget—and still forgot to get an amplifier. You don't have enough cable, you didn't need the video monitor, or the turntable, and you can't actually play or listen to music.

This scenario is uncomfortably akin to what has happened as America has "shopped" for an appropriate level of preparedness. We're on a national spending spree without knowing what we need or what we're trying to accomplish. We bought some port and border security, but not enough to make either system close to secure. We've invested in the public health system, but are not remotely capable of managing a major pandemic. We purchased radiation-detection equipment for police officers in most of our major cities, but the technology is not ready for prime time. The list goes on. There has been some progress, of course, but it's more or less without rhyme or reason, without a master plan. For about $200 billion we have a vast disconnected collection of what can best be described as "random acts of preparedness."

At the root of this disorganized profligate spending extravaganza are two basic problems that have plagued efforts to make the nation megadisaster-ready since 2001: (1) ill-defined goals, and (2) a virtual absence of accountability.

As in the music system analogy, the federal government has yet to say what it is trying to accomplish—in *any* area of preparedness. The key homeland security agencies are simply asking Congress to fund scores of security and preparedness programs without a clearly defined set of goals. And Congress, for its part, hasn't demanded that the agencies define their goals, describe the benchmarks for reaching those goals, or clarify how the nation's readiness will be enhanced by the programs it's being asked to fund.

We just can't seem to settle on a set of meaningful goals for preparedness. We need objectives that can be measured, benchmarked, and, with some degree of confidence, counted on to actually lead to an improved state of readiness for a megadisaster. Part of the problem is that we have still not defined the term "megadisaster" or the objective criteria that separate it from typical emergencies and local disasters. The Stafford Act, first enacted in 1988 to amend the 1974 Disaster Relief Act and amended in 2000 to give guidance around federal intervention in large-scale disasters, offers something of a definition, although it is expressed in general, highly subjective language:

> Any natural catastrophe (including any hurricane, tornado, storm, high water, wind driven water, tidal wave, tsunami, earthquake, volcanic eruption, landslide, mudslide, snow-storm, or drought), or, regardless of cause, any fire, flood, or explosion, in any part of the United States, which in the determination of the President causes damage of sufficient severity and magnitude to warrant major disaster assistance under this Act to supplement the efforts and available resources of States, local governments, and disaster relief organizations in alleviating the damage, loss, hardship, or suffering caused thereby.

This definition is far too general to provide guidance for planning purposes. Better would be something like this:

A *megadisaster* is a catastrophic, high-consequence event that (a) overwhelms or threatens to overwhelm local and regional response capacity, and (b) is caused by natural phenomenon, massive infrastructure failure, industrial accident, or malevolent intention. Indicators of capacity overload include the following:

- **Inability to manage immediate rescue of endangered survivors.**
- **Significant backlog of victims unable to get appropriate medical care or other essential support.**
- **Inability to protect vital infrastructure or significant property damage.**
- **Uncontrolled societal breakdown.**

As for the accountability question—in more than thirty years of working in public health, I can't remember anything resembling this current lack of accountability in a government program for any purpose. The lack of accountability starts with Congress.

In spending on and oversight for homeland security and bioterrorism, there are more than eighty committees and subcommittees that have some piece of the action. No single entity seems to have a clear picture of precisely what we're trying to accomplish or how to monitor the dollars being spent. And no congressional committee or existing federal agency is particularly interested in relinquishing its piece of the homeland security and preparedness pie. This is about power, visibility, and the control of money—sensitive issues for most elected officials.

After funds are appropriated, they are distributed to the relevant federal agencies. This list of agencies is very long; it certainly includes the Department of Homeland Security and all of its constituent agencies (Customs, Transportation Security Administrations, FEMA, et al.), Health and Human Services (Centers for Disease Control, Food and Drug Administration, and many more), and the Coast Guard. Unfortunately, many of these agencies that should be working closely together have trouble even communicating with each other.

Even before the Department of Homeland Security was created in 2002, many agencies within the Department of Health and Human Services wanted a share of the new resources, each according to its existing purposes. The National Institutes of Health develops new vaccines against biological weapons, for instance. The Centers for Disease Control works to improve bioterrorism disease surveillance and control, as well as other aspects of public health preparedness. The Department of Justice, for its part, detains and prosecutes those suspected of terrorist-related crimes, converts older communications technology to new, and assists state and local programs such as the Regional Information Sharing System, USA Freedom Corps, and State and Local Anti-Terrorism Training. The list goes on.

From the federal government, a good portion of the money is transferred to states, which in turn allocate the funds to local governments and relevant state agencies, special projects, and the like. Importantly, at each step along the way, the lack of accountability back to the source—Congress—is exacerbated. Moreover, a survey of state homeland security directors by the National Governors Association Center for Best Practices found that over half felt the parameters attached to the monies provided to states by DHS lack a sufficient focus on disaster prevention and response. The rigid restrictions on spending, which do not allow for information sharing and hiring additional personnel, prevent achieving a higher level of security. The federal guidelines are, in fact, sometimes unyielding about meaningless process directions and curiously silent on substantive input about actual enforcement of disaster readiness.

To add to the problem, we're really not talking about programs and investments that would help us prevent disasters, or minimize their consequences. For the most part, such programs are not included in homeland security budgets. Yet, prevention efforts, like improving safety in high-risk industries or funding reinforcement of structures in earthquake-prone regions, are as important to preventing high-consequence industrial accidents or minimizing damage from natural disasters as securing the borders is to preventing terrorism.

No government body is actually tracking and coordinating these safety or preventive measures. There is no framework goal yet for fixing what's broken or strengthening what's weak. It's all about responding to the latest media exposure or outburst of concern from a particular organization or a governor in a state where a major problem has come to the fore, very much like the new attention being focused on Northern California's unstable levees, or on the Northeast's lack of hurricane readiness.

How do we justify this disorganized, ad hoc process for spending such huge amounts of money on goals that, though vital to the national interest, are vaguely defined and poorly served by a system that just doesn't work? Perhaps one reason we have paid so little attention to accountability has something to do with basic human nature. The attacks of 9/11 totally shocked an unsuspecting nation and broadsided our national psyche. We could not have been more vulnerable. Although a relatively small cadre of national security and law enforcement staff was working on the prevention and interdiction of terrorism before September 2001, the American public wasn't thinking about international terrorist attacks on U.S. soil. Even worse, as we later learned from the exhaustive investigations of the 9/11 Commission, there was significant reason to act on evidence that Al-Qaeda was planning to attack the U.S. We were simply incapable of follow through.

Once the horror of the attacks had sunk in, most Americans, including elected officials, felt an overwhelming need to react. The president declared a "war on terrorism" with the almost unanimous consent of the Congress and nearly total concurrence of the American people. Congress passed resolutions and appropriated dollars, and we were off and running. Both the excursions to "fight terrorism overseas" and the rush to "prepare" for whatever might be next began as a mad dash—truly desperate manifestations of the need to *do something.*

The problem is that we started pouring dollars into highly complex new national initiatives without thinking through much of what we were doing. There's an unfortunate analogy here to our conduct of the wars in Afghanistan and Iraq, where we're still debating how many troops we *should have* committed and what an exit strategy *should have* looked like. We gave the White House and the Department of Defense a blank check. And so it goes in disaster preparedness and homeland defense, where we are initiating programs, mandating compliance, and spending lots of money without understanding what is needed, how much it would actually cost, or how it would be tracked.

The examples of how money has been spent, and wasted, are outrageous. And I'm not the only one who is shocked. Former congressman Christopher Cox, who now heads the Securities and Exchange Commission, told *60 Minutes:* "It's pork barrel. It's the kind of distribution of funds that Washington always makes when politics comes before substance."

What concerns me is not that Missouri now has 13,000 new hazmat suits, one for every single officer in the state. It is that no one in

Washington has oversight of local expenditures like this. Aside from reporters who happen to be following the story, there seems to be no agency consistently checking on the money flow. It is a bottomless pit, and there doesn't seem to be any prescription for how to do better in the future. Spending money on equipment we don't really need doesn't make us any better prepared, as a nation.

Following are some egregious examples of what states have done with the money allotted to them. Without risk assessment tools that help determine where to distribute funds or a method of controls to monitor results, the system depends on the elected representatives who are most dogged in using their persistence and clout to bring home the bacon.

- Two years ago, officials in Alaska were not sure what to do with $2 million in federal money after DHS officials rejected their proposal to buy a jet to "defend, deter, or defeat opposition forces" and to provide "security and transportation" for the governor. Alaska is second only to Wyoming in per capita funding received—three times the amount New York has received over the past two years. The Northwest Arctic Borough, a desolate area of 7,300 people, used $233,000 to buy radio equipment, decontamination tents, headlamps, night-vision goggles, bullhorns, and rubber boots.

- In 2005, American Samoa received $105 per capita in DHS funds, compared with New York, which was $10.13.

- Los Angeles County spent $57,045 to pay Hollywood extras to act as patients in a bioterror drill, as well as thank-you gifts for the actors including $10,000 in gift certificates, $13,600 for pens, digital thermometers, and bags to hold the gifts, plus thousands for transportation and food.

- Estes Park, Colorado, with a population of 5,790, spent $88,405 on gyms and personal trainers for volunteer firefighters.

- Des Moines, Iowa, bought traffic cones.

- Senator Mitch McConnell from Kentucky added $24 million to the military construction bill for "unrequested projects."

- The State of Louisiana paid just under $1 million prior to Hurricane Katrina to a consulting firm to put on four simulation workshops of a catastrophic hurricane hitting New Orleans. Not only were the workshops costly, the first one had about 300 people, the next two 100, and the last 80. FEMA attendees were the smallest group at each one.

- Bennington, New Hampshire, population 1,450, spent nearly $2,000 for five suits designed to protect against chemical weapons. The police chief said, "I don't see any specific threats. It was just something they offered, so we figured we'd get on the bandwagon."

- New Jersey spent $174,804 in 2002 DHS grants on ten new garbage trucks. The Department of Justice approved the expenditure to remove debris and contaminated materials after an attack.

- New Mexico's homeland security director resigned after she was accused of poor performance including the desire to award a no-bid contract to an unsolicited sole source for training exercises.

- Prosecutors in one Maryland county used DHS money to install an office security system.

- The Columbus, Ohio, fire department bought bulletproof dog vests for its canine corps.

- Officials in Pennsylvania are generally mum on homeland security spending. State and regional emergency management coordinators have decided, for the most part, that it is too dangerous to provide a detailed accounting of where the money is going, either for equipment purchases, training, or administrative costs. Citing security reasons, the Pennsylvania Emergency Management Agency, which must approve all expenditures, declined a request from the Associated Press under the state's right-to-know law to detail expenses since 2003.

- Tiptonville, Tennessee, a town two hours from Memphis with a population of 7,000, received $183,000 in funding to buy a Gator all-terrain vehicle, a defibrillator for use at high school basketball games, and protective suits for the volunteer fire department.

- South Carolina receives the least money per capita, $6.47.

- Senator Jim Johnson, a Democrat from South Dakota, added $26.8 million to the military construction bill for nonessential items.

- Converse, Texas, used its DHS security trailer to transport riding lawnmowers to the annual lawn mower races A state audit reported that overseers of the state's program have no way of knowing whether local governments were spending counterterrorism money wisely.

- A Virginia volunteer fire department purchased a boat for $350,000.

- Mason County, Washington, spent $63,000 on a decontamination unit no one has been trained to use. In 2005, it had been sitting in a box in a warehouse for a year.

- Washington, D.C., has received $145 million from DHS, but has spent less than 10 percent of it. Some of it has been spent on leather jackets for metropolitan police officers. A summer jobs program got $100,000, some of which went to developing a rap song about preparedness. Another $100,000 went to send sanitation workers to Dale Carnegie to learn how to deal with panicky customers.

- Wyoming, the state with the smallest population, receives more than $38 per person in antiterrorist financing, more than any other state and seven times the per-person amount for New York. Cheyenne received $809,627 in fiscal year 2003, but so far has spent less than half of it. Of the money used, 70 percent went to one item: a mobile command post for the state Office of Emergency Management. Meanwhile, no money has been spent on twenty-one of the thirty budgeted projects. Some of these appear directed less at terrorist threats than at everyday operations: Pine Bluffs is spending $10,000 of its $26,200 on a portable generator and an additional $4,000 on medical equipment including catheters, blood pressure cuffs, and gauze.

Federal agencies funding preparedness programs need to ensure that this irrational pattern of spending is stopped. Appropriate guidelines and real oversight will make a difference. In the meantime, the preparedness expenditures since 9/11 are an expensive embarrassment that have done almost nothing to improve true readiness. Who bears responsibility?

8 · Barrier 2
Failures of Imagination:
It's *Always* in the Details

The inability to effectively forecast difficult challenges and absorb critical details undermines both planning for and response to megadisasters. Learning to imagine the consequences of situations before they happen is an essential element of true preparedness.

Imagine how events might unfold in an avian flu pandemic. Public officials will likely institute widespread school closures as part of a strategy to reduce spread of the infection. This is because children are known to be potent carriers of influenza. From a pure public health perspective, this step is a reasonable way of attempting to slow the spread of a disease for which we do not have adequate vaccine or antiviral medications to treat individuals who become severely ill. Schools may well have to be closed for weeks on end, essentially throughout the peak impact period of the pandemic. But what happens when schools are closed? Who watches the children?

Group day-care arrangements won't do, since that would defeat the purpose of keeping children away from each other. Many parents would have to stay home from work to watch their children, perhaps threatening family income. Employers of homebound parents would lose employees and face productivity declines. Other employees may already be absent because they have developed flu symptoms themselves and need to stay home. The ripple effect on the economy could be substantial and devastating.

Everyone in each family would be pretty much confined to the house. Activities may be limited and we could certainly presume that stress levels at home would be high, particularly if there are growing concerns about income. These factors could contribute to increased rates of family violence and child abuse. Although the original policy to close schools was predicated on solid public health theory, we need to consider what steps might be needed to alleviate the economic, psychological, and social stress of extended home confinement.

Consider another example of imagining consequences, this time in the business sector. In early 2006, I spoke with a group of corporate leaders interested in business continuity during a serious pandemic. Many representatives from large multinational companies were there to hear from experts and share ideas. I was fascinated by a particular challenge presented by a major investment banking firm with a large worldwide client base. Over the past several years, the company had increasingly outsourced a variety of customer services to its call centers in India.

Recently, the company had been concerned about a disease outbreak focused in India that would significantly impair its ability to maintain staffing at the call center, with all kinds of unhappy consequences for the business. The company's concern was valid. In fact, it is easy to imagine a public health directive in India during a pandemic that would require closing of nonessential places of business. The company came up with a twofold solution: (1) maximize the ability for call center employees to work remotely from their homes if necessary, and (2) establish alternate sites in other regions, fully ready to go in the event of an emergency. These preemptive strategies would be very difficult to establish once a major pandemic took hold. Imagination and innovation are critical elements of successful planning.

Not every contingency can be anticipated, however, even by smart and creative planners. A high official in the Louisiana governor's office recently told me that they were getting reports of unusual deaths among cattle herds in the southwestern corner of the state. The local authorities attributed this phenomenon to a dramatic increase in mosquito populations in the standing floodwaters left in the aftermath of Hurricane Rita, which hit a few weeks after Hurricane Katrina. The official looked at me and said, "So, how do you think mosquitoes are killing our cows?" I tried to consider what infectious diseases might be carried by mosquitoes with lethal consequences for the cattle. I couldn't come up with any. "So, tell me," I said. He smiled, apparently pleased to have stumped me, and responded: "The mosquitoes are so thick that swarms of them fly into the nostrils of the cows and suffocate them." I didn't tell him this, but I could have thought for the next month and probably not come up with that explanation.

The law of unanticipated consequences always applies in disasters. The only hope is to keep them to a minimum and be able to solve problems as they emerge.

Imagination Training

In general we do not do a very good job of anticipating consequences or developing strategies to prevent or mitigate the outcomes that could have been predicted but weren't. Training might be an answer. I just wish it were more effective than it currently is. Disaster training is, generally speaking, a strange business, with little consistency in the management of exercises, a lack of real standards, and no way of objectively measuring outcomes.

In one form or another, "disaster rehearsals" are theoretically designed to help emergency service agencies, government bodies at all levels, and even entire communities improve their ability to function effectively during an actual crisis. Whether it's a short, several-hour "tabletop" discussion in a conference room about a hypothetical epidemic, or a major drill in a community involving emergency workers in full hazardous-materials gear working with mock victims of a hypothetical chemical spill, the principles are similar. The details of an unfolding disaster are laid out sequentially. At each stage, participants are asked what they think, how they would react, whom they would call, and what they would do. If the drill is conducted properly, participants have no advance notice of the scenario.

In a typical tabletop discussion focused on an outbreak of a highly contagious or infectious disease, the scenario might open with information that a single individual appears at a local emergency room with an unusual cluster of symptoms. Then a second hospital reports several similar patients. When the eighth patient, say a nurse from the first hospital's emergency department, is reported with the same rash, high fever, and cough, the local public health officer is called in and a determination is made that, indeed, something is happening that will require urgent investigation and the immediate introduction of emergency containment protocols.

At each phase of the exercise, participants are asked about what they would do in their official capacities. Someone would be representing the mayor, for instance, receiving ongoing reports of the situation, having to decide when to go public and what to say when she does face an increasingly concerned press. Another player might be the infection control officer of the first hospital who will need to make isolation decisions or activate emergency protocols to contain disease spread in the hospital. Yet another participant is the deputy director of the city emergency management office, and so on.

As the situation develops, participants learn how to assess and assimilate new information and come up with potential options for responding to ongoing developments. At each stage, players should be urged to think broadly, to step "out of the box" and anticipate what could happen. And if the drills are successful, three important outcomes emerge. First, key disaster response planners have a chance to familiarize themselves with existing guidance on establishing large-scale "incident command systems." Second, working relationships among agencies and sector leaders develop that would otherwise have to be sorted out in the heat of an actual crisis. Third, participants learn to struggle with critical details of real-life situations that reveal shortfalls in existing disaster plans. For instance, in the disaster scenario involving an outbreak of a communicable infectious disease accompanied by severe respiratory distress, the facilitator may say, "OK. It is thirty-six hours after the initial reported case and every isolation bed in every hospital throughout the city is occupied with very sick patients. But there are three hundred patients waiting for admission in the emergency rooms. What do you do now?"

In such a case, the drill participants will refer back to the disaster plans and find out whether this particular turn of events has been anticipated or not. If so, the ensuing discussion will describe how the hospitals would implement their plans to handle such a contingency. If not, after the drill, hospital officials will ideally return to their institutions and make sure that this planning deficiency is addressed. But it doesn't always work this way. Too often the scenarios are limited in scope or expectations of participants are too low. Sometimes, high-ranking officials do not attend, never gaining the opportunity to learn how they would function in an actual disaster.

Understanding the Challenges of Disaster Planning

Why would the hospitals *not* have considered a contingency plan for an overflow situation in the event of a major disease outbreak? Several factors might be at play. The institution may have thought about the possibility of a massive outbreak, but lacked the resources to develop a truly functional response plan and consciously decided to defer dealing with that issue until some later time—which usually means "never." Or they may have thought that they would just transfer patients to another hospital, not considering that every facility in the community would be similarly overwhelmed. Often people responsible for disaster planning do not consider the possibility of a disease spreading so rapidly that their facility would be overwhelmed almost immediately. They just cannot imagine a situation that dire.

The failure to imagine key details or outcomes that may be particularly difficult to manage is a problem that undermines meaningful situational forecasting generally, well beyond the area of disaster response planning. *New York Times* columnist Thomas Friedman wrote about this concept in May 2002, when he called on President Bush to imagine a different kind of war on terrorism that involved reducing our dependence on oil imports and setting a better example as a global citizen. He said:

> The failure to prevent Sept. 11 was not a failure of intelligence or coordination. It was a failure of imagination. Even if all the raw intelligence signals had been shared among the F.B.I., the C.I.A. and the White House, I'm convinced that there was no one there who would have put them all together, who would have imagined evil on the scale Osama bin Laden did.

Many "failures of imagination" have changed the course of human history, from the notorious failure of the American government to believe the intelligence reports about the full extent of Hitler's "final solution" to more recent failures in Iraq.

As our societies grow more complex, the challenge of thinking through all relevant contingencies, imagining the full range of possibilities (hard as they may be to believe), and acting or planning effectively is a difficult challenge. But it is an essential skill for disaster planners. If nothing else, disasters are often a nonstop cascade of unanticipated events against a backdrop of chaos and danger. Responders—including ordinary citizens, as well as professionals—must be able to function in an environment of uncertainty.

More "Teachable Moments" from the Katrina/Rita Annals

Successful disaster response often depends on how well responders appreciate and manage details. Remembering that responders will need a place to sleep, or that emergency vehicles will need fuel, or that evacuees may need lifesaving medications are all part of effective planning.

Looking back on the Katrina debacle, many crucial details either were in the planning documents relegated to gather dust on shelves or never thought about in the first place. New Orleans, like every other city in the nation, had a copy of the National Response Plan on how to organize an incident command system, including details that lay out a "critical chain of command" structure to manage a disaster. Unfortunately, there is little evidence that officials absorbed or referred to this document before or during the crisis. A key finding of the White House report on Hurricane Katrina, "A Failure of Initiative," was that government on all levels, and notably local officials, "failed to activate plans in an efficient and timely way including evacuation and calling for military assistance."

New Orleans had an evacuation plan that was, at best, incomplete. It certainly was not tailored to the needs of all its residents. The White House report rightly criticized New Orleans Mayor Ray Nagin for failing to complete the mandatory evacuation, a point underscored by the evacuation plan's failure to accommodate the 100,000 people, almost a fifth of the city's population, who relied on public transit. A report issued annually beginning in 2002 by the Center for the Study of Public Health Impacts of Hurricanes at Louisiana State University had outlined many of these evacuation problems, including the transit issue. Local officials not only failed to execute the existing plan, they also ignored the details about the very public they serve. Had anyone thought of the special needs of hospitalized patients or the infirm during an evacuation?

Hearing stories from colleagues who transported very sick newborn infants from the hospital in rowboats or observing the hundreds of patients and frail elderly awaiting transportation under dire circumstances on the tarmac of New Orleans airport, I knew that sufficient thought had not been given to these kinds of challenges before the deluge. Truly heroic actions of highly dedicated medical teams and unstoppable first responders and volunteers saved the lives of thousands of people. But better planning and more attention to detail *before* the storm would have made coping with all of these challenges much safer and considerably more effective.

One of the more flagrant examples of how details matter pertains to the ability of emergency workers to communicate reliably during the early phases of a major disaster-response effort. This is exactly what did not happen in New Orleans in the hours and days after the storm. The lack of radio communications interoperability among parishes' (counties') complicated rescue and evacuation efforts. One would think that, following the dangerous lapses in communication during the World Trade Center terrorist attacks, when fire and police officials could not communicate with each other or in the stairwells of the burning towers, this problem would have been rectified in major cities around the nation. Sadly, this has not been the case. A report by the 9/11 Commission concluded firefighters in the south tower perished because they had faulty or antiquated equipment and were unable to hear the police radio transmissions warning of the building's imminent collapse. Federal agencies and Congress are still struggling, years after 9/11, to find ways to achieve workable interoperability for emergency communications.

A well-reported example of failed imagination involved New Orleans nursing homes. All are required by law to have an emergency evacuation plan, and they did. But the plans called for evacuating residents *to other nursing homes.* When the big storm and floods hit, 80 percent of the nursing homes were damaged, and flooding made them inaccessible. That's why only 21 percent, or some sixty nursing homes, evacuated before the storm and the rest did not. Planners had never imagined that so many facilities would be simultaneously affected. Once the nursing home operators understood the severity of the situation, they did not have an adequate fallback plan—an omission that had fatal consequences.

In early 2006, I spoke to a group of emergency response and relief workers at a meeting in Alexandria, Louisiana, about the special needs of children during and after a major disaster. In the audience were a number of extraordinarily dedicated people who went from emergency rescue jobs directly into the daunting task of organizing the massive shelter system the state needed to care for thousands of evacuees still widely dispersed throughout a number of states.

Following my talk, one of the social workers who had been involved early on told us, "One evening I walked into the shelter we had just set up in Hammond [Louisiana]. I looked around and noticed something that made me pretty uncomfortable—lots of babies in cots with their moms or dads." Prolonged overcrowding in a makeshift shelter is bad enough, but as a pediatrician, I was particularly concerned about the idea of infants' sleeping in a narrow cot with a parent. There are too many reported cases of accidental suffocation of infants under such circumstances.

The relief worker continued: "Then, I realized, we had forgotten to get cribs in the shelters. Getting the cots was the main goal and we finally did that. But no one remembered that we'd need cribs for the babies."

Planners need an open mind, an intuitive sense of what *could* happen, and the wherewithal to come up with solutions that are realistic and achievable. Ideally the *planners* would have realized before the disaster that shelters need cribs. Failing that, the next best option would have been for *responders* to find and distribute the cribs rapidly as possible once the need was recognized. In this regard, Louisiana officials were, often enough, truly resourceful and persistent. They found the suppliers, cajoled FEMA, and acted before getting permission from the bureaucracy. As Dr. Kathleen Tierney, an expert in the social dimensions of disaster management who directs the Natural Hazards Research and Applications Information Center at the University of Colorado at Boulder, has said, "The most important quality emergency responders and managers need to acquire is the art of improvisation. More and more, the ability to improvise and to act on those ideas is the difference between a successful response and a failed one."

When planning for the potential onslaught of Hurricane Rita in September 2005, emergency officials in Texas noted that many bus drivers who were supposed to transport citizens from the flood-prone areas of New Orleans simply did not show up for work. They were worried about the safety and security of their own families. Whereas New Orleans planners "failed to imagine" this possibility, Houston officials addressed the issue in their own evacuation. Encouraged to take their families on the bus, virtually all the Houston bus drivers showed up for duty. The drivers didn't have to be concerned about the whereabouts or safety of their loved ones.

On the other hand, Houston officials "failed to imagine" that the thousands of people evacuating the city by road would need fuel. As a result, cars ran out of gas and clogged the highways, making egress virtually impossible. After twelve hours at a dead stop on the highways, many families returned to tough out the storm at home rather than face it on the open freeway. In the end, the storm weakened and diverted before it hit Houston.

Not everyone is suited for this kind of planning work. Having spoken with many disaster-response planners, in and out of government, I have often thought that we need to open up the planning process to a wider range of individuals who bring different experiences and insights to the table. That could mean bringing in some public transportation workers, military logistics specialists, older citizens, and teachers. And we need to train planners to be big thinkers with open minds and a lot of imagination.

9 · Barrier 3
Missing and Misplaced Leadership:
Who's in Charge?

As the nation passes the fifth anniversary of the 9/11 attacks—and a year following the devastation of Hurricane Katrina—we still do not have a leadership structure capable of seeing the nation through a megadisaster. The "good" leaders we do have, in the military, in local agencies, and even scattered throughout FEMA itself, are tangled up and disempowered in dysfunctional bureaucracies or sidelined by politics and policies that make little sense and undermine our ability to respond effectively when big disasters strike.

Inappropriate appointments of unqualified individuals, the functional dismantling of FEMA, and terrible confusion about the roles and responsibilities of federal and state agencies as well as the military in major disaster response have all helped create an environment in which the federal government's ability to lead the country through a major disaster has virtually collapsed.

Unqualified Appointees, Time and Again

Cronyism is nothing new to Washington. But the current Bush administration has taken the art of crass patronage to an all-time high, with dire consequences in many key agencies, none more critical than the nation's ability to protect the homeland and respond to major disasters. Rewarding political loyalists and major donors with high-level positions in the Department of Homeland Security, including FEMA, and the Department of Health and Human Services has had predictable consequences: stunningly inept, ill-qualified, and ill-prepared "leaders" have been trusted with some of the key decision-making jobs in the agencies charged with securing our future well-being, directly affecting the country's ability to prepare for and respond to public health emergencies and major disasters.

Should we be taking such a chance, for example, with the post of assistant secretary for immigration and customs enforcement? Before landing this appointment, Julie L. Myers was a special assistant to the president for presidential personnel; she also led enforcement operations at the departments of Justice and Commerce. She now runs the largest investigative office in DHS, and the second largest in the U.S. government, with more than 15,000 employees and a $4 billion budget. Myers's experience does not match the vast obligations of her position. Even the *National Review* noted her high-level political connections (her uncle is Richard Myers, chairman of the Joint Chiefs of Staff) and questioned her appointment.

Or take the appointment in mid-2005 of Jeffrey Runge, MD, to the senior DHS position dealing with bioterrorism. Dr. Runge is an astute emergency medicine physician who had previously done an exceptionally good job directing the crash-testing program at the National Highway Traffic Safety Administration in the Department of Transportation. But he had no known experience whatsoever in the field of terrorism or bioterrorism. Jeffrey Runge is a smart professional and said to be a quick learner. That's a good thing. The question is, why didn't the DHS secretary seek out an individual with an appropriate background of expertise to take on the senior medical position in the agency charged with overseeing the nation's capacity to interdict and respond to terrorism and the use of weapons of mass destruction? The fact is that specific expertise actually matters. Nobody would go to the world's best cardiac surgeon to have a brain tumor removed. It doesn't make sense that an emergency medicine specialist who is now a world expert on automotive safety runs the bioterrorism shop at Homeland Security.

The U.S. Department of Health and Human Services, the lead agency when it comes to many aspects of terrorism preparedness, pandemic flu planning, and a host of other public health emergencies, made one of the most seriously inept appointments of the Bush administration. One of Washington's worst-kept secrets, and a source of regular derision among professionals and journalists in the know, was former HHS secretary Tommy Thompson's appointment of Stewart Simonson to be assistant secretary for public health emergency preparedness at HHS at the beginning of Bush's first term. Simonson, a former political adviser and Amtrak lawyer, had worked for Thompson while he was governor of Wisconsin. Many of the experienced Public Health Service professionals he would be directing were stunned. How could someone with no previous experience in any way related to bioterrorism and public health emergencies be appointed to such a key slot? After all, this job carries one of the most heavy-duty emergency response portfolios in the entire federal government. This inexcusable mismatch between job responsibilities and background made Simonson one of the least qualified political appointees in recent memory. After sustaining withering criticism, from outside and inside the agency, Simonson finally submitted his resignation in March 2006.

Simonson wasn't the only questionable appointee in HHS. The deputy secretary, Alex Michael Azar II, was general counsel of the department from 2001 to 2005, and is credited with playing "a key role in the public health response to 9/11 and the subsequent anthrax attacks." His previous incarnation was as a private practice attorney involved in white-collar criminal defense, government ethics, congressional investigations, and administrative law. He served as associate independent counsel during the first two years of Kenneth Starr's Whitewater investigation. These experiences hardly qualified Azar to be given such a major post at HHS, where knowledge about health care, policy decisions, and implementation about sound health strategies are literally a question of life and death for Americans.

A Disempowered and Demoralized FEMA

The now-notorious case of FEMA's former director Michael Brown was the most public example of hubris gone wild. Is it possible that President Bush thought that nobody would notice that a horse show organizer was running the country's disaster-response agency?

Michael Brown came to FEMA in 2001 unqualified and unprepared, landing there through his close association with Bush's campaign manager and longtime associate, Joseph Allbaugh, Bush's first FEMA director. Allbaugh left the position for far greener opportunities as a lobbyist, but he was also very unhappy that his agency was being absorbed into the new Department of Homeland Security. He was said to have completely lost interest when he learned that the director of FEMA would not have direct access to the president. Brown then ascended to the top job at FEMA, with little concept of how to lead the agency, advocate successfully for its agenda, or manage a large-scale disaster.

But the problem was never just Brown himself. He was part of a more complex problem within the federal government's disaster preparedness apparatus. To his credit, Brown fought to reverse the inevitable changes in the reporting hierarchy that diminished FEMA's effectiveness. But Brown lost those battles, as the *Washington Post* and others have reported in embarrassing detail. Buried deep within the Homeland Security bureaucracy, Michael Brown was incapable of getting the administration to turn its focus from terrorism back to an all-hazards approach to preparedness—which takes into account the full range of potential disasters. Even when he was right, he became increasingly marginalized and ineffective.

In a hearing following Brown's dismissal, Republican lawmakers expressed their dismay. Representative Christopher Shays

(R-Connecticut) told Brown, "I'm happy you left. . . . You weren't capable of doing that job." About the administration itself, Shays said, "I have come to the conclusion that this administration values loyalty more than anything else . . . more than competence or frankly more than the truth." Shays wasn't the only one. Senator Trent Lott, who lost his own home in Pascagoula, Mississippi, said that "FEMA was overwhelmed, undermanned and not capable of doing its job" with Brown at the helm, noting "Michael Brown has been acting like a private, instead of a general." It's much worse than that, however. "Heck of a job, Brownie" helped cement a sense of gross American incompetence in the eyes of the world.

Before the Bush administration got its hands on FEMA, the agency had garnered well-deserved global respect under the leadership of the consummate disaster-response professional, James Lee Witt, who reported directly to President Bill Clinton during his terms in office.

President Carter established FEMA by executive order in 1979, in a consolidation that brought together a number of agencies charged with emergency response under one roof, including the Federal Insurance Administration, the National Fire Prevention and Control Administration, the National Weather Service Community Preparedness Program, the Federal Preparedness Agency of the General Services Administration, and the Federal Disaster Assistance Administration activities from the Department of Housing and Urban Development. FEMA also took over responsibility for civil defense from the Defense Department's Defense Civil Preparedness Agency. The early FEMA grew out of what had been a predominantly top-down culture, and as James Lee Witt testified in 2004, it took nearly fifteen years before FEMA got it right. The hallmark of Witt's tenure was to create a partnership between local, state, and federal agencies with an enhanced ability to communicate, train, prepare, and respond. Witt aimed—and in large measure he succeeded—to take the organization in a new direction "where the needs of the stakeholders and employees were valued and heeded."

Among the many successes of the Witt-led FEMA was the response and recovery following the 1994 Northridge, California, earthquake, which miraculously took few lives. FEMA played a hands-on role in seeing that major institutions that had not been retrofitted to meet new seismic standards were rebuilt to code. This included a $900 million investment in UCLA, one of the country's leading research and teaching medical facilities, and the retrofitting of high schools, hospitals, elementary schools, and other public buildings. Witt was also responsible for increasing the scope of the National Earthquake Program, which spent 80 percent of its funding on evacuation planning and disaster mitigation in high-risk parts of the country. And in an important step toward enhancing the preparedness of both businesses and individuals, Witt launched Project Impact, a public-private partnership that provided seed money to local communities to foster preparedness planning. Under President Bush, many of these programs have been reduced in scope, sent to other agencies, or stripped of funding.

In March 2003, FEMA became one of twenty-two agencies incorporated into the new Department of Homeland Security, which was "tasked with responding to, planning for, recovering from and mitigating against disasters." This change of status was highly disruptive. FEMA has ten regional offices and approximately 2,500 employees; it depends on the support of some 5,000 disaster reservists, who are called into action to respond to specific events. Its annual budget, which varies from year to year, is roughly $1 billion (the FY 2006 budget request was for $994 million). That number swells substantially if Congress appropriates money for a particular disaster, as was the case with Katrina, with some $60 billion approved overall for disaster relief. Many in DHS maintain that FEMA's roles and responsibilities, in effect, have remained the same since the move. But others disagree. The "redeployment" of FEMA stripped the agency of its direct connection to the president and relegated it to "stepchild" status within DHS, as Michael Brown testified to Congress after he was fired.

Michael Brown's early and persistent pleas to keep FEMA

independent from the new Department of Homeland Security resulted in a severe bureaucratic backlash from DHS. FEMA was punished, compromising the integrity and effectiveness of the nation's disaster-response agency.

Not until five days after Katrina made landfall did the federal government take the lead role—but without a leader. Secretary Michael Chertoff was neither seen nor heard. A former U.S. judge for the Third Circuit Court of Appeals prior to his appointment, the secretary had been in office for only some eight months, and had virtually no experience in disaster management. In a March 21, 2006, article in the *Washington Post,* Dana Milbank reported a telling observation about Chertoff: "he's a model technocrat in a position that sometimes demands a commanding leader." Michael Brown so disdained the flagrant disempowerment of FEMA (and the disconnection of its director) that, when it was clear that the situation in New Orleans was much worse than anyone realized, he violated the new regulations, bypassed the DHS hierarchy, and called the White House directly. His urgent briefings apparently did not reach the president, who was said to be traveling and making political speeches in California, unaware of what was happening in New Orleans.

Within FEMA, senior professionals with vast experience had left in frustration. That process began under Joe Allbaugh, Bush's first political appointment to head FEMA. According to Bill Lokey, the operations branch chief of the response division, morale at headquarters since Katrina has dropped to abysmal levels. Lokey says, "We have lots of tremendously talented people, but they've been kicked in the butt, and they are very discouraged." Some of the senior staff who wanted to stay at FEMA and had the courage to speak up were shown the door or marginalized by politically appointed staff who made a practice of overriding or ignoring the senior professionals in the agency. This situation could turn around now that a permanent and experienced chief is in place.

In 2006 the White House struggled to correct its course and identify leaders for FEMA with appropriate credentials, but much of the damage had already been done. One senior disaster-response professional, with expertise at the local, state, and federal levels, described what it was like to be the recipient of blistering criticism from all quarters during and after the relief effort: "There is plenty of blame to go around, but many of the problems we faced were 'everybody's' problems, not just ours."

Identifying, hiring, and orienting qualified personnel could take a year or more. It will take time to undo and repair bad decisions made during crises, poor relationships with local response organizations, and ill-conceived structural changes within the agency. And as for the vanishing pool of response professionals at FEMA, one official summed it up in a conversation we had in January 2006. He said, "The entire eighth floor is empty." I asked, "What does that mean?" He looked away and told me, "So many left, our headquarters is like a ghost town. I can't even count how many key vacancies we have now." He continued: "Until recently, the secretary's office was telling us to keep 15 percent of the vacant positions permanently open as a cost-saving strategy. Now we've been told to fill them all, ASAP." He and his colleagues knew that some kind of restructuring of FEMA was imminent. "No one knows what's going to happen," he said, "but nobody believes it will be good."

In early April 2006, the *New York Times* ran a front-page story reporting that more than half a dozen senior, highly experienced disaster managers from across the nation had turned down White House requests to consider taking the job of FEMA administrator. Almost all of the potential candidates cited concerns about the basic structure of the agency; none were convinced that things could ever improve in the current context of FEMA having been swallowed up in the Department of Homeland Security. Within ten days of the story's publication, President Bush offered the job to acting director David Paulison, an experienced former fire chief from Miami. He accepted, and was confirmed the following month.

Two months later, Secretary Chertoff issued a terribly misguided report outlining the new distribution of homeland security dollars to all states. Declaring, in effect, that New York—which has the

New York Stock Exchange, the George Washington and Brooklyn Bridges, the Empire State Building, Ellis Island, three of the world's great art museums, Lincoln Center, the nation's largest subway system, among other major sites—has "no national monuments or cultural icons" that might serve as yet another terror target, the federal government cut homeland security dollars to the city by 40 percent. Chertoff's agency also took a gratuitous slap at the internationally acclaimed New York City Police Department's counterterrorism unit. In one fell swoop, Michael Chertoff demonstrated an astounding misunderstanding of terror risk analysis and a serious lack of judgment in terms of assessing the capabilities of the nation's most effective urban counter-terror programs. Calls for his dismissal began to resemble the sound of rolling thunder.

The Role of the Military in Large-Scale Disaster Response

If the challenge at hand in a megadisaster is managing the complex task of moving large numbers of people out of harm's way or providing highly organized emergency rescue resources under a central command, the single entity that comes to most people's minds is the United States military. The military represents the only sector in U.S. society with the history, expertise, and experience to design and manage large-scale logistics. When called into service in modern-day disasters, the military can serve ably in a wide range of critical roles, including evacuation strategies, traffic management, deployment of essential supplies, and emergency medical response. As Vice Admiral Richard Carmona, the U.S. surgeon general, puts it: "There is no other organization or entity in our society—other than the military—that has the experience and know-how to provide support and oversight of major catastrophic events."

Colin Powell, the former chairman of the Joint Chiefs of Staff and former secretary of state, acknowledged that certain corporations have the capacity and wherewithal to accomplish massive logistic coordination of materials and services on a daily basis. He correctly observed that companies such as FedEx, UPS, and Wal-Mart have made high-level logistic management of materials and people a way of life—and a successful business model. But for large-scale emergency operations, the trained units of the nation's armed forces offer the ability to think and plan "to scale."

"What you really have in the military that is of enormous use— and does not exist in civilian life—is command and control," said Powell during our conversation in the early spring of 2006. He also contended that the hard-core logistics capabilities are almost always found in the National Guard (controlled by the governors) and in the Army Reserves. Active-duty forces need this kind of support when they are on specific missions, but when they are not so engaged (which is most of the time) that expertise can potentially be deployed in a major domestic emergency.

These forces, said Powell, are "uniquely qualified for a major domestic emergency. The military is about effective leadership, major communications capabilities, and real-world logistical experience." He added: "We have experience in taking charge"—precisely the missing ingredient in the civilian management of many very large-scale domestic emergencies.

Still, it is not necessarily easy to determine just when the military should be called in to assist or oversee response to a major emergency. Part of the solution is for the military—and FEMA, for that matter—to establish clear relationships with state and local disaster-response organizations well before an actual emergency. Both General Powell and former FEMA head James Lee Witt emphasize this point. Under Witt, FEMA made it a priority to build solid relationships with the key players in local disaster agencies so that everyone would know each other's strengths and limitations. Local agencies would realize when more resources were needed and whom to call for assistance at the next level of government, particularly FEMA or the Department of Defense.

Powell believes that successful military response also depends on early assessment of a situation *before* the formal call for help is issued. The general recalled the Los Angeles riots of 1992. Racial tensions were boiling over and the local authorities were unable to prevent an accelerating breakdown in social order. Colin Powell knew the chances were good that federal troops would be called in, though when was unclear. Not waiting for the official call, the former chairman of the Joint Chiefs of Staff began making plans to be ready when the official order came: "I didn't wait until I got called. I knew who was going to go and I alerted the troops. The Army wanted to send troops from Fort Ord, California. I had to remind them that there was a Marine Division in Camp Pendleton [and] I could get them there in 40 minutes—and then we'd bring in the 7th Division from Fort Ord. I knew exactly what I would do and had alerted the commands before I ever got the order."

This, I thought, was leadership of a kind we did not see enough of in the Gulf just before, during, and immediately after Katrina and the great flood. Timing is always a critical issue. But there are important legal limitations to "calling in the troops." These principles apply specifically to when and how federal troops are deployed in a domestic situation of any kind. Under the Posse Comitatus Act of 1878, the military is generally prohibited from enforcing domestic laws. However, additional stipulations may enable the president or Congress to authorize domestic use of military forces under specific circumstances, such as quelling domestic unrest or responding to terrorism.

The Robert T. Stafford Disaster Relief and Emergency Assistance Act, passed in 1988 and amended in 2000, spells out in detail how federal assets may be used to assist in a domestic disaster. The governor of a state must make the request for federal assistance directly to the president, clearly stating that the state and local response capacities are overwhelmed. But, for any number of reasons, a governor may delay calling the president. Sometimes a delay may be attributed to inadequate understanding of conditions on the ground or overconfidence in the state's ability to handle the emergency. And under certain circumstances politics plays an unwarranted role. Politics may have influenced how and when Kathleen

Blanco, the Democratic governor of Louisiana, put the call in to the Republican White House during the unfolding disaster of Hurricane Katrina. By the summer of 2005, partisan rancor between the two parties was already at a fever pitch. How this actually affected the response to the crisis is still not clear.

The double threat of Katrina and Rita forced the largest migration of Americans—well more than a million—since the Dust Bowl of the 1930s. If there were ever a time to involve the military's know-how in organizing large movements of people in a short time, this was it. Instead, elected officials and emergency managers with limited experience in large-scale logistics took responsibility for a massive operation they were not equipped to handle.

Even very large disasters in the past have been managed better than we saw in the fall of 2005. A few months after the April 1992 Los Angeles riots, Hurricane Andrew, a ferocious category 5 storm, made landfall in south Florida. The devastation affected about 300 square miles of residential communities from Coral Gables to Homestead. While not nearly on the scale of Katrina, which laid waste some 100,000 square miles and flooded New Orleans, Andrew's destruction was certainly swift and brutal.

At the time of that storm, my organization, the Children's Health Fund (CHF), had been in existence for nearly five years. We were already using mobile medical units to take health care to medically needy children in several states. These units seemed an excellent way to provide care in a major disaster zone, so when Andrew struck, I called CHF co-founder Paul Simon to suggest that we help in the relief efforts. I was particularly concerned about access to health care for many indigent people, mostly immigrants, who lived in and around Homestead, Florida, where Andrew had rendered several essential health clinics inoperable.

I thought our mobile units would work well in that environment and Paul agreed. Led by a dedicated young pediatrician, Dr. Alan Shapiro, our team and a fully equipped medical unit left the next day, driving straight through to south Florida. We arrived some four days after the storm. For the next month, the team worked alongside colleagues from the Department of Pediatrics at the University of Miami School of Medicine. We were incredibly busy seeing children in desperate need of medical care, but in the larger scheme of the overall disaster, we were a relatively small cog in an impressive response operation led, for the most part, by the U.S. military. Civilian organizations and other governmental agencies were involved and critical to the operation's success, but the Army was an enormous presence. They surveyed damage, managed logistics, established field hospitals, and controlled traffic. Not only did the military *look* like they were in charge, in fact, they provided essential resources and leadership in time of need and thus helped avert the kind of chaos that followed Hurricane Katrina.

General Powell, who was responsible for deploying the military forces to south Florida following Andrew, was certainly pleased with the job his troops did when they finally got to the scene some three days after the storm. But he was deeply frustrated that it took so long to get there: "Florida played 'mumbley peg' for about two days—no matter what we told them. And we told [Governor] Lawton Chiles that 'you can't handle this' and it [still] took him three days to realize it was beyond his capacity. Then he finally called for help, and we went racing in and stabilized things." What I know now is that, although Powell waited for the legal go-ahead before sending in the troops, he was on the case *before* Andrew made landfall. In effect, the military had been put on alert and a defense coordinating officer assigned a day before the storm hit.

This experience came to mind when Lieutenant General Russel L. Honoré took charge in New Orleans on September 2, four days after Katrina hit. Everything seemed to change when Honoré arrived on scene. New Orleans had taken on the terrifying look of urban anarchy and wholesale human suffering—all in plain sight. Honoré brought order, logistic expertise, and, most importantly, hope for the citizens who remained in the flooded city. He represented leadership at its finest, but the big question is what took him so long to get there.

It's fair to consider *why* there are persistent problems with the functional interface between military and civilian resources in disaster planning and response. Part of the answer is the utter lack of experience of many civilian officials in the management of very large-scale operations. Elected leaders or political appointees may not know what they don't know. And why would they. They should not be expected to have had the kind of experiences or training to make them capable of handling, say, the evacuation of a major American city—or the aftermath of a terrorist attack using a weapon of mass destruction.

Colin Powell underscored this point: "It's a problem of civilian organization and . . . you see this in the federal government. You have people in these agencies who have no concept of organizational leadership. They are for the most part lawyers or political appointees who got their jobs because they needed a job or they were being rewarded." He went on: "I'm not picking on lawyers . . . but [even] Michael Chertoff [Homeland Security secretary] was picked because he is a good guy . . . but [he] has never done anything like this. He doesn't have the experience base."

When the military should become involved, for how long, and whether there are agencies and other responders that can draw on the military model to improve the quality of disaster response around the country are just some of the questions that should be resolved about the military's ongoing role in disaster response.

Still, not all disasters require the military, something President Bush doesn't seem to grasp. On October 5, 2005, the president was holding a rare live news conference. In response to a question about planning for a pandemic influenza crisis, the president offhandedly noted that he would possibly deploy armed U.S. military troops to enforce urban quarantines during such an emergency. The statement understandably provoked a public outcry, my own included. *Yes,* the military should have a key role in evacuations or logistic oversight during a major catastrophe, but it should not be seen as a federal police agency brought in to enforce a local quarantine under the direction of the president of the United States.

NIMS: A Command-and-Control Model

Since September 11, as we have wrestled with the idea of securing order in a chaotic and unpredictable world, the Bush administration has moved increasingly toward an all-out command-and-control approach. The whole point of Homeland Security Presidential Directive 5, which established the National Incident Management System (NIMS) in 2003, was to reassert chains of command and clarify relationships among agencies participating in the mitigation of and response to disasters.

NIMS is a theoretical framework upon which to establish an operational response plan. Every state and local official with primary responsibility for emergency management is required to fulfill its training mandates by September 30, 2006, taking the requisite courses offered by a host of consultants around the country. If local jurisdictions do not comply, they jeopardize their eligibility for federal preparedness funding or grants.

NIMS is based on "incident command," a thirty-year-old management style very much out of synch with current management practices. James Lee Witt said as much in House testimony in March 2004, when he noted a return to the top-down command-and-control model he had successfully moved the agency away from in the 1990s. Witt believed strongly in the concept of collaborative planning and response among local and federal professionals. He emphasized the notion of empowering leadership on-site, where the disaster was playing out.

Kathleen Tierney at the University of Colorado–Boulder has pointed out that while NIMS provides a single point of reference and common terminology, "in and of itself, NIMS is insufficient to ensure that we are prepared." She explained: "The problem we in the research community see is the over-focus on NIMS as the solution to disaster management. Mandating that every organization that participates or wants to participate in disaster response must comply with NIMS ignores the deeper issues of high-level strategy, policy, and decision-making that must also be addressed."

One career emergency manager is skeptical of the role of NIMS in enhancing local preparedness. "Remember," he says, "most problems with emergency management are 'management' problems, not problems of skills and resources available at the time of a disaster." In other words, leadership remains the critical factor to success.

Informing the Public

The ability to communicate effectively to the public, the media, and the responder teams during and after a major disaster is an essential quality of leadership. Messages delivered by real leaders under such conditions are effective and always credible. Often, they will be inspiring as well. In fact, keeping the public informed, engaged, and confident during a crisis is one of the most important functions of effective leadership.

No matter how other aspects of Rudolph Giuliani's tenure as New York City's mayor are remembered, he was universally recognized for his presence of mind and his sense of purpose, which were a source of considerable strength for the city after 9/11.

And just weeks after the attacks, I traveled across New York State with Hillary Rodham Clinton, less than one year into her first term as the state's junior U.S. senator. She wanted to meet with citizens from all walks of life, as well as public health and emergency response professionals. People were still bewildered and anxious. But Senator Clinton's presence was galvanizing and reassuring. She had information, she listened carefully, and she responded honestly—connecting with people in a time of lingering crisis.

But contrast the style and messages of Giuliani and Clinton with those of so many other public officials after the 9/11 attacks and during the anthrax crisis that followed. Tommy Thompson, then the secretary of health and human services, used his bully pulpit to reassure citizens disingenuously, promulgate inaccurate information, and undermine public confidence. As the *Washington Monthly* reported in September 2002:

More than any other government agency, the CDC's mission is to get accurate information to the public as quickly as possible, so that public health officials and citizens can respond appropriately. The main avenue of dissemination is through the news media. Bush's decision to marginalize the agency's press office in favor of Thompson and his close minions interfered with this mission. Reporters couldn't get their calls returned and as a result, complained *New York Times* medical reporter Lawrence K. Altman, produced stories that were "often conflicting and occasionally inaccurate." In other words, by centralizing authority, the Bush administration ensured that the public got information that was unreliable and slow in coming. In the absence of reliable information, the public succumbed to national panic.

The sad reality is that we seem to overuse inarticulate, ill-informed political appointees to "lead" or manage crisis planning and response and to underuse competent, skilled leaders even when they are available.

Where's the Surgeon General When We Really Need Him? (Or, the Inexplicable Marginalization of Richard Carmona)

One of the more perplexing phenomena recently has been the virtual disappearance from public view of the highly qualified U.S. surgeon general—Vice Admiral Richard Carmona. Surgeon General Carmona is a physician, a former combat nurse, trauma surgeon, and public health leader who brings great experience and insight to the position he has held since August 2002. Unfortunately, he's been kept almost completely out of the public eye. According to more than one highly placed administration official, the surgeon general is kept under tight control, with the White House monitoring his public appearances and writings.

The surgeon general has many duties, not the least of which is to protect and advance the health of the nation by educating the public, advocating for effective disease-prevention and health-promotion programs and activities, and providing a highly recognized symbol of national commitment to improve the public's health. He also provides leadership and management oversight of HHS's emergency preparedness and response activities through command of the United States Public Health Service. Unfortunately, Dr. Carmona has had to work very hard during his tenure as surgeon general to obtain the resources needed to get the job done. He points out that the Public Health Service is the seventh uniformed service—in addition to the Army, Air Force, Marines, Navy, Coast Guard, and NOAA—but when it comes time to mount a public health offensive, his team has to scramble to gather the personnel, equipment, and transport they need to accomplish the task.

When a U.S. Army division is told by the president, "We need you in Iraq next week," its commander doesn't need to go shopping to find supplies and planes, says Dr. Carmona. An operational package comes together including the full inventory of troops, planes, water, food, and fuel. The same is not true for the Public Health Service. "We have to do that on the fly. During Katrina, for example, we were dealing with private contractors, not military planes, until we finally got the Air Force involved."

Because of his long experience in the armed forces as well as in public health, Richard Carmona's perspective on the role of the military in disaster response is unique. While he believes strongly that first response for an event must always be local, he notes that it is imperative for everyone to understand—and carry out—their respective roles. Local governments need to press harder to get citizens to respond, state government leaders need to be prepared to weigh their own strengths and limitations, and the federal government needs to do a better job of saying what it is prepared to do and to do it effectively and efficiently.

As his talks about good health to the nation suggest, Dr. Carmona believes in the power and responsibility of the individual:

The person at home needs to accept some responsibility for their health, safety and welfare, whether it is dealing with obesity or preparing for disaster. You are obligated as a citizen to have some knowledge as to how to protect yourself and your family. The government will help you, and provide you with information, but don't blame the government if you fail to act.

According to 2003 and 2004 surveys conducted by the National Center on Disaster Preparedness, 75 percent of Americans trust the surgeon general for accurate and reliable information, a higher rating of trust than the president's, who garnered 65 percent in 2003 and just 59 percent in 2004.

During the anthrax scare in 2001, the public would have been well served by the calm reassurance of Dr. Carmona, an expert and leader with relevant experience and actual knowledge. Instead, it got Secretary Thompson, a public health novice and blustering political appointee. Now, as we face the possibility of pandemic flu, it would make particular sense for Surgeon General Carmona to be at the helm, discussing the government's plans to prepare the country for what could be the worst public health catastrophe of our times.

Small-Town Living: Does Preparedness and Response Work Better on the Community Level?

The answer is twofold: maybe and sometimes. We shouldn't assume that everything automatically works better in smaller towns. My friend Mark Makuc is a lifelong resident of Monterey, Massachusetts, which has a population of about 900. He left for college, majored in history at Brown University, and returned to his hometown soon after. He has a great family and is about as civic-minded as anyone I've ever met. He manages properties for second-home owners, runs the local library, and has been part of the leadership of the local volunteer fire department for more than a decade. Mark has taken many of the available emergency system training programs offered by the state as well as by FEMA.

One unusually mild January afternoon, Mark and I were chatting in my driveway about my old Toyota pickup truck, climate change, and a little local politics. But we got into the subject of emergency response. I asked Mark what the setup for emergency responders was in this area. He replied that Monterey has a volunteer fire department consisting of fifteen members, plus a chief and assistant chief. The police department has two full-time officers and four part-timers. The problem, Mark says, is that "the police officers and firefighters don't really communicate all that well. I mean, we have radios on the same frequency, but it's the human aspects of communication where things are not working so well. They are always having feuds over this or that." And, he added, "When we respond to local emergencies, there is still a lot of confusion over who exactly is in charge."

And when it comes to local fire departments cooperating with each other even on basic fire calls, Mark shook his head. "Well, there are some communities we work with—and some we don't. Of the five surrounding local fire departments, we don't trust two of them." He gave me the example of a plane crash on a mountainside near Monterey:

When we got the state police, or MEMA [Massachusetts Emergency Management Agency], or FEMA and whoever else had jurisdiction over that plane crash, it became what is known in this line of work as a "cluster." At the actual crash site, state police threw up roadblocks and turned away firemen who were responding to the rescue of known survivors, even though an accident scene is supposed to be under the jurisdiction of the fire chief or his incident commander until the victims are rescued. But other authorities are interested in the crash site as an accident investigation and even a potential crime scene.

In that particular situation, I was on the mountaintop along with my own firemen, a neighboring town's firemen, paramedics from the New York State Police, Civilian Air Patrol, and a couple of other agency representatives. We worked together pretty well, but in the parking lot at the base of the mountain, the State Police, MEMA, and everyone else spent a lot of time feuding over access to the scene, jurisdiction, and other matters. There was a mix-up with the evacuation. What should have taken fifteen minutes to get the helicopter on its way to the nearby Level 1 trauma center instead took an hour or more. In the heat of the moment, decisions are often made and carried out by the strongest personality instead of by rational logical thinking.

The bottom line is that as soon as the state and federal authorities get involved, as has happened in our town with the plane crash, searches, and a tornado, the question of "who is in charge" becomes even more confusing.

I had wrongly assumed that interagency relationship issues were more likely to occur in bigger cities, where turf wars and bureaucratic confusion were part of the ongoing challenges in emergency response. In truth, we cannot be too sanguine about the ability of any particular local response system to function effectively, especially in a major disaster. Local resources can quickly be overwhelmed. Responders may or may not be properly trained or experienced—and response quality may vary widely from one town to the next. Even the existence of cordial working relationships among neighboring agencies may not be there when it needs to be.

The Other Sector: The Role and Impact of Voluntary and Nongovernmental Organizations (NGOs)

Disasters bring out a wide range of human response. My sense is that most people try to help neighbors and strangers in times of distress.

The most effective nongovernmental and voluntary organizations are just structured, scaled-up versions of this desire of people to help each other in times of need. This is as true for the thousands of faith-based groups as it is for the major nonprofit organizations that make up the volunteer sector of American society. The American Red Cross (ARC), the Salvation Army, and Save the Children are all examples of such organizations that have broad operational structures akin to those of a corporation or government agency. In the case of the ARC, founded more than 125 years ago, a federally 3authorized charter requires it to play specific roles, like sheltering people rendered homeless during a disaster.

The American Red Cross has more than 800 locally supported chapters throughout the country, as well as a national presence in Washington, D.C. In responding to Katrina and the subsequent floods, the Red Cross alone raised $2 billion—approximately 60 percent of all dollars donated by Americans for the relief efforts—and mobilized nearly a quarter of a million volunteers. While Red Cross efforts assisted hundreds of thousands of people in one way or another, the problems encountered were legion. Attempts to locate appropriate shelter sites were often slow and failures to appreciate the full scope of needs of evacuees were frequently reported. Accountability for relief funds was a major problem. Checks for $1,000 or more were given to individuals with little proof of need, and the organization did not keep consistent records to prevent issuing multiple checks to the same family or individual.

Complaints about poor coordination with local and state organizations and other relief agencies were also lodged against the ARC. On September 28, 2005, for instance, *USA Today* reported that the ARC was evicted from a DeKalb, Georgia, shelter. Vernon Jones, the county executive, claimed that "victims were treated like cattle" by the organization's volunteers, who seemed totally overwhelmed and unable to deliver needed services.

Red Cross volunteers also reported problems in offering their services to the victims in makeshift shelters that were being established across Mississippi and Louisiana. Sometimes, in the midst of a major emergency, when well-meaning volunteers arrive on the

scene without required skills, it is difficult to verify their back-
grounds, find suitable tasks for them, and keep tabs on what is
happening. On the other hand, many motivated, highly skilled
individuals were dismayed to discover how difficult it was to find
productive roles in shelters controlled by the ARC.

Brad and Sharon Harmon were two such volunteers. Within
days of the disaster in the Gulf, they left their home in Sacramento,
California, and traveled on September 12 to Brookhaven, Mississippi, where the Red Cross told them to go. Brad is a physician and
Sharon a nurse. They hoped to help some of the thousands of evacuees who had been injured during the storm, or who had left New
Orleans without their prescription medications and whose chronic
medical conditions were deteriorating. When they arrived in
Brookhaven, the Harmons were told that there were some 3,500
evacuees in the area, when in fact there were between 8,000 and
10,000. Many displaced families were sleeping in their cars in parks
or in the surrounding woods: the majority had been there for a
week or more. During the day, they would flood the ARC shelters
seeking supplies, money, and medical care. Brad's original assign-
ment was to rotate around twenty-three ARC shelters in five Mississippi counties, to oversee medical care being delivered by nurses.

Meanwhile, thousands of physicians were volunteering to come
to the region from around the country, but neither ARC nor the
federal government could figure out how to coordinate or deploy
this willing and able army of medical personnel. One colleague told
me of her experience in trying to volunteer. "I was on God knows
how many useless national conference calls with officials from the
U.S. Department of Health and Human Services." She continued:
"This went on for weeks—and they never got it organized."

Brad and Sharon Harmon struggled to make sense of the state
of affairs in the Mississippi ARC shelters. Sharon had this to say
about it:

On our first day . . . we were told that we had a "situation"
developing at the Red Cross Complex, where checks were
being distributed [by the Red Cross]. We found a number of

physicians from the University of Indiana. They had set up an area . . . meeting the immediate needs of [evacuees] already at the shelter. The complex was surrounded by people and cars lining the streets for at least half a mile . . . There were at least 8,000 people who had gathered there . . . very upset [having] gotten there the night before . . . A riot was developing because people had been without food and water all night and [by 10 a.m.] the temperature was already in the 90s, with tremendous humidity. The National Guard was . . . up and down the hill. There was much heat exhaustion, thirst, hunger, people without their insulin and heart medications, women who were pregnant and children who were not attended. We needed shade, but there was none available.

As the situation worsened, it became clear that the Red Cross management team had not anticipated how much food and water was needed, and the National Guard troops were not much help on this score. Sharon asked the National Guard for water and food, but they informed her they were just there for security. In the meantime, Brad had rounded up some volunteers to identify the sickest people on the hill and take them in the Red Cross van to a little makeshift area he had created with some of the other doctors to do what they could. Sharon reported: "The number of sick began to overwhelm the doctors and nurses . . . Brad told the head of the Red Cross to get those people off the hill by whatever means they had . . . It was a dangerous situation." That day, the National Guard, as ill-prepared and disconnected as it seemed to be, held this very volatile situation in check. When the Guard troops were inexplicably pulled out over the next few weeks, the security concerns at the ARC shelters became, according to the Harmons, "too dangerous to stay."

The longer I spoke with Sharon and Brad and read their reports, the more horrified I was. Two weeks into the crisis, around the time the Harmons went to Brookhaven, the ARC had already raised millions of dollars. Its leadership was supposed to have had experience handling large-scale situations like this. Apparently not.

And according to the Harmons, even the local police were not helpful to the Red Cross workers who had barely tried to establish working relationships with any of the community officials.

I spoke with Dr. Harmon months later. He was back in California and had had time to reflect on his experiences in the Gulf trying to work with the ARC. "I was stunned to see how poorly the Red Cross organized the care of evacuees in the shelters. First of all, these were sick, hungry, and very traumatized people, many quite desperate. The effectiveness of the Red Cross was markedly impaired by their inability to ensure basic security for the evacuees and for those of us who came to help." To make matters worse, the Red Cross seemed completely disorganized in its distribution of money to the evacuees who were crowded into the shelters. Brad called the situation "not well thought out and disturbing." Mostly, Brad said, it was "horribly frustrating to witness the inefficiency of the Red Cross in utilizing the . . . expertise they potentially had available to them."

Brad concluded: "In our experience, both FEMA and the Red Cross were themselves disasters. The system just did not serve the evacuees. In the end, the Red Cross was overwhelmed by the medical needs that they seemed unable to anticipate. The sad thing, too, is that the media just missed this whole story." He wondered aloud if this would just happen again, when the next megadisaster struck. I couldn't help but wonder the very same thing.

In addition to the large, beleaguered not-for-profit organizations, thousands of much smaller volunteer groups and even individuals showed up to help throughout the devastated region. They came from every part of the United States, traveling in cars, vans, buses, and tractor trailers. They brought food, water, toys, blankets, tents, over-the-counter medications, everything that might be needed. These very well-meaning people came and did what they could. And they were typically compassionate, generous lifelines for countless families and individuals who had lost everything. What's particularly amazing is how much local communities embraced members of these smaller organizations. They fed volunteers and, when possible, put them up in churches along the Gulf coast. From their outpouring of support, one had the feeling that if a major disaster struck in the Midwest or up north, Mississippi and Louisiana volunteers would return the favor.

In stark contrast to the way the ARC functioned, many faith-based organizations came during the acute phase of the relief effort and have remained for the long-term recovery. Some are working alongside local projects, including those connected with rebuilding efforts, such as Habitat for Humanity. Habitat is one of the more effective organizations that focuses on tangible results; it is famous for getting volunteers to build houses for needy families, encouraging the eventual occupants to join in the process. Many other organizations came to help and stayed. The Lehigh Presbytery Helping Hands Katrina Working Group from Allentown, Pennsylvania, for instance, is still there, sustained by fund-raising from its congregation and rotating church volunteers who travel to the D'Iberville area of Mississippi to help rebuild homes and serve survivors. In the end, organizations like this can do a lot of good, often succeeding where the large charities fail to connect with local communities. But this is not always the case.

Several inherent problems impair the ability of small NGOs to function optimally in a situation like the post-Katrina Gulf. First there is the question of scale. In a megadisaster, there is a tendency to misunderstand the true impact of the disaster and the level of aid needed for relief and recovery. For example, Habitat for Humanity does a great job of engaging volunteers to build houses, but it can only build hundreds of houses—and in the Gulf after Katrina, *hundreds of thousands* of houses were needed immediately to replace those that had been destroyed. My own organization, the Children's Health Fund, uses mobile medical units to provide health care for medically underserved children; we care for approximately 125,000 patients a year. But in the United States there are more than *10 million children* who have difficulty gaining access to health care.

Neither Habitat nor the CHF can solve the problems we're addressing by simply expanding services. In responding to a megadisaster or addressing a large-scale chronic societal problem, like childhood poverty or poor access to medical care, it takes the commitment and resources of government to make a definitive impact. It simply cannot be accomplished by the private or voluntary sectors alone, no matter how dedicated or skilled they may be.

The government has *almost* gotten it right with its federally funded community health center program. Conceived by physician activist H. Jack Geiger in the late 1960s, these comprehensive, community-based health programs serving the most medically underserved populations have flourished under all administrations in the last thirty-five years. More than a thousand of these facilities are now in rural and inner-city communities throughout the country, but they still serve only a small fraction of those communities where they are very much needed.

Smaller nongovernmental organizations play another crucial role as innovators. They often develop model programs that help people in myriad ways, such as using mobile medical units and school-based health-care programs to bring health care to remote, impoverished populations. In an ideal world, government would use these successful programs as models for large, governmental interventions. If only it worked that way. The inside joke in the world of nongovernmental social programs is that America is addicted to demonstration projects, but it is unable to sufficiently expand those that prove to be workable and effective. Sometimes, government-funded private sector organizations can be useful in ensuring the quality and scale of service programs in remote areas. One of the most effective of these is John Snow Inc. (JSI), headquartered in Boston, which helps make quality public health programs available in eighty-four countries around the world. JSI's president, Joel Lamstein, has a strong commitment to quality and oversight, and JSI focuses specifically on helping indigenous local organizations improve their internal capacities to function more effectively.

Jeff Sachs, the Columbia University economist and author of *The End of Poverty,* has developed highly effective strategies to lift villages in Africa out of desperate, grinding poverty. The principles are simple—good seed, fertilizer, water conservation, and anti-malaria mosquito nets—and the costs are minimal: $300,000 can literally save a village. He is raising millions in a project called the Millennium Promise, but that sum still represents a drop in the bucket of what is needed. Jeff recently suggested, only half-jokingly, that we create a "Department of Scaling Up" at the university. Its sole purpose would be to figure out how to get successful model programs recognized and embraced by government, and then replicated on a mass scale. I understood what he meant.

Quality control is another concern regarding the work of small NGOs, especially in post-disaster environments where needs are intense and there is little organized oversight. There really is no system for evaluating the quality or outcome of services provided. In addition, it is difficult to control the information these groups deliver. I have seen, for instance, examples of very bad medical practices under the auspices of volunteer organizations and even individual medical providers who had no idea what they were doing. Of equal concern are faith-based organizations that exploit charitable work to promote their particular religious doctrines. I've seen flagrant examples of this in Ethiopia and Guatemala, following disasters where aid workers from religious charities insisted on prayer rituals before passing out food. This kind of proselytizing is the worst kind of exploitation. While it is generally unusual, I know it happens. Controlling the message and the methodologies of small nongovernmental organizations is difficult and imperfect. In the current political climate, distasteful and exploitive practices may be overtly promoted by a government that has tacked strongly to the ideological right.

In most cases, the work of nongovernmental organizations and individual volunteers in the aftermath of disasters is vital and effective. And while the volunteer sector is an essential partner in effective disaster-response efforts, along with government, first-responder organizations, and citizens themselves, the challenges they face of responding to scale, ensuring quality and keeping ideology out of the relief work remain unresolved.

10 · Barrier 4
The Strange Psychology of Preparedness and Why the Public Isn't Buying

One of the most enigmatic realities of reaching a better state of effective readiness in the United States is the difficulty of "selling" the preparedness message to the general public. Many factors may be responsible for this situation, including a failure of citizens to understand the importance of their own roles in responding to emergencies. What many people do not realize, though, is that the very first actions, in the moments following *any* emergency—from an automobile accident to aspirating food and choking in a restaurant—may determine whether a life is saved or lost. It is the behavior of people in the immediate vicinity of the victim that count. These are the true first responders. Typically, though, in most communities, emergency medical personnel can be on scene a few moments later.

Even more sobering is the fact that in a large-scale disaster, the average citizen can actually end up being a responder for an extended period of time—perhaps days—if the usual emergency response systems are overwhelmed or incapacitated. The cavalry may simply not be on the way any time soon. That's why individual and family preparedness planning is so crucial in disaster readiness.

So why isn't that happening, especially in the post-9/11 and post-Katrina environment?

My colleagues and I first began studying public opinion and behavior concerning disasters and terrorism within months of September 11, 2001. We developed comprehensive surveys that covered a number of issues, from concern about further attacks to how confident people were that the government could effectively prevent or respond to terror or disasters in general. We learned a great deal about what people think about disasters and how they responded to a growing appreciation of risk and vulnerability in our society.

Still, I hardly needed a survey to know how people are responding to the "preparedness message." At every talk I give across the country on the subject, I always ask, "How many of you consider yourselves 'prepared' for a major disaster?" I never get more than two or three raised hands. It makes no difference whether I am speaking with medical professionals, students, or lay groups. When I press them, I often hear one of the following comments:

- *It's not very likely that anything will really happen, and, if it does, it won't happen to me.*
- *I'll just call "911."*
- *I don't know what to do.*

The fact is that few Americans have complied with the recommendations made by any number of organizations promoting basic, prudent steps to ensure their safety in the event of a megadisaster.

Though surveys show the public is concerned about the potential for future disasters, this awareness does not seem to translate into enhanced preparedness planning. Even an executive order from the president for citizens to prepare fell on deaf ears. The American public remains stubbornly unprepared. Patricia McGinnis, the president and CEO of the Council on Excellence in Government, recently commented, "It is surprising that while people across the country were moved to open their hearts and wallets to help the victims of Katrina, they were not moved to *prepare themselves and their families* for a major emergency. What is it going to take? If Katrina didn't spur the public to action, what will?"

The question is fair enough. Only about four in ten Americans report having a family emergency preparedness plan that all members of the family know about—a modest improvement over previous years. Of those who report having a plan, less than a third say they have all or some of the major elements that are part of an emergency plan (such as two days' supply of food and water, a flashlight, a portable radio and spare batteries, emergency phone numbers, and a meeting place).

On the other hand, citizens who do have a complete family emergency plan are more than twice as likely to be familiar with the emergency or evacuation plans at their children's schools. They are also more likely to be familiar with the emergency evacuation plan in their community, and they feel better prepared to withstand another terrorist attack. And being prepared means different things to different people, depending on what the "event" is. Approximately six out of ten people feel personally "very prepared" or "prepared" for a natural disaster or emergency weather event in their community, but just about a third feel prepared for a terrorist attack.

The same was true for people's views of their community's response plans. More than half of the American public think their community has an adequate response plan in place for natural disasters or emergency weather events, compared with just 37 percent who believe their community has an adequate response plan in place for a terrorist attack. More people (almost four in ten) are familiar with their community's natural disaster plans than with their terrorism response plans (fewer than a quarter).

Even before the stunning revelations about the response to Hurricane Katrina, the American public's faith in its government was steadily declining. In the summer of 2005, and for the first time since September 11, 2001, less than half of the American public expressed confidence in the government's ability to protect their community from a terrorist attack. This figure has been consistently decreasing, from a high of 64 percent in 2003 to 42 percent in 2005, according to polls conducted by the National Center for Disaster Preparedness (NCDP) at Columbia University and the Marist College Institute for Public Opinion.

And yet, more than three-quarters of Americans remain concerned there will be more terrorist attacks in the United States. No matter whether they live in a small community or a large city, or in which region of the country, nearly one in three Americans believes an attack will happen within a year. We are, it seems, almost universally concerned about a repeat of 9/11 or worse.

The American public feels less safe than it did in 2003 or 2004. And these are not just reflections of a general anxiety about the future. We are worried about the government's ability to:

- Protect nuclear power facilities (only half are "confident" or "very confident," down from 63 percent in 2003).
- Prevent the detonation of radiation-contaminated "dirty bombs" (37 percent are "confident" or "very confident," down from 40 percent in 2004 and 49 percent in 2003).
- Protect public transportation, like buses and trains, which has been on a downhill slide, as well, recently showing only 37 percent expressing confidence—down from 43 percent the year before.

Public pessimism extends to the public health arena as well. Confidence in the health-care system's ability to respond effectively to a biological, chemical, or nuclear attack remains unchanged at 39 percent from 2004. But that represents a steep decline from 2002, when more than half held out hope for an effective response.

Interestingly, our studies have found that in nearly all areas of confidence and perception, African Americans are more pessimistic about the competence of government than whites and Latinos. They have little confidence in the government's ability to protect the places where they live, or that they would receive a fair share of money to prepare for future terrorism.

Perhaps not surprisingly, Republicans have been more optimistic about our state of readiness than either Democrats or Independents. Three-quarters of Republicans think the United States is prepared for a future attack (compared with half of Democrats and less than two-thirds of Independents). For a party generally skeptical about what government will do, Republicans are far more confident than Democrats and Independents that the government will protect where they live (62%, 40%, and 43% respectively). They feel safer than before September 11 (37%, 12%, and 18%); and they believe far more often than Democrats or Independents that their communities are receiving their fair share of the money intended to prepare us for future attacks.

Why Aren't Americans Listening?

Although recent trends in preparedness planning and public messages have been moving increasingly toward an all-hazards approach, the survey findings suggest that this strategy, which is now supported by government, the Red Cross, and other readiness organizations, may not be the most effective. In theory, the approach—helping people survive any kind of disaster—makes sense. However, people are not buying the notion that, for instance, hurricane planning will help much in a terrorist-caused smallpox attack or nuclear detonation. They may be right.

One problem may be that people are less likely to follow a complicated and expensive recommendation. A good example of this is the contrast between planning for "all-hazards" readiness and the much more onerous recommendations for quarantine in the event of a pandemic flu. While general disaster readiness calls for a three-day supply of food and water, some government officials are suggesting that in the event of a pandemic, people may be directed to stay at home for two weeks—or more. If we are already having difficulty persuading people to prepare for the possibility of "shelter in place" (at home) for three days, suggesting a two-week stockpile would be an uphill battle.

Well-meaning guidance can become intimidating and off-putting to the general public. I think about my own daughter living in a very small New York City apartment and wonder where she would even begin to find the room for everything she would need for two weeks of isolation. And low-income families, even if they had the room, may well not be able to invest in a two-week stockpile of necessities.

Moreover, if individuals are not well informed, or believe that the information they are receiving won't do any good, they are not likely to take action. The examples from the nuclear terror scenario are a case in point. It is the job, then, of those responsible for public communications on disaster readiness to reassure people that survival is in fact possible and to provide reliable, accurate information that can save lives.

The credibility of the messenger is also essential. In 2003, the Rand Corporation's disaster-readiness experts took the U.S. government's Ready.gov website to task for providing inaccurate and inadequate information to citizens about how to survive a nuclear blast. Unfortunately, once the accuracy of information coming from an organization or government is proved to be of questionable validity, it is difficult to correct.

The same was true for the Department of Homeland Security when it promoted using duct tape to seal off a safe room in homes in the event of a nuclear or nerve gas attack. Whether the information itself was actually correct or not became irrelevant, once it became fodder for late-night comedians. Peter Sandman, a noted expert at Rutgers University on credibility of communications, explains: "In communicating risk information, trust and credibility are a spokesperson's most precious assets. . . . Once lost, they are almost impossible to regain." The central point is clear: bad messages and noncredible messengers breed loss of confidence in government.

Have Americans Ever Responded to Preparedness Messages?
(A Short History)

Americans' propensity to "miss the message," or to hear it but not be moved to act, is not a new phenomenon. Last year, I asked David Berman, a senior policy analyst at Columbia's National Center for Disaster Preparedness, to look further into this issue. I was interested in the historical perspective on how Americans have responded to crisis in general, and to calls for public readiness for major threats in particular.

The results of David's research were surprising. It had been my impression that in response to the surprise attacks on U.S. Navy ships in Pearl Harbor on December 7, 1941, the entire nation mobilized. In my view, December 7 and September 11 had a great deal in common. On both days the nation suffered violent surprise attacks by hostile foreign elements, resulting in a rapid, overwhelming reaction among the public as well as an enormous response from the national government, including declaration of war.

Following September 11, we also reorganized government (the creation of the 180,000-employee U.S. Department of Homeland Security), attacked Al-Qaeda strongholds in Afghanistan, and invested hundreds of billions of dollars in a controversial incursion in Iraq. And the government urged citizens to "prepare" for more terror attacks through DHS's Ready.gov and America Prepared campaigns. Both programs were barely noticed and there is no evidence that either actually improved public preparedness.

Most Americans assume that after Pearl Harbor, we went to war, we geared up our military machine, *and* we took to the streets—and the beaches—to watch for enemy aircraft overhead and U-boats off the coasts. And it turns out that this was mostly true, but not entirely. If one takes a close look at surveys of the American people done by the Gallup organization since the early 1940s, a more nuanced picture emerges.

Record numbers of Americans—mostly young men—joined the

military. In all walks of life, in every part of the country, patriotism prevailed and we went off to fight enemies on three continents. What's more, some 300,000 women joined the military forces (with a quarter of them serving overseas), and millions more became the predominant workforce in the industries vital to the Allied war effort. The shipbuilding industry alone employed some 200,000 women in 1943, compared with only 36 in 1939. Out of concern that resources might be limited because of the war effort, the government urged citizens to plant vegetable gardens on their own property. Over 20 million Americans complied, growing as much as 40 percent of the produce consumed during the years of World War II.

But what about *individual preparedness*? While the years of America's engagement in the war produced enormous patriotism and willingness to risk one's life in battle and reinvent the entire U.S. workforce to sustain the economy and the military campaign, that fervor did not actually materialize in individual actions to protect the homefront. Gallup surveys showed that just after Pearl Harbor and at the beginning of World War II, when people were asked if they knew where to go in the event of an air raid, 35 percent could give a correct answer; 58 percent said they had not given the question any thought. When individuals were asked if, beyond regular employment, they were doing any work in civil defense programs such as air raid watches or first aid, just 9 percent said they were. Communities were supposed to establish civil defense programs as the primary means for protecting themselves from further Pearl Harbor–type attacks on the homeland. Despite aggressive campaigns to persuade the public to join these programs, by February of 1942, almost three months after Pearl Harbor and the entry of the U.S. into World War II, just 23 percent of respondents participated in a civilian defense program. In 1943, when asked if they had to make any "real sacrifice" for the war effort, only 2 percent said they had volunteered as air wardens, in civilian defense, or with the American Red Cross. In other words, civil defense was not seen as a priority in the culture of national sacrifice that prevailed in civic life during the years of World War II.

During the Cold War years, growing tension between the former Soviet Union and the United States manifested itself in a hair-trigger standoff between the superpowers: at its peak, more than 50,000 nuclear weapons were poised for launch from one side or the other. By the late 1950s, 64 percent of Americans felt that nuclear war was possible. Despite this, the trend of public unpreparedness continued throughout the Cold War. In 1953, participation in civil defense programs fell to 4.5 percent. Even when informed that civil defense officials suggested it would cost only $200 to build a "reasonably safe air raid shelter," just 2 percent said they were likely to build one in the next year. In 1954, when asked about a hypothetical war with the Soviet Union and a subsequent air raid alert in their town, only 6.5 percent of the public said they would follow instructions of civil defense wardens; 4 percent said they would report for civil defense duty. Nearly a fifth (19 percent) said they did not know what they would do or they would do nothing.

In 1960, as the nuclear arms race intensified, only 11 percent of the public had done anything to prepare for a nuclear attack. While 71 percent favored a law requiring every community to build a public bomb shelter, only 21 percent had ever given thought to building a home bomb shelter. And when asked, as they had been seven years earlier, if they would consider paying $500 to build a home bomb shelter, 61 percent said they would not. A year later, in 1961, only 2 percent of the public said they had made any changes to their home to protect against a nuclear weapons attack. When Gallup asked the question again a month later, this time with an emphasis on "plan"—Do you *plan* to make any changes to your home to protect against a nuclear weapon attack?—just 12 percent said yes and 1 percent said they already had, even with tax breaks for home shelter construction and broad public awareness campaigns.

Not even the Cuban Missile Crisis of 1962, with a global nuclear war looking imminent, moved the American public to prepare: only 4 percent of the U.S. public said they had engaged in safety- or survival-related activities. During that period, described as the closest the U.S. had come to a third world war, public preparedness did not improve. In 1963, at the same time as 24 percent of those polled described the danger of world war as the second most important problem facing the country (after communism in the United States with 31 percent), only *2 percent* called fallout shelters the most important priority. Amazingly, 41 percent—the highest percentage of any choice—selected it as the least important.

Although tensions eased once that crisis was deflected, and treaties were hammered out between the superpowers, the nuclear arsenals never materially diminished and the threat of annihilation remained. When in the late 1970s and early 1980s tensions between the U.S. and the USSR intensified, a number of activist organizations rose up to warn the public about the risk and threat of nuclear war. Physicians for Social Responsibility (PSR) and International Physicians for the Prevention of Nuclear War (IPPNW), for example, played key roles in developing this public message and advocating in Washington and internationally for a reduction or elimination of the world's nuclear arsenals. PSR's modus operandi was particularly effective. Physician members of the organization, well informed about the explicit consequences of nuclear detonations on civilian populations, blanketed the country, speaking graphically as doctors about the impact of a nuclear blast on the specific community they were addressing at the moment. The effect was predictable. The media paid attention and the public was appropriately horrified at envisioning what might actually happen.

But during those times of heightened awareness about the potential for nuclear devastation, individuals still did relatively little in the way of preparing for a possible disaster. There is no evidence to support any significant degree of "public uptake" of the civil defense and preparedness message coming from government or prompted by the dire warnings of activist antinuclear groups. That lack of interest in civil defense was, to a certain extent, seen as a positive sign by antinuclear activists who were busy reinforcing the notion that civil defense strategies would be totally ineffective in the face of an all-out nuclear conflict between the United States and the Soviet Union. As an active member of the Physicians for Social

Responsibility, I participated in this campaign, even mocking the absurd images of "duck and cover" civil defense exercises that had been widely promoted for schoolchildren during the early years of the Cold War.

H. Jack Geiger, who co-founded PSR, had this to say recently about those efforts:

> During the intensity of the anti-nuclear work of the 1980s, people recognized the fundamental futility of being able to really do anything in the event of a nuclear war with the Soviet Union. And that was good for what we were trying to do, which was point out the futility of civil defense and the necessity for ending the arms race and the conflicts that brought us to the brink of war. We were saying that the fabric of the society would be irreparably torn by a global nuclear war and the solution was avoiding this conflict, not trying to survive in the aftermath.

We face a very different situation today, however. The nuclear scenarios we're worried about are not nation-destroying, massive attacks involving hundreds or thousands of nuclear-tipped, high-grade weapons. We're more concerned now about a *single detonation* in a *particular place* under circumstances that would be truly terrible, but, for many, survivable. Perhaps there's a certain degree of residual skepticism about Cold War preparedness that continues to sustain resistance to preparing for large-scale terrorism, especially that involving a nuclear device.

On a certain level, then, the failure of Americans to take seriously the preparedness message in the post-9/11 and post-Katrina environment is historically consistent with other times in our contemporary history. We seem to respond reasonably well initially to patriotic calls to battle, but we do not respond to more passive messages of preparing for the next attack or megadisaster. Perhaps the "battle-cry appeal" deeply resonates with our sense of rugged toughness in a crisis. Is there something a little "wimpish," perhaps, in carrying around a whistle, a flashlight, and a bottle of water "in case something happens"?

Stages of Change

If disaster preparedness campaigns are to be successful in changing the public's understanding and acceptance of their individual roles, those designing these materials need to understand how people normally modify their behaviors. One of the most helpful theoretical constructs for doing this is the "Stages of Change" model, originally described by Dr. James Prochaska, director of the Cancer Prevention Research Consortium and professor of clinical and health psychology at the University of Rhode Island, and his colleagues. Prochaska's model may help explain why Americans still seem so unwilling to take the necessary steps to improve their own readiness for major disasters. It may also help in developing a new perspective on how to create a *culture of readiness* that enhances public reception of the preparedness message.

Prochaska's model tracks the phases, from denial through action, that people pass through in modifying behaviors that pose health threats, such as smoking or substance dependency. One of his key points is that most treatment programs for people who smoke or who are addicted to drugs or alcohol are "action-oriented"; that is, people are instructed to "do things." However, as many as 80 percent of smokers and substance-dependent individuals are simply not ready to engage in any kind of action plan. Successful interventions for such persons may require understanding and assisting people to progress through the stages of change to a point where they are ready to accept an action-oriented strategy. Prochaska describes five stages of change:

Pre-Contemplation

In clinical-care settings, this stage refers to denial or complete lack of interest in changing what might be a health-threatening behavior. People in this stage are difficult to treat and not receptive to the advice of a physician or other professional. This perspective may describe the frame of mind of people who were shaken and distressed by 9/11—and perhaps Katrina—but did not think such catastrophes could ever happen to them. Public exhortations around readiness may not make a dent.

Contemplation

At this stage, people are beginning to recognize that there is a problem. They may weigh the pros and cons, and become more curious about what they might actually be able to do in the event of a major emergency. They will have acknowledged the fact that this is something potentially worth their investment of time and resources. But they're still not ready to "do something."

Preparation

In this stage, there's a real opening. People will begin to discuss disaster readiness with their families; perhaps talk to colleagues about emergency procedures in the workplace. This is the moment when more specific information should be made available to people who are about to get considerably more engaged.

Action

This stage is the ideal state for making inroads. At this point, people want to know what to do. They will engage. This is the moment when resources and information should be available and the hard sell for the campaign will have the greatest likelihood of being accepted and acted upon.

Maintenance and Relapse Prevention

For patients attempting to stay tobacco-free or stick to a diet, this phase is crucial. Special support and attention are needed to keep people from relapsing into former habits. A similar phase may be experienced by people who initially heed preparedness advice, perhaps soon after 9/11 or in the aftermath of a major natural disaster. Over time, particularly if no further events occur, interest in readiness lapses. Food stocks may go out of date and people misplace the lists of emergency family contact numbers. Here, strategies for sustaining interest in readiness will need to be devised. Ultimately, the goal will be to *normalize readiness,* making preparedness planning as routine as smoke alarms and seat belts.

In terms of disaster readiness and Prochaska's stages of change continuum, Americans hover somewhere between contemplation and preparation, but clearly are not yet ready to take action. This insight should be driving our national strategies to enhance preparedness engagement among citizens. At the moment, we may be aggressively pushing a very active agenda for a population still not ready to hear it.

IV

Making America Safer:
What We Need to Do Now

11 · Introducing Change

There is a temptation to reach broad, unsettling conclusions about the state of the nation's preparedness for megadisasters and then suggest a precise set of prescriptive fixes. And though I will offer a version of just that, some of these fixes will almost certainly be imperfect because many of the key issues that influence strategic proposals are almost always "in motion." Last year's threat analysis may be made obsolete with new intelligence—or more sophisticated climatic information—suggesting new risks or downplaying old ones. Bureaucratic barriers to preparedness, while seemingly unrelenting, are rarely static. And important new legislation may even be waiting in committee, redrafted to respond to new pressures or insights. The point is that to make sweeping proposals in an area this complex is tricky and uncertain.

Still, there are ways to prepare for megadisasters that will always be relevant. I'm thinking about the overwhelming need to have a well-functioning health-care system that can take care of the day-to-day needs of the population as well as respond effectively to bioterrorism or pandemics. Likewise, there are basic problems that are simply blatant and persistent, such as the failure of the radio communications systems of different emergency response agencies to operate on similar wavelengths—a problem on 9/11, after Katrina and still not solved today.

Part of the challenge in making recommendations to improve preparedness is that many of the key concepts, such as "safety" and "prepared," are relative terms. One person's perception of and response to a given risk may be very different from another's. And what makes the public *feel* secure is markedly different from an objective measure of what makes a society actually prepared to respond to large disasters.

The psychology of emotional or behavioral reactions to threats is complex terrain, as is made abundantly clear in David Ropeik and George Gray's compelling book, *Risk: A Practical Guide for Deciding What's Really Safe and What's Really Dangerous in the World Around You.* These social scientists compare the mathematical probability of occurrence for many threats across a range of categories including natural events, environmental exposures, and animal attacks. They assert that "risk is the probability that exposure to a hazard will lead to a negative consequence."

But other far more subjective factors actually affect people's behaviors. Ropeik and Gray offer an interesting illustration. Think of how people abandoned air travel immediately following 9/11, even though the chances of dying in an automobile accident remained far greater than the risk of being involved in a fatal plane crash. Subjective perceptions of safety, not actual probabilities and crash statistics, determined behaviors.

Greg Thomas comments on the fear of terrorism in his book *Freedom from Fear:* "the threat of terrorist attack is no greater—and in many cases is significantly less—than the threat of harm posed by the risks we take in our everyday lives." Nevertheless, getting prepared should both satisfy objective benchmarks and help people to actually feel secure.

That said, the specific measures adopted to improve the response to major disasters must be objective and rational. Effective planning must gather reliable data and establish clear benchmarks or best practices that can be tested and replicated. Unfortunately, few of our current policies and protocols, whether concerning terror interdiction or megastorm response protocols, are based on such evidence and rigorous testing.

Instead, the Bush administration's policy decisions regarding preparedness are too often based on a kind of "threat anxiety" generated by the most recent disaster or the latest media buzz about pandemics or earthquakes, instead of an objective analytical assessment of specific threats. Security protocols at airports, regulated by the federal government, may reflect this. Since the 9/11 attacks used hijacked jetliners, extraordinary investments were made in procedural changes for airport screening, onboard security, and the like. An estimated $3.4 billion was spent on airport and airline security in 2005, compared with $320 million in the year before 9/11. So far, there is little objective evidence that the specific programs have been worth the investment.

If you think it's been worth the investment, because there have been no jetliner hijackings since 2001, don't be so sure. In July 2004, the *Seattle Times* published an article reviewing 100 media reports of airport security breaches since 2002 when the Transportation Safety Administration took over responsibility for safeguarding passengers and aircraft. Breaches included missed knives, martial arts weapons, explosives, and even handguns. People have slipped passed screeners and "disappeared in the crowds." And failures continue to be identified at many of the more than 400 commercial airports in the United States on a regular basis. We've been more lucky than prepared.

We are heavily invested in airline and airport security systems that do not work as well as we may have hoped *and* we've shortchanged other essential issues, like border and port security or improved technology for communications systems vital to postdisaster response efforts. Our overall patterns of determining preparedness priorities and distributing funds to support these efforts have become more reactionary and impulsive than rational and balanced. This also was repeated when the administration began to catch on to the possible threat of a pandemic flu: the Department of Health and Human Services put all available hands on this issue, often at the expense of other vital programs. Several sources at two different agencies within HHS told me similar stories: orders came from the office of the secretary of HHS to direct all discretionary funds to programs dealing with avian flu, literally diverting them from other pressing needs.

In thinking about what needs to change about the country's approach to preparedness, it is tempting to focus on the most obvious areas of concern or the recommendations most likely to actually be implemented. For instance, it certainly makes sense, in my view, to extract FEMA from the Department of Homeland Security and designate a special leadership role in disaster response for the U.S. surgeon general. Indeed, those are among my own recommendations.

But these are the easy issues. Far more difficult, however, is the grueling work of examining and addressing the pertinent underlying issues that genuinely interfere with long-term, meaningful improvements in the level of national preparedness. A federalist system that sends money, but no leadership or relevant guidance, to states, the dysfunctional state of the nation's health-care system, an inexplicably low level of public participation in personal preparedness measures, lack of governmental accountability, and an absolute dearth of credible leadership are all examples of the major structural challenges that need to be addressed.

No matter what, we need to disavow any misbegotten sense that getting better prepared somehow replaces or precludes taking care of other important societal needs. This is a false and dangerous trade-off that must be recognized and avoided. The U.S. has more than sufficient resources to both improve readiness *and* ensure health-care access for all, mount effective campaigns to eradicate tobacco use, promote essential medical research, and so forth. Furthermore, many of the most important recommendations to reduce the risk of major catastrophes or improve disaster-response capacity may have enormous general benefit for society.

12 · International Models: Who Does It Right? And Who Doesn't?

Over the past decade and a half, terrorism and natural disasters have appeared in all corners of the world, from the sarin attacks of 1994 and 1995 in Japan to the great tidal wave that swept across the Indian Ocean in December 2004, to the devastation in a remote corner of Pakistan following the 2005 earthquake, and the suicide bombings in London, Madrid, and Amman, Jordan. Sometimes countries have responded to these disasters in ways that have seemed both efficient and heroic. Other times, the response efforts were clearly and tragically overwhelmed. The popular belief is that in general, poor countries with few resources will respond poorly, wealthier countries more effectively. This may be generally true, but Cuba's response to Hurricane Ivan in September 2004 was a model of efficiency, with a very successful evacuation of low-lying regions and no reported loss of life. A year later, the world's most affluent nation responded to Hurricane Katrina with a display of systemic incompetence that became an international embarrassment.

No single country has all the answers, but important ideas can and should be drawn from the lessons of previous disasters. Increasingly, there are opportunities to discuss response models developed in one country that are applicable in another. One good example is the expansion of the International Ship and Port Security code (ISPS), which has established uniform standards for port security throughout the world. Nations see this code as a means to improve security, and also enhance and facilitate global commerce.

The U.S. government has a mixed record of learning from international experiences with disaster prevention or response. While delegations travel to other countries to visit with disaster-response officials, these opportunities seem, at best, sporadic and random. In contrast to the federal government, some American cities have a good understanding of what is to be gleaned from the experiences of other nations and make it their business to develop relationships with counterparts in other parts of the world. Ray Kelly, New York City's police commissioner, recently told me, "We have regular and effective communications with our colleagues overseas, especially in Great Britain." He continues: "As for the federal government's engagement in such activities, I've heard about very little going on in this particular arena."

How countries respond to the challenges of increased terrorist threats, natural disasters, and crumbling infrastructure depends a great deal on the kind of society and political systems under which they are governed. Liberal democracies must find the right, delicate balance between openness and secrecy, between civil rights and individual restraints—important factors that may affect the efficiency of counterterrorism strategies or the ability to solicit citizen cooperation during a crisis. Totalitarian states, on the other hand, are far less constrained by respect for privacy or the specter of people's refusing to comply with government orders during a catastrophic event.

For the rest of the world, the painfully visible lack of response to Hurricane Katrina dramatically changed the perception of U.S. competence in planning for or coping with disasters.

"In belated recognition of the depth of the crisis, Washington swallowed its pride and asked for blankets, food and water trucks from the EU and NATO, and beds and medical supplies from Canada."

From "Empty, Ruined and Desperate,"

the *Guardian* of London, September 5, 2005

"Day by day this week the world has watched a mounting horror in the United States. . . . No part of the world is entirely immune from the effects of a disaster on this scale. The damage to oil production in the Gulf of Mexico is expected to be felt in the petrol prices, and the cost of damage to insurers will be passed into premiums the world over. If the disaster had struck a different part of the world, appeals for aid would have been made. America is expected to look after its own, which it will. But it might appreciate some gesture of sympathy. Even the most powerful turn out to be frail in the face of nature."

From the *New Zealand Herald*

(Auckland), September 3, 2005

"The best he [President Bush] can do is a brief flyover of the region and a belated visit, hurriedly put together only because of the protests. . . . After siphoning off 200 billion USD of their hard-earned cash to finance his illegal act of butchery overseas, he turns his back on them, leaves them to wallow in the sewage, to lie rotting in the streets and to starve to death. . . . It appears the man is as inept at governing his own country as he is at conducting foreign policy."

From *Pravda*

(Moscow), September 2, 2005

"We have seen a society in collapse. . . . There has been gigantic failure here . . . The weakness of the levees was known, the danger of hurricanes was known, but plans to improve the

levees and to deal with a major flood were clearly inadequate. . . . At the same time, the picture of thousands of desperate people, many of them poor and black, left to fend for
themselves in an anarchic city speaks volumes about a society
dangerously polarized between the privileged classes and a
marginalized underclass."

From the *Edmonton* (Alberta) *Journal*,

September 3, 2005

The fall in the nation's reputation certainly seemed precipitous.
During the Clinton administration, FEMA, under the leadership of
James Lee Witt, had so many inquiries about new programs and
strategies that Witt created an international office just to handle the
stream of visitors and partner agencies. More than a hundred countries signed partnership agreements with the United States, including Armenia, Romania, Russia, Mexico, Canada, and Japan. FEMA
professionals were actively engaged in sharing information, ideas,
and training with their counterparts from other nations. Then
came two Bush appointees, Joe Allbaugh and Michael Brown, inexplicably determined to undo eight years of hard work.

James Lee Witt tells of the time when President Bush was making his first official visit to Mexico to meet with President Vicente
Fox. Witt called Joe Allbaugh, then the new FEMA director, and
said, "Joe, I see President Bush is going to Mexico. Now would be a
great opportunity for him and President Fox to expand the agree-
ment that FEMA has with Mexico on haz-mat exercises, earthquake and other preparedness issues of interest to both nations."
Allbaugh told Witt they were eliminating all those programs, that
they weren't going to be doing that international stuff anymore.

But Witt had an entirely different point of view. He thought that
the disaster preparedness and response work that FEMA was doing
was great policy for the State Department, a kind of "grown-up
version of the Peace Corps" that engendered extraordinary good-
will. Witt told me, "Now, disaster planners from these countries
e-mail me and they say, 'What happened to America? What

happened to FEMA?' and I don't know what to say." By 2006, few of the partnership agreements that Witt's office established were active, and much of the funding that supported shared training exercises has dried up.

Still, as recently as late 2004 and early 2005, in the immediate aftermath of one of the world's most devastating tsunamis, and following the earthquake along the Pakistan-India-Afghanistan border in 2005, the U.S. military was one of the first to respond, securing the devastated regions so that international aid workers and NGOs could arrive and establish their outposts. But that was the military doing what it does best—hardly a test of FEMA and its capacity to function effectively during a major disaster.

Even if FEMA is no longer as actively supportive as it had been previously of ongoing exchange with international partners about preparedness planning, there is much that first responders and academic and government leaders can learn from other countries, though no other nation's system is perfect.

Engaging Citizens and Organizing Government in Israel

Whatever challenges it faces, the Israeli government has attempted to ensure that the Israeli public—described as the "most prepared in the world"—knows what to do, where to go, and how to respond to large-scale emergencies. This level of preparedness has been complex and costly. The Israeli government issues gas defense kits (GDKs) to all citizens in preparation for chemical or biological attacks. They have established an elaborate emergency broadcast system and the means for public emergency announcements through cell phones and other notification systems. All schools, senior-citizen homes, and hospitals have disaster contingency plans, and each public building and private residence is required by law to have a mandatory "safe room" where circulation of outside air— and possible toxins—is significantly reduced.

One of the more innovative programs developed by the Israelis was to print a comprehensive section on disaster preparedness in the yellow pages of the phone book. The text is scenario-specific and updated regularly. The government has also developed websites and videos that increase awareness, engagement, and information-sharing among its citizens. Finally, Israeli students practice for emergency situations on a regular basis and soldiers visit each school annually for a lecture on preparedness. If a bioterror attack were to actually occur, Israel's Home Front Command (HFC) would go door to door to pass out medications and instructions. Engagement in disaster preparedness and response has made Israelis a crucial asset in a country's war against terrorism and aggression in general.

But just how prepared is the Israeli public? While the GPKs are available, they would help only *if* there was ample warning of a nerve gas attack and *if* individuals actually had their masks with them at the time of the attack. Under normal daily conditions, neither condition is likely. Further, only about a third of schools were found to have sufficient shelters. And just like the United States, Israel has been erratic in its preparedness spending. In the late 1990s, the U.S. provided Israel with $100 million for counterterrorism equipment, of which only 60 percent was spent. Some of this money was intended to help Israel purchase equipment to enhance port security. This never happened.

Israel has also learned that keeping stocks of medications for chemical and biological attacks is expensive and sometimes impractical. When the effectiveness date of the medicines passes, Israel does not always replace these stores, especially during times of a diminished perceived threat. This was the case just prior to the 1998 tensions with Iraq. As a result, the U.S. had to provide Israel with an emergency $57 million for upgrading medication stockpiles.

Israelis do have a sophisticated understanding of the psychosocial aspects of preparedness. Boaz Tadmor, a former colonel in the Israeli Defense Forces and director of the medical services in the Home Front Command, talks frequently of the need to build real preparedness from the ground up. Tadmor believes that training people to think and behave appropriately in any kind of emergency situation serves the community better than focusing on specific skills.

Another deservedly well-respected aspect of Israeli readiness is the functioning of its health-care system under emergency conditions. To begin with, universal access means that the Israeli medical system does not have to contend with uninsured people seeking care during an emergency. And medical personnel train and drill regularly to improve response to major emergencies. Furthermore, since Israel's health-care system is run by a three-part collaborative consisting of the military surgeon general, the head of the national medical organization, and the minister of health, it is a seamless operation. When an emergency is declared, operations move effortlessly into full emergency mode. This process has no equivalent whatsoever in the United States.

Japan: Conceptualizing and Responding to Terror

Culturally, the Japanese have had a hard time conceptualizing and responding to terrorism. In Japan, there seem to be two states of being: war and peace. Terrorism, being a middle state, is viewed more as a crime than as an idea or principle against which war can be declared, which is what the Bush administration did in response to 9/11. The Japanese typically view terrorism as a result of government failure—the unmet needs of the poor, oppression of a minority, or some other failed policy. And among legislators the topic of terrorism is rarely overtly discussed.

Because of this perspective, the Japanese tend to place greater priority on individual and group rights, particularly if restrictions on individuals or groups are seen as unwarranted. This outlook was a leading factor in the Japanese government's failure to stop the Aum Shrinrikyo cult's sarin gas attacks in 1994 on an apartment complex and in 1995 on the Tokyo subway. If the United States suffered from a failure of imagination on September 11, so too did the Japanese by failing to see Aum Shrinrikyo as a terrorist organization rather than a fringe religious organization.

Unfamiliar with how to deal with chemicals and unable to identify the toxin, Japanese transit officials actually exposed themselves to the poison gas, allowing trains to continue running for almost an hour and a half after the cars had been contaminated. It took the Japanese military nearly two hours after the attack to identify the agent as sarin, and another hour to share the information with other agencies, including some of the local hospitals.

The phenomenon of poor communication—and even competition—among agencies in Japan is well known and is partly responsible for some of the key lapses in the aftermath of the sarin attack. This same kind of problem was also evident after the Kobe earthquake in 1995, when the local governor did not want to contact the national support agencies for essentially "political" reasons.

Following the sarin attacks, the Japanese government created an interesting program worth considering in the United States and other countries: a national disaster center in Tokyo, which includes a disaster-oriented hospital that serves as an educational facility for first responders and medical professionals. This was an innovative development in a country where disaster-response training is not regularly seen as an important agenda item for most elements of the health-care system.

Like the United States, Japan's medical system is variable in quality, resources, and disaster readiness. During the usual course of business, the two nations generally have a strategy of "just in time" inventory management, which means that, for mostly economic reasons, critical supplies are generally not stockpiled but replenished as needed. This approach saves money and storage costs on a day-to-day basis, but it would not work and could be dangerous in a large-scale biological disaster such as pandemic flu, when it will be difficult, if not impossible, on short notice to obtain ventilators, face masks, intravenous tubing, and other critical supplies.

United Kingdom: Rethinking Disaster Preparedness

Perhaps more so than from any other nation, the U.S. has learned a great deal about disaster readiness from the United Kingdom. With similar societal values and legal systems, and close political ties, the U.K. experiences with the Irish Republican Army (IRA), the Underground bombings in 2005, and the foot-and-mouth disease response in 2001 serve as legitimate case studies in reducing the risk of major emergencies for U.S. policymakers. Periodic joint conferences including U.K. and U.S. emergency preparedness leaders have encouraged information sharing and planning between the two countries.

There are also interesting legal and statutory parallels between the two nations. In the U.S. the 2001 Patriot Act (reauthorized in March 2006) gives the federal government wide investigative and detention powers as part of the "war against terrorism." Although they were ultimately not successful, Republican and Democratic lawmakers mounted considerable resistance against passage—and reauthorization—of the act, because of concerns that certain provisions violated constitutional guarantees of privacy and the right to due process of law.

The struggle to constrain the intrusive authority of the Patriot Act has an instructive precedent in the U.K.'s Civil Authorities (Special Powers) Acts of 1922, passed in Northern Ireland. The acts provided substantial emergency powers to quell violence and limit civil liberties. One of the legislation's key premises was that "lesser" rights could be suspended in favor of protecting more important rights such as life and property. As such, the state could take any measure it deemed necessary to protect its interests, however it chose to define them. Many of the provisions of the acts would have been deemed unacceptable under previous legal precedent. However, by establishing terrorism as a new context and justification for undermining certain civil rights, the acts became the law of the land. The acts remained in place until 1973, when they were finally repealed.

Great Britain has come up with some very practical methods of mitigating terror attacks. During the height of the conflict in Northern Ireland, the IRA made a point of attacking visible symbols of political and economic power in London. The April 1992 bombing of the Baltic Exchange in central London prompted a series of strategies to reduce the likelihood of severe bombing damage to key buildings. Responding to persistent bombing threats, London built many secure office buildings that are set back from the street and flanked by planters lined with reinforced concrete and lead; city planners have also created a "ring of steel" around the city center to enhance the general level of security.

All of these concepts are being incorporated into the protection of key infrastructure in cities throughout the United States, particularly New York City and Washington, D.C., where substantial attention is now paid to the physical security of important government facilities. Similarly, in New York City efforts are being actively pursued to ensure that the rebuilding of lower Manhattan, site of the destroyed World Trade Center, incorporates security designs in part derived from successful examples implemented in the U.K.

Canada: Epidemic Containment

Canada was widely praised for its containment campaign in response to the 2003 outbreak of the virus-caused Severe Acute Respiratory Syndrome (SARS). In particular, Canadian officials created an integrated strategy of disease-containment guidance, specific protocols for hospitals and health-care workers, and highly effective public messages. The entire system worked exceedingly well and could serve as a possible model for U.S. pandemic influenza planning.

One of Canada's most important strengths in successfully managing the outbreak of SARS was its robust public health system, meaning the agencies and programs that oversee population-based health assessments, disease surveillance, disease prevention, and health maintenance. Through the development of the SARS response initiatives, Canada's entire public health system was assessed and upgraded. In May 2003, the government established the National Advisory Committee on SARS and Public Health with a mandate to assess the ongoing public health needs of Canada's people and, most importantly, look at lessons learned that could be applied to future outbreaks.

These lessons were so important that Canada has become an essential resource for any nation now wanting to examine its own state of readiness for major infectious disease outbreaks. The problem for the U.S. in attempting to emulate Canada's approach is that the American public health system has been substantially degraded by inadequate funding and erratic attention for the past several decades. Since 2001, the struggle to rebuild the basic system and simultaneously develop a capacity to respond to large-scale public health crises has been an overwhelming challenge.

The fact that Canada has long had a superb public health infrastructure and universal health care greatly facilitates the process of ensuring the timely delivery of health services during an emergency. Emulating Canada's ability to rapidly mount an effective response to an epidemic threat like SARS in 2003 is a terrific idea. But for the United States, that process would ideally begin with fixing the foundation of its dysfunctional and costly health-care system. Until this is done, most proposals to upgrade the system's disaster-response capacity will be essentially "patchwork and Band-Aids."

China: A Powerful Lesson in Disaster Mitigation

If there were a contest to determine the best example of disaster mitigation in the past 100 years, one of the finalists would surely be the Qinglong district of China, where a major earthquake occurred in 1976. This is a tale of two cities, from the point of view of preparing for a natural disaster—or not.

The earthquake that struck in the very early hours of July 28 basically destroyed the city of Tangshan. On the Richter scale, sources outside China recorded a level of 8.2—a phenomenally powerful quake. The Chinese government said that the magnitude was no more than 7.8. What is not in dispute was the extent of physical destruction of the built environment and the human toll. The disaster claimed more than 240,000 lives and injured another 165,000 people. The people of Tangshan had no warning and had done virtually no preparation in anticipation of a giant quake.

The catastrophe was historic in scope and the human toll unbearably large. But the amazing part of the story has to do with Qinglong, a community not far from Tangshan. Qinglong suffered the same earthquake that morning, but for reasons that are not clear, Qinglong had been warned about the potential for the earthquake some two years earlier. The local government, as well as the population, had taken those admonitions very seriously. City officials developed intensive educational programs about preparing for earthquakes; they introduced modern monitoring for early warnings, building reinforcement, and other strategies. When the early signs of disruption began, such as the sudden appearance of muddy water in the community's wells, schools began holding classes outside and the educational programs intensified.

The death toll in Qinglong on July 28? One—a man died of a heart attack.

The lesson is overwhelmingly important: mitigation, education, and planning work. Perhaps officials from some of the major earthquake-prone American cities should make a site visit to China. We've got a lot to learn.

Russia: Insights from a Terrible Tragedy

The New York Police Department has been a leader in seeking insight and interchange with its counterparts in other countries.

Since 9/11, the department has stationed or deployed officers around the world, from the U.K. to Israel to Russia to Singapore, to absorb best practices and provide intelligence for the city. After the London Underground bombings, for instance, NYPD detectives were dispatched that day to work with colleagues in Great Britain on the investigation and follow-up.

In October 2005, I hosted a conference at Columbia University on children as targets of terrorism and invited Mordecai Dzikansky to speak. Dzikansky is a fascinating NYPD officer who is often deployed to Israel. But he had also been to Russia to study the Beslan school incident in 2004. Dzikansky's firsthand experiences provided a critical perspective to the conference attendees quite different from the information gleaned from media accounts or legal study. He had actually visited the school where the tragedy unfolded and had spoken with Russian agents who were there at the time. Since then, Dzikansky has shared the insights he gained on the ground in Beslan with colleagues in the NYPD's counterterrorism units, making an invaluable contribution to the city's process of preparing for the possibility of a similar attack against a school in New York.

Sweden: Enforcing Security Measures
Where No Threat Is Perceived

In Sweden, the public and the government alike do not view port security as a high priority on the overall agenda of national security. Nonetheless, bowing to pressure from global trading partners, notably the U.S., Sweden is more or less reluctantly following the new International Ship and Port Security (ISPS) code for securing its ports. However, the code is an ongoing source of frustration to policymakers and enforcement agencies. Swedish officials are having difficulty adhering to its provisions and have assigned only four national inspectors (two of whom are part-time) to enforce the security provisions of the code. Moreover, Swedish Customs and Coast Guard have no official role.

It remains to be seen how very minimal levels of Swedish compliance with the ISPS will affect attitudes regarding shipping of materials from that nation to U.S. ports. This is of particular interest in the aftermath of the 2006 uproar over the proposed management of a number of American shipping ports by Dubai Ports World. One of the consequences of that controversy has been a much more intense focus on international shipping in general. Given the current inadequacy of U.S. port security, that increased attention is, in my view, a positive outcome.

Mexico: Creating a National System of Civil Protection

After the earthquake that devastated Mexico City in 1985 and killed as many as 10,000 people, the Mexican government developed a unique system of civil protection, including a center of excellence in disaster warnings and response. Staffed by an outstanding team of scientists and experts, the National Disaster Prevention Center was created to monitor potential natural disasters that might affect metropolitan Mexico City. This is a model that might well be emulated in any number of U.S. cities, including New York, San Francisco, Los Angeles, and Seattle, sites of potential multiple hazards. In Mexico City schools, students drill for both fires and earthquakes, creating a culture of preparedness that promotes an "all-hazard" perspective. In contrast, most U.S. schools focus almost exclusively on fire drills.

Europe: Levees as They Should Be

On June 8, 2004, more than a year before Hurricane Katrina hit the Gulf, Walter Maestri, emergency manager for Jefferson Parish,

Louisiana, expressed to the *New Orleans Times-Picayune* his concerns about the repairs desperately needed by the fragile levee system protecting his parish and the city. Appeals for money and resources to fix the levees had been repeatedly rebuffed. Here's what Maestri said:

> It appears that the money has been moved in the president's budget to handle homeland security and the war in Iraq, and I suppose that's the price we pay. Nobody locally is happy that the levees can't be finished, and we are doing everything we can to make the case that this is a security issue for us.

Whatever the reason, the U.S. focus on vital levee systems has been abysmal. European nations take an entirely different approach. Well-designed water control systems and state-of-the-art levees are based on sophisticated science and engineering principles. Rotterdam's Maeslant storm surge barrier is one example of such a design. After the 1953 flood, the Dutch Rijkswaterstaat, the equivalent of the U.S. Army Corps of Engineers, chose to protect the country from flooding that takes place every 10,000 years, at a much higher threshold than in New Orleans. That said, many of the systems in place are old and in need of repair. But in countries like the Netherlands, Great Britain, Italy, and Germany, the general condition of the systems and the urgent repair or redesign needs are identified and, by and large, met. These problems are met with governmental response that is far more constructive than we've seen in the U.S.

Since we cannot dependably prevent terrorism or natural disasters, it behooves us to diligently explore experiences and strategies developed by others, both the successful and the unsuccessful, as we plan new approaches to enhance the security, resiliency, and preparedness of the United States.

13 · Rational Preparedness for an Uncertain Future: A Nine-Point Plan

There is no simple road map to repairing what is wrong with the state of megadisaster preparedness in the United States. Much as we might be tempted to put the onus of national readiness on a single agency or a particular individual, the challenges extend far too broadly across every sector of society. As I have pointed out, many key federal agencies are dysfunctional, nongovernmental organizations are struggling, and citizens are disengaged. Even more troubling, our safety-net systems—particularly health care—are on the ropes. At the same time, appropriate congressional oversight of the national preparedness agenda is impaired by an arcane committee system that is actually hindering our ability to prepare the country for large-scale disasters. And with two years remaining in his second term, President Bush has repeatedly failed to provide competent, credible leadership in defining or implementing a preparedness agenda for the nation.

In the pages that follow, I propose a nine-point plan to help address the major impediments faced in attempting to make the nation more prepared to prevent, mitigate, and respond to megadisasters. The chart below highlights the essential theme for each point.

**Preparing America
A Nine-Point Proposal**

1. Reconvene the 9/11 Commission to address the definitions, benchmarks, and accountability of prevention (including counterterrorism programs) and preparedness efforts.
2. Extract FEMA from the Department of Homeland Security and return all public health response functions to the Department of Health and Human Services.
3. Establish the U.S. surgeon general as the "public health czar" with wide authority over public health disaster response.
4. Restore and codify professionalism in federal disaster-response agencies.
5. Clarify and expand the role of the U.S. military in planning for and responding to megadisasters.
6. Develop a "rapid-fix" strategy to improve readiness of the health and public health systems to respond to large-scale disasters.
7. Create a "new millennium infrastructure initiative" to address dangerous inadequacies in national infrastructure.
8. Strengthen regulations to improve the security and safety of industries that pose potential disaster threats.
9. Upgrade programs to engage citizen participation in national preparedness.

The descriptions of five potential megadisasters contained in chapters 2, 3, 4, 5, and 6 were meant to illustrate some of the risks we face from terrorism, natural disasters, public health crises, and other persistent threats. In each case, specific proposals to reduce the risks or lessen the effects followed the scenarios. The nine-point plan lays out a set of ideas that will help us to find a prudent, comfortable level of preparedness, without breaking the bank, turning the nation into a paranoid, overregulated armed camp, or avoiding the myriad unresolved issues we face. Clearly there is still plenty of room for open debate about disaster preparedness, and many experts will have other opinions about priorities and direction. That's fine. But let's get started soon.

1. Reconvene the 9/11 Commission to address the definitions, benchmarks, and accountability of prevention (including counterterrorism programs) and preparedness efforts.

So far, the Department of Homeland Security has not demonstrated sufficient ability to produce clear definitions or direction for enhancing the country's overall state of readiness. The department continues to struggle with organizing itself around a cohesive mission and is rapidly losing the confidence of the American people.

One might be tempted to consider changing the leadership, including the secretary, of DHS. That would not be an unreasonable suggestion. But the problems go far deeper into the structure and basic rationale for creating the new cabinet-level department in the first place. The challenge now is to take another hard look at how the country intends to prepare for whatever threats might materialize in the coming decades.

Sorting through this challenge will take a highly focused effort involving a smart, experienced multisector group of Americans who can operate without constraints of party affiliation or ideology. The 9/11 Commission should be reconvened for this purpose, even if its charter needs to be appropriately revised. During the commission's tenure, its bipartisan leaders, Thomas Kean and Lee Hamilton, drew unconditional praise for their leadership, for their respect for the many Americans who appeared before them to provide testimony, and for the thorough, uncompromising manner in which they fulfilled their difficult mission. The conduct of the commission—and its ensuing recommendations—won praise and support from many citizens, as well as leaders of both political parties. There hardly exists a better forum to tackle the job of understanding preparedness, helping establish a national guidance document, and rethinking the structure and mission of DHS, in general.

The 9/11 Commission would have a significant head-start in tackling many of the issues raised concerning the structure and function of the current departments and agencies charged with homeland security responsibilities. Many of the original recommendations made by the commissioners deal directly with some of the most pressing homeland security concerns. So it would seem a natural and efficient process of moving them to permanent status with an expanded agenda and increased authority.

Bob Kerrey, former 9/11 Commission member, U.S. senator, and Nebraska governor, now president of the New School University in New York, said, "Perhaps a re-engaged 9/11 Commission should focus on the specific problem areas in preparedness that would, if fixed, have substantial other benefits to society. I'm thinking of areas like the public health system concerns and deficits in emergency communications that must be able to function more effectively during crises. Fix those and there will be many secondary benefits in normal times, too."

The commission should be given full subpoena powers to conduct proper and thorough investigations and gain essential information. And it should be charged with clear responsibilities.

a. High on the commission's to-do list would be a mandate to **address how Congress oversees national preparedness and homeland security.** With more than eighty congressional committees and subcommittees having jurisdiction over some aspect of homeland security or preparedness, it is virtually impossible to establish accountability and coordination of oversight. Can this be changed? Perhaps so, but the powers within the legislative branch will not likely relinquish authority voluntarily. Nonetheless, with so much at stake, Congress needs to evaluate potential options for streamlining the process of overseeing relevant legislation and appropriations.

The commission should be prepared to recommend mechanisms to modify these unwieldy structures and ensure accountability. Charles Tiefer, professor of law at the University of Baltimore and former solicitor of the U.S. House of Representatives, thinks that this complex challenge can be met. Citing precedents in jurisdictional simplification and restructuring of congressional oversight from the energy crisis during the 1970s, Tiefer would take on the Senate and House structures separately, beginning with the latter. He also supports the notion of establishing consolidated "select committees," replacing two or more existing jurisdictional bodies in the process. This approach worked with the Kefauver Committee of the early 1950s on organized crime and in another effort created to deal with labor racketeering. Tiefer says, "That [model] seems an idea particularly worth trying for bioterrorism."

b. **Recommending accountability standards** may be the commission's greatest challenge. With respect to homeland security and preparedness for disasters, there is a long and complex chain of decisions and actions between federal guidance (the legislative process and presidential or secretarial directives) and state, local, and agency-based strategies and protocols. Assuming that greater clarity can be achieved in defining preparedness goals, along with establishing relevant benchmarks to assess progress in reaching defined goals, a culture of accountability from one end of the process to the other would help root out the enormous waste and inefficiency in the system.

The accountability question has at least two distinct aspects. The first task is to ensure that we understand what goods and services we are buying with public dollars and making certain that we are actually getting what is needed, at a price that makes sense.

Second, and equally important, accountability cannot be simply diverted downstream. When the federal government determines what the nation needs to prepare for a pandemic flu, for example, there are major roles that state and local communities need to play. But the money to support state and local preparedness strategies cannot be wished into existence by the federal government. Congress and the agencies it authorizes must be clear that sufficient funds are in fact available to prepare for and cope with a national public health crisis. Otherwise, states and local organizations cannot fulfill their obligations and the federal guidance becomes instead an enormous financial burden, one that is virtually impossible to meet.

c. **Recommending new priorities for reducing the threat of terrorism in the U.S.** would be one of the most important functions for the commission. Current measures to improve the nation's capacity to prevent or interdict terror attacks in the United States are inadequately delineated, randomly prioritized, and lacking in appropriate accountability. Much of this was supposed to have been delegated to the Department of Homeland Security by direct authority of the president of the United States. However, the new department has neither the credible leadership nor the structure to fulfill these critical responsibilities.

   The White House itself seems disengaged, unable to grasp the agenda or the urgency of these concerns. Like DHS and the Department of Health and Human Services, it continues to play a catch-up game, buffeted by whatever incident or issue is grabbing the disaster headline of the day. Airline security, pandemic flu, Katrina response, port security, immigration and border policies each takes its turn at center stage; none are suitably resolved. Challenges are dealt with superficially and sequentially, at high levels of authority, precisely where competent multitaskers with vision, intelligence, and experience ought to be. The one bright light in the Bush administration may be Frances Townsend, the president's homeland security adviser. She has been brutally honest and highly organized in her assessments of need and priorities, although getting control of the DHS bureaucracy is another matter.

Beyond these goals, the independent commission should also (1) recommend a new national security agenda, balancing the nation's need to simultaneously revamp and enhance coordination and capacity of intelligence agencies; and (2) define and prioritize enhancements to port, airline, and border security, and secure critical industries. All of this, admittedly, should be the work of existing government agencies. Perhaps this will be possible in the not too distant future. For now, Americans remain at a level of risk that should not be tolerated.

We need the 9/11 Commission, redefined and empowered right now.

2. Extract FEMA from the Department of Homeland Security and return all public health response functions to the Department of Health and Human Services.

Creating a new department of the federal government to oversee homeland security in the aftermath of 9/11 may have made sense. However, swallowing up twenty-two agencies (including FEMA) was a significant mistake. DHS should continue to focus on its primary responsibility—addressing the threat of terror in the country—and leave FEMA to its own strengths: preventing, preparing for, and responding to disasters.

As head of FEMA during the Clinton administration, James Lee Witt reported directly to the president and his office held cabinet-level status. Witt was in charge of the federal response to major disasters. He developed and maintained a highly developed network of experienced, competent disaster-response professionals who worked closely with state and local counterparts well before disaster actually struck. FEMA nurtured these relationships in order to minimize the possibility of nasty surprises in federal-local interactions in the aftermath of an actual disaster. That relationship needs to be restored as quickly as possible.

Another dysfunctional plan gaining momentum in the Department of Homeland Security is the effort to assert control over the public health response to disasters, taking them away from the

Department of Health and Human Services. This needs to be stopped. Health and Human Services has the expertise and the mandate to oversee any kind of health or public health crisis, whether natural or manmade. The current efforts to undermine this expertise by moving oversight responsibility to Homeland Security add confusion and promote disorganization.

3. Establish the U.S. surgeon general as the "public health czar" with wide authority over public health disaster response.

The surgeon general of the United States should always be a physician and should be clearly designated as the nation's principal health authority during any major public health disaster. If the position is properly filled, as it currently happens to be with Dr. Richard Carmona, there is no other individual more capable of making effective decisions and maintaining public confidence during a crisis.

During a crisis, the surgeon general would ideally report directly to the president of the United States and work closely with the FEMA director. The surgeon general's responsibility in a mega-crisis would encompass the entire federal public health response, including military public health-care assets, once a disaster has been federalized.

Even during periods of relative calm, the country needs to have a recognized public health czar who can help develop strategies for disasters and oversee the development of new technologies or pharmaceuticals that could be important during an actual crisis. At the moment, for instance, there is no clear mechanism for resolving conflicts between the Food and Drug Administration's "business as usual" product approval and the "fast-track approval" of a new vaccine or technology that might be critical at the time of an act of terrorism or a natural disaster.

Bob Essner, the insightful CEO of Wyeth, puts it very well: "The country needs an experienced, empowered voice of credible authority to make sure that the public's health remains the main priority in determining what new drugs, vaccines or programs are needed at any given moment. This would be a valuable role at all times—and especially so in preparing for major public health disasters." This role is precisely what the surgeon general could and should be able to fill.

4. Restore and codify professionalism in federal disaster-response agencies of the U.S. government.

Hiring unqualified cronies in an agency's leadership positions negatively affects the competency of the agency and demoralizes the experienced professionals who work under them. Both FEMA and the Department of Health and Human Services have been severely undermined by the placement of ill-qualified individuals in positions of authority.

New legislation for agencies having to do with national security, homeland security, and public health should incorporate language that requires the cabinet secretaries responsible for these agencies to delineate explicit job descriptions for each position deemed essential.

5. Clarify and expand the role of the U.S. military in planning for and responding to megadisasters.

The U.S. military is not a perfect machine. Its bureaucracy is enormous and the interface between military and civilian leadership can be fraught with conflict and confusion. Still, the U.S. military is better prepared to manage large-scale disasters, strategic planning, and crisis logistics than virtually any other sector of American society. Even recognizing the limits imposed by the Posse Comitatus Act, the Stafford Act, and other relevant legal constraints, it is clear that the military has been both underused and misused in modern U.S.

disaster management. This needs to be addressed.

The country must now revisit the rules of military involvement in domestic disasters from any cause. Local and state governments are of course the first responders to a disaster. But they need to have a better, more consistent grasp of the mechanisms that are in place for calling in military support—either at the National Guard or the federal level. Large-scale civilian population movements, such as rapid evacuation in anticipation of a major storm or exodus from a nuclear detonation site, would benefit greatly from military expertise and experience. Likewise, military forces could be called in to manage large-scale rescue efforts in the aftermath of a major catastrophic event, or to maintain civil order in cases of extreme social breakdown.

Additionally, the military has had significant experience in training personnel to respond to deployment of nontraditional weapons, particularly chemical, biological, and nuclear weapons of the kind that terrorists might use. Civilian authorities, including public health agencies, health-care provider organizations, and first responders would benefit from these training protocols. To date, very little organized knowledge and expertise transfer from the military to their civilian counterparts has actually taken place. Clarifying, defining, and formalizing a role for the U.S. military in planning for and responding to megadisaster needs to be a high priority.

6. Develop a "rapid-fix" strategy to improve readiness of the health and public health systems to respond to megadisasters.

The serious, debilitating problems with the U.S. health-care system represent a huge burden on the nation's ability to cope with a major public health crisis. As discussed earlier, tens of millions of uninsured Americans, a fragile hospital system, and ongoing resource shortages in public health agencies create an almost impossible situation for disaster-response planners. In a recent conversation, U.S.

Surgeon General Richard Carmona spoke about the fragile state of the American public health system:

> If there was anything good that came from 9/11, it was the recognition that the public health infrastructure nationally had eroded to the point that it was very dangerous. The manifestations of 9/11, the anthrax after that, Katrina and other natural disasters and possible impending man-made disasters have brought this to our attention and we need to do something about it.

Unfortunately, very little of this very complex challenge lends itself to rapid solutions. These problems have been literally decades in the making and are now fully ingrained in American society.

Still, there are short-term strategies that can provide an improved safety net, especially in the event of a national emergency. Some of these ideas have been activated in recent disasters, notably Hurricane Katrina. U.S. military mobile field hospitals, for example, can be deployed and assembled quickly in diverse settings. FEMA is looking to develop civilian mobile field hospitals that, unlike military facilities that are equipped to treat only adult soldiers, can treat anyone from babies to the elderly. These self-sufficient major medical facilities rival the capacity and functionality of a typical medical center.

On the health-care personnel side, there are also systems outside actual military medical teams. These include the highly trained regional disaster medical assistance teams (DMATs), as well as the U.S. Public Health Service and the new Medical Reserve Corps. These teams of trained medical personnel can augment the professionals available to serve in acute-need areas. Their role, however, is usually limited in scope to the immediate crisis response. Generally, they are not dispatched for long-term medical assistance.

I recommend instituting the following short-term proposals to address some of the more important critical lapses of the health-care system with respect to planning and response:

a. **Design an "emergency access to care" strategy to be activated when the president declares a national public health emergency.** This program would recognize the need for immediate access to health care for anyone in the United States, once an emergency state was declared. It should be emphasized that the state of emergency should be declared as early in the crisis as possible. If the World Health Organization confirms the existence, for example, anywhere on the planet, of a new form of lethal avian flu transmissible among humans, the U.S. would initiate its own state of emergency. At that point, public service announcements regarding unfettered access to the health-care system for people with possible influenza would be issued and emergency funds to cover evaluation and treatment of otherwise uninsured individuals would be instituted. This program could readily be managed under the Medicaid infrastructure in a mechanism successfully employed after the attacks of September 11, 2001.

Admittedly, such an undertaking would be expensive. But if we experience a full-blown avian influenza pandemic, some 15 million out of the nearly 46 million currently uninsured people would likely become sick or symptomatic or carry the virus. The longer it takes for these individuals to be diagnosed and, if possible, treated, the greater the chances of accelerated spread of the disease. The greater the disease toll, the more people in hospitals and out of work, the greater the economic toll. A *relatively* modest investment made to ensure full access to health care for everyone during the crisis could turn out to be a small price to pay, as social investments go.

Once a vaccine is available to prevent the contracting of avian flu, the government would set up stations where everyone would have access to appropriate immunizations. But we are still many years away from having the right vaccine and the capacity to make any vaccine rapidly enough in the face of a pandemic. So, in the short run, it is very much in society's interest to make sure that anyone, regardless of insurance status, has good access to the system.

b. **Fast-track the continuing decentralization of critical diagnostic laboratory capacity.** Our ability to respond quickly to a major infectious disease, whether caused by bioterrorist agents or not, depends on the ability of clinicians and laboratory diagnosticians to recognize potentially problematic organisms as quickly as possible, report those findings, and deal with the disease or virus at its source. As Stephen Morse, an infectious disease expert at Columbia's National Center for Disaster Preparedness, has pointed out, the rapid flow of timely and accurate information between the point of care—an emergency room or hospital bed—and a laboratory is essential. The Laboratory Response Network is a national network of 140 laboratories that provides increasingly sophisticated levels of diagnostic analysis. For the LRN to be effective, Morse notes that it must (1) better educate clinicians to know what samples to gather, and where and how to send samples to maximize the diagnostic effectiveness; (2) be sustainable, so that capacity can be expanded and investments made in sensitive equipment and personnel without concern that funding will dry up in any given year; and (3) improve communications between laboratories and epidemiologists to help facilitate the diagnostic process.

c. **Develop an "emergency supply pipeline" to ensure availability of critical hospital and public health supplies.** In nearly any megadisaster, supply chains for vital goods would be substantially disrupted if not halted altogether. One scenario I did not address earlier is the threat of very large solar storms (coronal mass ejections), which could theoretically obliterate significant components of the worldwide electrical grid. Such an event, while not likely—and certainly not preventable—would result in a rather immediate shutdown of economic engines and vital supply lines.

   And in a pandemic, as Dr. Michael T. Osterholm, director of the Center for Infectious Disease Research and Policy at the University of Minnesota, has pointed out, the net consequences of disease-containment policies that limit travel and shut down commerce, coupled with a growing demand for essential goods and services, would be unimaginable shortages in nearly every community.

To counter what could be devastating disruptions in manufacturing and supply lines, two possible strategies should be considered:

- **Community-based stockpiling of locally anticipated necessities for a several-week period during a pandemic, when goods and supplies may be relatively unavailable.** While supplies may be needed for substantially longer, planning for even a limited period of deprivation would be extraordinarily difficult and costly, well beyond the capacity of most communities without significant federal help. It would be reasonable to begin by establishing federal guidelines to assist states and local communities in assessing their needs. From there, decisions about the process and extent of stockpiling could be made with sufficient analysis and relevant data.

  The federal government, in fact, has a robust program of stockpiling large caches of medical supplies, including antidotes, antibiotics, and disposable supplies. These materials are loaded on jumbo jets, strategically positioned around the nation, ready for dispatching to areas in acute crisis. The problem with the program, called the Strategic National Stockpile (SNS), is that during a pandemic or other nationwide public health emergency, there is hardly enough supply to cover even a small portion of the affected areas. The SNS would be rapidly overextended, then exhausted. Some states and cities are also involved in stockpiling, at least on a limited basis.

- **Convene a special White House panel of economic and manufacturing experts to discuss and plan for disaster-based disruptions in these essential areas.** Such a panel or commission would be mandated to understand the conditions that would produce major disruptions, and to develop strategies to help communities and the nation as a whole to get through a major crisis.

In general, the disaster planning and response process has made little use of the expertise and innovation of major corporations. Corporate leaders need to be actively engaged in the process.

d. **Develop a "National Alternative Care Strategy" focused on (a) reduced standards of care and (b) developing guidelines for citizens to care for themselves and their families, to the greatest extent possible, at home.** Federal and state initiatives already exist to develop "alternate standards of care" models for downgrading the quality or intensity of care administered during a major public health crisis. These need to be developed more fully and disseminated so that public health workers know what their roles are.

Americans are not used to the notion of reduced levels of care, but much would change under extreme conditions. Even the idea of "battlefield" triage would be a difficult adaptation, for medical personnel as well as patients. For emergency planning to be successful, both medical personnel and patients need to know that these shifts in prioritizing the sick and delivering treatment are possible.

Another important new concept should be organized soon: home care in the event of a major biological attack or pandemic influenza. In these instances, it is possible that family members will need to care for individuals who are relatively sick, including those who might in other circumstances require hospital care, including some level of intensive care and/or isolation. The protocols for such home care have yet to be developed. These would include basic, comprehensible instructions for management of supplemental oxygen, certain types of mechanical ventilators, isolation techniques, feeding tubes, and other procedures that the vast majority of nonmedical civilians are hardly accustomed to thinking about, under any circumstances.

During a national public health emergency, it is entirely possible that family members would not only be caring for the unfortunate victims of a weapon-borne biological agent or a virulent avian flu virus, but for other individuals with more routine illnesses and injuries. In other words, day-to-day health care would go on as usual, even during a biological emergency. Heart attacks, strokes, and accidents will continue to happen. Children will develop pneumonia and ear infections. People with severe chronic illness such as diabetes, kidney disease, and emphysema who might otherwise have benefited from hospitalization may have to be tended at home by a family member. In some instances, home health assistance from community or volunteer agencies might be available; at other times it will be whatever the family is able to do. Contingency preparedness planning for a health-care emergency should include the development, distribution, and marketing of a system of care based on a new understanding of the role and capacity of ordinary people in managing under extreme conditions. It can be done, but will require a good deal of thought, sufficient resources, and innovative engagement of the American public.

e. **Fully fund a national hospital preparedness plan.** To date, funding available to support necessary upgrades in the network of hospitals around the U.S. is grossly inadequate. More than 5,000 hospitals receive less than $500 million a year to prepare for major national emergencies. According to Dr. Tara O'Toole, director for the Center for Biosecurity at the University of Pittsburgh Medical Center, it would take approximately $5 billion to appropriately upgrade the U.S. hospital system and $1 billion a year to sustain adequate preparedness. While this is not insubstantial, it represents a very small fraction of what is currently being expended on homeland security. Furthermore, the general benefits to hospitals and the health-care system as well as to the U.S. response capacity in any megadisaster would be incalculable.

f. **Expand investment in global health.** The United States remains exquisitely vulnerable to many threats that originate from remote corners of the earth, like the possibility of a deadly pandemic. There will be no stopping it once it breaches the boundaries of the local outbreak.

The far better outcome would surely be containment on a local level. Critical elements of an effective plan to avert a pandemic include managing domestic poultry, including separation from wild birds, identifying and containing diseased animals, isolating infected people, plus ensuring adequate supplies of vaccine and efficient mechanisms to deliver appropriate treatments. Currently, very few of these critical elements exist where they really count: in the remote villages of the developing world where people subsist under the worst imaginable conditions.

Many of the most worrisome dangers that Americans face originate in other parts of the world. Hemorrhagic fevers of Africa and the drug-resistant strains of malaria, HIV, and SARS all represent deadly threats that can and have grown out of the outposts of where poverty and hunger afflict fully one-sixth of the world's population. That's why the U.S. homeland security strategy must incorporate a healthy boost in support for global health programs—and any feasible efforts to reduce the burden of poverty and disease worldwide.

7. Create a "new millennium infrastructure initiative" to address dangerous inadequacies in national infrastructure.

Responding to the urgent call of the American Society of Civil Engineers for significant investment in infrastructure repair, Senators George Voinovich (R-Ohio), Thomas Carper (D-Delaware), and Hillary Rodham Clinton (D-New York) have introduced a bill to establish a National Commission on Infrastructure in the U.S. The commission would study current and future infrastructure needs, and issue a report to Congress in 2009 that will detail the legislation necessary for the next five, fifteen, thirty, and fifty years. The lead time for this long-term study means that serious infrastructure improvements could be delayed for many years. The federal government needs to identify the most critically unsafe structures and allocate investments right away to correct these problems. Based on U.S. Department of Transportation estimates an investment of $1.6 trillion over five years could mean as many as 5 million jobs created. It is a win-win proposition, and Congress must push this through and quickly.

An important component of the infrastructure agenda is the bolstering of buildings, key structures, and utility systems to enhance resistance in the event of major natural disasters. As detailed in chapter 3, earthquake reinforcement strategies are a prime example of this kind of effort.

8. Strengthen regulations to improve security and safety of industries that pose potential disaster threats.

In chapter 4, I raised concern about the safety and security safeguards that need to be in place to reduce the possibility that a major chemical spill involving a highly toxic substance or a meltdown in a nuclear power plant could endanger hundreds of thousands of people. Regulations guiding safety and security measures are extremely variable, to say the least. Many of these protocols are heavily influenced or totally developed by the industries themselves, leading to inherent conflict between costs and public safety concerns.

The key to increased safety in our most dangerous industries is an active engagement among state and federal authorities, industry leaders, and informed citizens to create and sustain a culture of accountability and knowledge about the hazards in and around our communities. As detailed before, a protective web of right-to-know laws, serious safety regulation, rerouting of dangerous substances, regular preparedness testing, and substitution of safer substances and technologies when possible are all part of the package of initiatives essential to safeguard the public.

9. Upgrade programs to engage citizen participation in disaster preparedness.

There are many plausible reasons why so many Americans have not acted on the preparedness message. But we need to get beyond the analysis and provide solutions to this substantial challenge. Citizens have a crucial role to play in ensuring that the country reaches an acceptable level of preparedness for natural, accidental, or terrorist-driven disasters. The other key notion is that citizens (individually, in families, and as community members) represent one component of a five-way partnership, along with first responders, nongovernmental organizations (including health-care facilities and response organizations), the private sector, and government.

The nation needs to revisit the overall strategy for improving the public receptivity to the preparedness message. The government and industry need to do more to tap into the wealth of resources in marketing and academia that will translate to better uptake of the readiness message among U.S. citizens. Clinically tested strategies such as the "Stages of Change" model provide substantial guidance in terms of public readiness to hear messages that have an improved likelihood of prompting desired actions.

There are also substantial lessons to be learned in the fields of marketing and advertising where successful campaigns drive sales in highly competitive markets. The government has not yet focused enough on these success stories. Even the campaigns such as Ready.gov that have involved some input from marketers or even the Ad Council have not yet resonated with the public. We need to establish a national initiative, operating on a short time line, to assemble experts in academia, social, and commercial marketing and other relevant fields to recast the campaign to enhance citizen readiness.

Government leaders responsible for appropriations also need to understand that this effort cannot be done on a shoestring. The U.S. government established the Citizen Corps program in 2004 to mobilize communities to form citizen councils that bring together local officials, first responders, and community members to work together to prepare for disasters. Grants from DHS go to the states, which are then obligated to send at least 80 percent of the award to local governments. In 2004 the total made available by DHS was just $35 million. While the concept and some of its early results are positive, a huge gap exists between the level of need and the amount of resources available to make preparedness happen *at the scale required.*

Finally, no matter what else is done, all citizens need to acquaint themselves with the basic principles of disaster readiness. Developing a family plan for who will do what in a disaster, stockpiling essentials, and learning about the particular risks that might affect one's own family or community are important first steps.

14 · Final Thoughts:
Coping and Resiliency in a Dangerous World

It seems to me that part of our problem in the enormous challenge of public engagement in preparedness has to do with some level of inflexibility or denial among Americans in general. Maybe we are terribly stuck in Prochaska's second stage of contemplation.

Perhaps we have become less adaptable to a changing environment than we might have expected. We may have intellectually appreciated that the United States was jolted into the real world of international terrorism on 9/11, but we just can't accept the implications of that reality. Life has been good for many Americans—and we're already overloaded with responsibilities and obligations. For those citizens who face economic or social challenges, survival really depends more on struggles other than worrying about more visits from Al-Qaeda. In either case, we just can't bear—or won't tolerate—any more burdens.

For the moment, though, the nation seems to be having trouble coping with the new world of threats, human-made and natural. We can't seem to prioritize, we aren't staying focused, and we seem to have little ability to successfully address multiple challenges. And there seems to be no end to the challenges confronting modern society.

I recall the extraordinary smallpox debacle of 2002. The White House had raised the prospect of this long-eradicated disease's being possibly reborn as a terrorist threat, as plans were being made for the U.S. to invade Iraq. As it turns out, the threat was never credible and few in the public health community bought into the possibility. To make matters worse, several deaths were attributed to administering the vaccine to people at risk for complications. Yet, before the plan was called off, enormous sums and substantial energy were invested in the development of a complex scheme to vaccinate millions of Americans, beginning with more than 500,000 health-care and emergency workers. This was just a very bad public health strategy, based on faulty intelligence that faded away when it was clear that public and professional response was dismissive and critical.

The country acts surprised at every new challenge, even those we've been warned of repeatedly. Our national preparedness judgment is clearly impaired and, as discussed earlier, our ability to imagine, plan ahead, and accommodate new realities have been incredibly limited. This is not evidence of a mature, competent society. To me, as a parent and a pediatrician, this is all eerily reminiscent of the behavior of a still-immature teenager.

When I was growing up, there were three particular stories my mother, Charlotte, was fond of retelling that shed light on the nature of our changing sense of risk and adaptation.

In 1945, we were living in Brooklyn, New York. My father was in the military and had been transferred to California, awaiting deployment to the Pacific theater. My mother and I followed some months later, traveling across country by train. As Charlotte tells it, I was a precocious fifteen-month-old child, already verbal and walking, and was thus allowed to stroll up and down the car chatting with strangers who, in my mother's highly revisionist recounting, seemed attentive and entertained.

A little more than a year later, we returned to the East Coast for a visit. This time, we were in a car driven by my grandfather, Nathan. I was about two and a half. Decades before seat belts or car seats, I roamed around the old car, an active toddler on a 3,000-mile family adventure. Front seat to back, from Grandma Rose's lap to just standing in the back seat chattering away. Apparently no one thought about the now well-known fact that in the event of an accident, or even a short stop, I could become a human missile—a grave danger to myself and others.

A few years later, in another trip back to New York on a propeller-powered TWA Constellation, I was five years old, and we were joined by my newly arrived little brother, Neil. Charlotte recalls a twelve-hour bumpy endurance test in a cramped cabin. One of the key distractions for the kids, though, was the opportunity to tour the cockpit. The pilot let folks look out through the front windshield and awarded "junior wings" to the children who visited the crew up front.

These tales from family lore are experiences likely shared by many others of my generation. But each of these experiences would be unthinkable today. No responsible parent would let a toddler wander unaccompanied around a train car filled with strangers. And it's unimaginably risky, not to mention illegal, to let children ride in cars without proper restraints. As for passengers of any age entering the cockpit of a commercial airliner today, that would be totally forbidden and for good reason.

The world changed. Our sense of vulnerability evolved, and so, too, did our behaviors and our sense of what is "normal." That is precisely how we need to view our collective adaptation to this new and unsettling new world of terror attacks and megadisasters.

I remember a conversation I had several years ago with a colleague who was evaluated in the emergency room for severe chest pains. He had been on the verge of a major heart attack that was caught in time. Emergency surgery was able to bypass the constricted coronary arteries and, in a few days, he was generally fine. My friend was a very busy physician. Before he was discharged, his surgeon and cardiologist came to pay a final visit in the hospital. They stood at his bedside, telling him about the new lifestyle and strategies he'd have to adopt to prevent another attack. They prescribed more sleep, less stress, an exercise regimen, a whole new diet, and a number of medications.

My friend complained to me that he "didn't have time" for everything his new life seemed to require. We both laughed—he a little more nervously than I. The fact is that he had no choice. If he wanted to live, he would have to absorb the new impositions of really caring for himself. He did just that. And he still enjoys his practice, works reasonably hard, makes time for his family, and travels with his wife.

America's situation at the moment is like that of my friend. Before 9/11 or Hurricane Katrina, we had no time or money to prudently and preventively prepare for disasters. For years we had evidence that Al-Qaeda had the United States in its cross-hairs. We had long known that federal intelligence agencies were ignoring important warnings that something terrible could happen at any moment. And for more than a decade we had been well aware that the levees protecting New Orleans from flooding were too fragile to withstand a category 5 storm. We just didn't—or couldn't—get our collective act together.

Now, we must. We have to invest the resources and time to enhance our ability to detect, prevent, and respond to catastrophes, whether natural, accidental, or at the hands of extremists wishing us harm. There is no choice.

Beyond Batteries and Go Packs:
Redlener's Eight Principles
of Disaster Preparedness and Survival

Readiness is a state of mind, as much as a stockpile of essential needs. A number of excellent websites and other resources provide complete survival guidance and lists of what individuals and families need to store or carry during a major disaster—and I'll recommend a few such resources at the end. But my discussion of personal preparedness is not intended to be an exhaustive list of what individuals or families might need to have at the ready in a time of emergency. I'm more concerned about a philosophy of readiness and resiliency that can be important in many kinds of stressful or complex situations. And some of the principles that I consider most important are not generally emphasized, or even included in many of the preparedness materials available to the public. Yet, how you think and your frame of mind in a high-risk situation may end up being more important than whether you have two or three days of bottled water in your car or—as U.S. Health and Human Services Secretary Michael Leavitt recently recommended for pandemic influenza preparedness—three weeks' worth of canned tuna fish under your bed. Both of these recommendations might be absolutely correct, but being really prepared is much more involved—and much more about mental readiness.

The Eight Principles of Citizen Preparedness

1. Stay healthy and fit. I cannot emphasize this enough. In a serious emergency, people need a good reserve of physical and mental strength to cope. Boarding up windows or moving belongings to a safe place in a short period of time may be physically demanding. Escaping from a dangerous situation may be physically and mentally taxing.

2. Develop a "citizen responder" state of mind. The Israelis, perhaps more so than others, believe that all citizens need to be ready to think about how they might react in a true disaster. One way for Americans to get insight and training about this concept is through their local Citizen Emergency Response Teams (CERTs), established by the U.S. government through the well-intended, if underfunded, Citizen Corps. The program familiarizes citizens with basic emergency response skills, teaching them how to be first responders until the official response agencies actually arrive.

3. Learn basic CPR and first aid. The American Red Cross and all of its local affiliates have long focused on teaching citizens basic resuscitation and first aid skills. Being able to take care of a person who is in serious medical distress or who has been injured is enormously useful on an everyday basis. Thousands of lives are actually saved each year by citizens who "know what to do." In addition to the actual skills acquired about resuscitation and trauma management, people gain real confidence in their ability to function in a major emergency or megadisaster.

4. Practice situational awareness. First described in the context of military air traffic control, situational awareness (SA) is also crucial in battlefield performance and for assessing environments that might pose any kind of potential hazard. For trained professionals, this becomes second nature. Secret Service agents guarding the president, for instance, have a high degree of SA when they are on the job. People who practice SA know what's going on around them. For civilians, this means being cognizant of movement and people in your peripheral vision, taking an instant inventory of what's happening around you; or rapidly verifying the locations of all family members in a crowd. SA also applies very much to your day-to-day environment: work, school, recreation, and so forth. If you work in a high-rise building, for instance, familiarity with emergency exits and procedures, knowing what it would take to get out of the building rapidly, and the like, are crucial elements in preparedness and disaster survival. Families traveling through busy airports, attending a county fair, or even shopping in a large mall can benefit from knowing where the children are, who's around, and what dangers might be in the environment.

5. Become "disaster informed" about your own community. Memphis, Tennessee, sits on top of one of the largest earthquake faults in the United States. Long Island, New York, is vulnerable to massive hurricanes with tidal-wave-induced flooding. It is important for citizens to be aware of the particular risks and hazards of their area. So, if you live in an area susceptible to (or long overdue for) a major earthquake, it makes sense to think about what you need to know in the event of such an emergency. For instance, it might be reasonable to consider bolstering the foundation of your house, or enhancing its ability to withstand a major quake. Similarly, people residing in coastal communities need to stay aware of potential storms and understand what would need to be done in the event of evacuation or other emergency measures.

6. Clarify your personal network. Most of the available disaster-response guidelines highlight the importance of making a "family plan," delineating who would do what in the time of an emergency. This does not go far enough. Individuals and families need to sit down and really think about who is dependent, fully or partially, on you. It might be an elderly relative in a residential facility, a neighbor with a disability, co-workers with particular challenges, and so forth. There may also be individuals *you* depend on for support and assistance. Based on your personal network list, think about two specific scenarios:

- What would need to happen in a situation where a *rapid evacuation* was necessary from your community of residence during the workday? What about at night? How would people leave? Where would they go? Who would be responsible for transporting those who need assistance? Who would pick up the children from school? And where would they go?

- What would be necessary to consider in the event of *mandatory quarantine*, directing people to stay at home or within their local neighborhood? How would people in your personal network stay in touch? Who would be responsible for making sure that the homebound senior next door got food and medications?

While there are many other possible situations that entail particular responses, these two examples will help you and your family think about certain key issues regarding who would need what within your own network. Be as specific as possible about functions that would have to be covered.

7. **Develop an emergency communications plan.** In many emergencies, telephone, Web-based, or cellular communications may be impaired, temporarily or long-term. Or regular telephone service may be fine, but electricity may be out. This would render "complex" phones (cordless, answering machine combinations, and so forth) useless. In those circumstances a very inexpensive telephone that simply plugs into the telephone wall jack—without requiring an electrical outlet—may work just fine. Cell phone systems might be down for calling, but working for sending text messages. Or cell phones may be working, but without electricity recharging may be impossible. Sometimes local phone service may be unavailable, but long-distance trunks may be working fine. It is conceivable that one phone carrier will be very impaired while a competitor is not. All of this suggests a few key actions to think about in advance:

- Keep at least one "simple" phone (one that doesn't need electrical power) in the house.
- Consider having one carrier for local calls, another for long distance.
- Keep several emergency power packs (which are now quite inexpensive) for each cell phone.
- Have a local, central contact person that everyone in your

personal network can reach to get status reports, updates on various issues, and other information.

- In case local lines are down, identify a central out-of-state contact who can serve as a backup "communication coordinator" as needed.
- Determine a distant gathering place that all members of your network know that can serve as a common destination, even if no communication is possible for an extended period of time.

8. Work on family resiliency. Very little is reliably predictable in this world. But I think I am on fairly safe ground in asserting that the potential for future terrorism, natural disasters, and major industrial failures is not about to diminish any time soon. It is important for families to come to grips with this reality in ways that do not result in a paralyzing paranoia or a persistent sense of doom that interferes with appropriate optimism about the future. Parents need to help their children put the news in context. With support and honesty that is appropriate to each child's *age and developmental stage,* parents need to help their kids see things in perspective, learning how to react with concern or even sadness—then to move on. One key to managing all of this successfully is for citizens to feel *empowered.* The antidote to situations that seem overwhelming is to establish a sense of control, reinforcing the idea that we are anything but helpless victims of madmen or megastorms. That's why active engagement of the whole family in disaster preparedness is a good thing. It says "we are doing something and we will control our own destinies."

These eight principles of preparedness should, in my view, precede and permeate the more concrete strategies for preparedness. But the details will matter, so having the battery-operated radio, the food and water supplies, and the flashlight ready may well be crucial. So, to get more of those essential details about preparedness planning, I recommend three good websites (and there are literally thousands of these):

- The American Red Cross guidelines, available on its website, www.redcross.org.
- Information that can be found at www.health.harvard.edu, Harvard Medical School's public access site.
- The website of the National Center for Disaster Preparedness, www.ncdp.mailman.columbia.edu.

In addition, these are two particularly useful publications:

Freedom from Fear, by Gregory Thomas (New York: Random House Reference, 2005).

What You Should Do to Prepare for and Respond to Chemical, Radiological, Nuclear, and Biological Terrorist Attacks: Pocket Edition Survival Guide. Prepared by the Rand Corporation (Washington, D.C.: Rand Corporation, 2004).

Notes

1 • Help on Hold, Lives at Stake

3 Operation Assist is the collaboration: Singer-songwriter Paul Simon, one of the primary performers for USA for Africa, "We Are the World," which focused world attention on the great sub-Saharan famines of the mid-1980s, and I created The Children's Health Fund together in 1987. On September 5, 2005, in the immediate aftermath of Hurricane Katrina, Paul and I traveled to the Gulf area to deliver mobile medical units to assist children in need.

5 Gregory Kutz, the Government Accountability Office: "Audits: Millions of Dollars in Katrina Aid Wasted," MSNBC, February 13, 2006, http://www.msnbc.msn.com/id/11326973 (accessed February 13, 2006).

5 A total of $24 million: Richard Sisk and James Gordon Meek, "Waste Disgrace," New York *Daily News,* February 14, 2006, http://www.ny dailynews.com/front/story/391269p-331809c.html (accessed February 14, 2006); United States Senate Committee on Homeland Security and Governmental Affairs. *Collins, Lieberman Hold Hurricane Katrina Hearing on Waste, Fraud and Abuse in FEMA's Assistance Programs* (Washington, D.C.: Press release from the committee, February 14, 2006).

6 This devastation surpasses: United States, the White House, *The Federal Response to Hurricane Katrina: Lessons Learned.* Chapter 1, Figure 1.2 (Washington, D.C.: GPO, 2006).

6 So much of the mess: Linton Weeks, "A Bus Tour of Hurricane Hell," *Washington Post,* February 18, 2006, http://www.washingtonpost.com/wp-dyn/content/article/2006/02/17/AR2006021702293.html (accessed February 18, 2006).

6   Only 2,700 of the 25,000: Eric Lipton, "Trailer Dispute May Mean Thou-
     sands Will Go Unused," *New York Times,* February 14, 2006,
     http://select.nytimes.com/search/restricted/article?res=F30716F6395A0
     C778DDDAB0894DE404482 (accessed February 14, 2006).

7   The cost of some: Spencer S. Hsu, "Waste in Katrina Response Cited;
     Housing Aid Called Inefficient in Audits," *Washington Post,* April
     14, 2006, www.washingtonpost.com/wp-dyn/content/article/2006/04/13/
     AR2006041302159.html (accessed April 14, 2006); Federal Emergency
     Management Agency, *Cruise Ships Leaving New Orleans March 1.* Wash-
     ington, D.C.: Press release, February 24, 2006; Jonathon Weisman, "$236
     Million Cruise Ship Deal Criticized," *Washington Post,* September 28,
     2005, http://www.washingtonpost.com/wp-dyn/content/article/2005/09/
     27/AR2005092701960.html (accessed September 28, 2005).

7   Congress ultimately approved: Sheila Grissett, "Shifting Federal Budget
     Erodes Protection from Levees," *New Orleans Times-Picayune,* June
     8, 2004, http://nolassf.dev.advance.net/newsstory/levee08.html (accessed
     April 10, 2006).

8   More than half of the evacuees: *Washington Post,* Kaiser Family Founda-
     tion, and Harvard University, *Survey of Hurricane Katrina Evacuees:
     Toplines* (Washington, D.C.: Kaiser Family Foundation, September
     2005).

2 • The American Health-Care System

23   More than a dozen major: For an in-depth discussion of bioterror and
     health care system preparedness spending, see Elin Gursky's *Epidemic
     Proportions: Building National Public Health Capabilities to Meet National
     Security Threats* (2005), a report to the Subcommittee on Bioterrorism
     and Public Health Preparedness; *Progress and Peril: Bioterrorism Pre-
     paredness Dollars and Public Health* (2004), a Century Foundation Report;
     and *Biodefense Funding: Where Has it Gone? How Has it Been Spent?*
     (2003), a Century Foundation Report.

23   A 2004 statement delivered: Janet Heinrich, *Public Health Preparedness:
     Response Capacity Improving, but Much Remains to Be Accomplished.* Tes-
     timony of the Director of Health Care, United States General Account-
     ing Office, Before the House Committee on Government Reform
     (Washington, D.C.: 2004), p. 2.

24   Shockingly, in many states: Trust for America's Health, "Ready or Not?
     Protecting the Public's Health from Disease, Disasters, and Bioterror-
     ism" (Washington, D.C.: 2005).

24   The number of manufacturers: Denise Grady, "With Few Suppliers
     of Flu Shots, Shortage Was Long in the Making," *New York Times,* Octo-

ber 17, 2004, http://www.nytimes.com/2004/10/17/health/17flu2.html?ex
=1145764800&en=12da1664fe05ea7b&ei=5070 (accessed April 21, 2006).
25 I had said repeatedly: Ibid.

3 • Natural Megadisasters

43 Two important studies: P. J. Webster et al., "Changes in Tropical Cyclone
    Number, Duration, and Intensity in a Warming Environment." *Science*
    309, no. 5742 (2006): 1844–1846; P. A. Hoyos et al., "Deconvolution of the
    Factors Contributing to the Increase in Global Hurricane Intensity," *Science* 312, no. 5770 (2006): 94–97; Kerry Emanuel, "Increasing Destructiveness of Tropical Cyclones over the Past 30 Years," *Nature* 436, no. 4
    (2006): 686–688.
44 More than 75 percent: PDC.Org, Pacific Disaster Center, March 1, 2006,
    www.pdc.org/iweb/definition.jsp (accessed March 1, 2006).
44 The U.S. Geological Survey notes: USGS.Gov, *United States Geological
    Survey,* www.earthquake.usgs.gov (accessed March 1, 2006).
45 San Francisco just marked: Suzanne Herel, "1906 Quake Toll Disputed,"
    San Francisco Chronicle, January 15, 2005, http://www.sfgate.com/cgi-bin/article.cgi?f=/c/a/2005/01/15/BAGL0AQK2U29.DTL (accessed January, 15, 2005).
46 The quake hazard: A subduction zone is the opposite of an ocean ridge,
    destructive plate boundaries where plates are believed to move down
    into the Earth's mantle.

4 • Terrorism

64 Some 6 million containers: U.S. House of Representatives, Subcommittee on Coast Guard and Maritime Transportation, *Hearings on Port Security: Shipping Containers,* 109th Congress (Washington, D.C.: GPO, 2006).
64 That amounts to 2 billion: AAPA-Ports.Org. 2006. *America Association of
    Port Authorities,* April 10, 2006, http://www.aapa-ports.org/industry info/portfact.htm.
65 And while the systems have grown: Stephen E. Flynn, "Port Security Is
    Still a House of Cards," *Far Eastern Economic Review,* January/February
    2006, April 10, 2006, http://www.feer.com/articles1/2006/0601/free/p005. html (accessed April 10, 2006).
65 The generally accepted threshold: Stephen E. Flynn and Lawrence
    Wein, "Think Inside the Box," *New York Times,* November 29, 2005,
    http://www.nytimes.com/2005/11/29/opinion/29weinflynn.html (accessed November 29, 2005).

250 / Notes

65 Conversely, at current inspection: Clark Kent Ervin, "Strangers at the Door," *New York Times,* February 23, 2006, http://www.nytimes.com/2006/02/23/opinion/23ervin.html (accessed February 23, 2006).

66 Flynn and Loy propose: Stephen E. Flynn and James M. Loy, "A Port in the Storm over Dubai," *New York Times,* February 28, 2006, http://select.nytimes.com/gst/abstract.html?res=F20C15F83D550C7B8EDD AB0894DE4044821 (accessed February 28, 2006).

66 Along both the Mexican and the Canadian borders: Bob Simon, "The Prince of Pot," *60 Minutes,* CBS, WCBS, New York, March 5, 2006; Will Weissert, "Portrait of a Mexican Drug Lord," *CBS News,* October 24, 2003, http://www.cbsnews.com/stories/2003/10/24/world/main579960. shtm (accessed March 5, 2006).

67 While some colleges: Kelly Heyboer, "Colleges Struggle to Meet Post-9/11 Demand for Arabic Language Classes," *New Jersey Star-Ledger,* October 3, 2004, http://www.nj.com/news/ledger/jersey/index.ssf?/base/news-7/1096778128132280.xml (accessed January 10, 2006).

67 At the end of 2005: John Diamond, "It's Not Secret, CIA Scouting for Recruits," *USA Today,* November 25, 2005, http://www.usatoday.com/news/world/2005-11-22-cia-recruit_x.htm (accessed January 10, 2006).

68 The agency now: U.S. Department of Justice, Office of the Inspector General, Audit Division, *Audit Report on the Federal Bureau of Investigation's Foreign Language Translation Program Follow-Up* (Washington, D.C.: GPO, 2005).

68 The same report: Ibid.

68 The CIA has reported: Linda Robinson and Kevin Whitelaw, "Seeking Spies," *US News and World Report,* February 14, 2006, http://www.usnews.com/usnews/news/articles/060213/13cia.htm (accessed February 14, 2006).

68 While they agreed on little else: The U.K., U.S., France, India, Pakistan, Russia, and China have declared nuclear capability. North Korea and Israel are also thought to possess nuclear weapons.

69 Despite the bilateral: Lester Haines, "Ukrainian Nukes Go AWOL," *The Register U.K.,* March 25, 2004, http://www.theregister.com.uk/2004/03/25/ukrainian_nukes_go_awol (accessed January 10, 2006).

69 One concern: Philip Hilts, "Tally of Ex-Soviets' A-Arms Stirs Worry," *New York Times,* March, 16, 1992, http://select.nytimes.com/gst/abstract.html?res=F10616FB345D0C758DDDAA0894DA494D81 (accessed January 10, 2006).

72 "The United States government": See, for example, the Nuclear Weapon Archive, August 27, 2003, http://www.nuclearweaponarchive.org (accessed January 10, 2006).

74 In addition to the: Betty Pfefferbaum, Sara Jo Nixon, Rick D. Trivis, et

al., "Television Exposure in Children After a Terrorist Incident," *Psychiatry* 64, no. 3 (2001): 202–11.

75 Few Americans have: "Duck and cover" were instructions meant to protect individuals against the effects of a nuclear detonation. The U.S. government taught "duck and cover" to generations of schoolchildren from the late 1940s into the 1980s. If children saw a flash, they were instructed to stop what they were doing, and get on the ground under some cover—such as a table, or at least next to a wall—and assume fetal position, lying facedown and covering their heads with their hands. Critics of the education campaign said the training would do little to protect students, and did no more than promote paranoia and unease.

5 • The Built Environment

81 Folsom Dam, built in 1950: County of Sacramento, *Multi-Hazard Mitigation Plan,* 2004. See Chapter 4.2, "Vulnerability Assessment." http://www.msa.saccounty.net/waterresources/files/DMA/Section%204-2%20 Vulnerability3rdFinal.pdf (accessed February 10, 2004).

82 While the urgent repairs: Dean E. Murphy, "Storms Put Focus on Other Disasters in Waiting," *New York Times,* November 15, 2005, http://www.nytimes.com/2005/11/15/national/15disaster.htm (accessed January 16, 2006).

83 The annual U.S. budget: U.S. Central Intelligence Agency, *World Fact Book,* March, 29 2006, http://www.cia.gov/cia/publications/factbook/rankorder/2001rank.html (accessed April 10, 2006).

83 Not only is repairing: "Report Card for America's Infrastructure." National Fact Sheet, American Society of Civil Engineers. http://www.asce.org/reportcard/2005/page.cfm?id=45 (accessed May 10, 2006).

83 "It's human nature": James R. Chiles, *Inviting Disaster: Lessons from the Edge of Technology* (New York: HarperBusiness, 2002), p. 260.

84 "It is the deadliest": David Kocieniewski, "Facing the City, Potential Targets Rely on a Patchwork of Security," *New York Times,* May 9, 2005, http://www.nytimes.com/2005/05/09/nyregion/09homeland.html (accessed May 9, 2005).

86 While the nonprofit research: "Collins' Revised Security Bill: An Improving Grade," *OMB Watch,* January 11, 2006, http://www.ombwatch.org/ article/articleview/3239/1/1 (accessed January 11, 2006).

86 In its 2004 report: David Lochbaum, *U.S. Nuclear Plants in the 21st Century: The Risk of a Lifetime* (Cambridge, Mass.: Union of Concerned Scientists, May 2004).

87 Without such increases: Edward S. Lyman, *Chernobyl on the Hudson? The Health and Economic Impacts of a Terrorist Attack at the Indian Point*

Nuclear Plant (Cambridge, Mass.: Union of Concerned Scientists, September 2004).

87 The environmental watch: Riverkeeper, *Riverkeeper to Address Concerns over Indian Point's Emergency Plans at NRC Meeting.* Press release, August 25, 2005, http://www.riverkeeper.org/campaign.php/indian point/the_facts/1116 (accessed January 12, 2006).

87 Persistent calls for action: Office of U.S. Representative Nita M. Lowey, "Lowey Urges FEMA to Reject Recertification of Indian Point Evacuation Plans," Press release, January 27, 2006, http://www.house.gov/apps/list/press/ny18 lowey/ipo12706.html (accessed January 27, 2006).

88 While safety advocates: "Issue Brief: Spent Fuel Security," *Union of Concerned Scientists,* October 16, 2001, http://www.ucsusa.org/clean_ energy/nuclear_safety/spent-reactor-fuel-security.html (accessed January 10, 2006).

88 One recent example was: "State Officials Blast EPA Charges." Associated Press, January 13, 2006. Available at WCBS-TV New York online: http://wcbstv.com/national/topstories_story_013215751.html.

89 In fact, the sole survivor: Ian Urbina, "Surviving Miner Says Air Mask Failed to Work," *New York Times,* April 28, 2006 (accessed May 4, 2006).

89 While there are differences: Marshall Hamilton, spokesman for the Mosaic Company, personal interview, Esterhazy, Saskatchewan, April 10, 2006.

6 • Special Populations, Special Needs, and Soft Targets

104 Approximately 23 percent: National Organization on Disability, *Report on Special Needs of Katrina Evacuees Project* (Washington D.C.: NOD, 2005), p. 2.

104 In a survey conducted: Ibid., p. 8.

109 However, the net result: "School Nurses Want More Terror Preparation," Associated Press, February 21, 2005.

110 A 2004 report: "Preparedness in America's Schools," The America Prepared Campaign, September 2004, http://www.workplaceviolence911. com/docs/20040916.pdf.

111 The military historian: Caleb Carr, *The Lessons of Terror* (New York: Random House, 2002).

111 And in their distressing: Michael Dorn and Chris Dorn, *Innocent Targets: When Terrorism Comes to School* (Canada: Safe Havens International, 2005).

112 In the fall of 2004: Nick Madigan, "Schools, on Alert, Step Up Security Measures," *New York Times,* October 9, 2004, http://query.nytimes.com/search/restricted/article?res=F30713F7395F0C7A8CDDA90994DC404 482 (accessed January 10, 2006).

113 In essence, Al-Qaeda's: Alan Cullison, "Inside Al-Qaeda's Hard Drive," *Atlantic Monthly,* September 2004, http://www.theatlantic.com/doc/200409/cullison (accessed January 16, 2006).

113 The USBP estimates: Susan Carroll and Billy House, "Border Patrol's 'Progress' Unclear," *Arizona Republic,* September 23, 2005, http://www.azcentral.com/arizonarepublic/news/articles/0923border-spin.html (accessed January 5, 2006).

114 The Chiricahua mountains corridor: Based on interviews by Christopher Farrell, director of research and investigations at Judicial Watch, of current and retired officials of the U.S. Border Patrol (April, July, and November 2005), the Department of Homeland Security (at least monthly contacts since September 11, 2001), the U.S. Army (July and November 2005), Cochise County Sheriff's Office, Pima County Sheriff's Office, and Tucson Police Department (April, July, and November 2005).

114 It is a fact that in June 2004: Julian Coman, "Arab Terrorists Are Getting into the US over Mexican Border," *Sunday Telegraph,* August 15, 2004, http://www.telegraph.co.uk/news/main.jhtml?xml=/news/2004/08/15/wmex15.xml (accessed January 6, 2006).

114 Many were released: An Associated Press investigation of the Bush administration's so-called "catch and release" policy revealed that the number of non-Mexican illegal aliens released on their own recognizance has increased dramatically: FY 2001: 5,251; FY 2002: 5,725; FY 2003: 7,972; FY 2004: 34,161. See Pauline Arrillaga, "AP Investigation: 'Catch and Release' Policy Frees Illegal Immigrants to Move About U.S.," *Associated Press,* July 5, 2005.

114 Tucson's ties to radical Islamists: A classified joint FBI-CIA analysis, "Arizona: Long Range Nexus for Islamic Extremists," reportedly details Tucson's role as a center for militant Islam. The analysis was mentioned in the 9/11 Commission report, and its declassification and release is being sought under the Freedom of Information Act.

115 For that, they seek readily available: The tri-border region served as the base of operations for terrorists carrying out the 1992 bombing of the Israeli embassy in Argentina and the 1994 bombing of the Argentine-Israel Mutual Association Jewish Center in Buenos Aires. A principal suspect in the 1997 Luxor bombings, as well as the 1998 East African bombings of U.S. embassies, Al-Said Hassan Hussein Mokhliss, used Ciudad del Este, Paraguay, as his hideout until January 1999, when he was apprehended.

115 This is a notorious destination: See Rex Hudson, "Terrorist and Organized Crime Groups in the Tri-Border Area (TBA) of South America" (Washington, D.C.: Library of Congress, 2003); and Jessica Stern, "The Protean Enemy," *Foreign Affairs,* July/August 2003, http://

www.foreignaffairs.org/20030701faessay15403/jessica-stern/the-protean-enemy.html (accessed January 16, 2006).

115 The tri-border area: Bartosz H. Stanislavski and Margaret G. Hermann, *Transnational Organized Crime, Terrorism and WMD*. Prepared as a Discussion Paper for the Conference on Non-State Actors, Terrorism, and Weapons of Mass Destruction, October 12, 2004, University of Maryland.

116 Arizona offers: According to twenty-seven-year veteran FBI agent James Hauswirth, Squad Five (international terrorism) of the FBI's Phoenix office was conducting photographic surveillance in the Arizona desert of suicide bomber training by persons affiliated with Sheikh Rahman (the "blind sheikh" behind the 1993 World Trade Center bombing) as early as 1994. See Peter Lance, *1000 Years for Revenge* (New York: HarperCollins, 2003), p. 209.

123 According to the National: "Reports on Incidents of Terrorism 2005." *National Counterterrorism Center,* April 11, 2006, p. ix.

123 "The interagency [counterintelligence] system": Thom Shanker, "The Struggle for Iraq: Security; Study Is Said to Find Overlap in U.S. Counterterror Effort," *New York Times,* March 18, 2006, http://select.nytimes.com/search/restricted/article?res=F20C14FB3550C7B8DDDAAOB44DE40448Z (accessed May 4, 2006).

124 Noting the 100th anniversary: John Ritter, "Disaster is coming to San Francisco . . . the question is when." *USA Today,* April 6, 2006, p. A1.

124 And according to: Erin Hallissy, "Are We Prepared?" *San Francisco Chronicle,* September 18, 2005, http://www.sfgate.com/cgi-bin/article.cgi?f=/c/a/2005/09/18/MNGK6EO3BJ1.DTL (accessed February 10, 2006).

7 • Goals and Accountability

137 Former congressman Christopher Cox: "Handouts for the Homeland," Steve Kroft Narr, *60 Minutes,* CBS, WCBS, New York, April 10, 2005.

138 Following are some egregious examples: Eric Klinenberg and Thomas Frank, "Looting Homeland Security," *Rolling Stone,* December 29–January 12, 2006, pp. 44–54; "Some Funds Spent on Gym Equipment, Personal Trainer," *The Denver Channel.Com,* August 2, 2004, http://www.thedenverchannel.com/3606181/detail.html (accessed January 10, 2006); Edward Wyatt, "As New York Fumes, Wyoming Says It, Too, Needs Antiterror Fund," *New York Times,* June 1, 2004, http://www.nytimes.com/2004/06/01/nyregion/01wyoming.html?ex=1401422400&en=5baf1dd81429e9d9&ei=5007&partner=USERLAND (accessed January 10, 2006); Dean E. Murphy, "Security Grants Still Streaming to Rural States," *New York Times,* October 12, 2004, http://www.nytimes.com/

2004/10/12/politics/12security.html?ex=1255320000&en=6fa47a5a422e9 376&ei=5088&partner=rssnyt (accessed January 12, 2006); David Bates, "Beyond the Sweepstakes Mentality," *Homeland Protection Professional,* May 2005, pp. 20–27; Steve Kroft Narr, "Handouts for the Homeland," *60 Minutes,* CBS, WCBS, New York, April 10, 2005; Raymond Hernandez, "More Money for the Cities Most at Risk," *New York Times,* September 14, 2004, http://select.nytimes.com/search/restricted/article? res=F50611F63D5D0C748DDDA00894DC404482 (accessed January 15, 2006); Marc Levy, "Officials Mum on Use of Homeland Security Funds," *Post-Gazette,* January 30, 2005, http://www.post-gazette.com/ pg/05030/450030.stm (accessed January 26, 2006); Rick Tucker, "The Cost of Safety," *Townhall.com,* November 26, 2003, http://www.town hall.com/opinion/columns/ricktucker/2003/11/26/160335.html (accessed January 26, 2006); Lawrence Morahan, "Politicians Use 9-11 to Justify Pork Spending, Watchdog Alleges," *CNCNews.com,* August 15, 2002, http://www.cncnews.com/pentagon/archive/200208/pen20020815b.html (accessed January 26, 2006); Shaun Waterman, "Lawmakers Cut $800 Million from Homeland Security Spending," *Washington Times,* May 4, 2005, http://www.washingtontimes.com/upi-breaking/20050504-083133-5796r.htm (accessed January 16, 2006); Charles Ornstein, "County Aims Anti-Terrorism Cash at Some Unusual Targets," *Los Angeles Times,* March 6, 2006, http://latimes.com (accessed March 6, 2006). Shawn Reese, "FY2003 and FY2004 State Allocations for Selected Homeland Security Assistance Programs," *The Library of Congress, Congressional Research Service,* August 16, 2004.

8 • Failures of Imagination

147 "The failure to prevent Sept. 11": Thomas L. Friedman, "A Failure to Imagine," *New York Times,* May 19, 2002.
148 Local officials not only failed: Spencer S. Hsu, "Katrina Report Spreads Blame," *Washington Post,* February 12, 2006, http://www.washingtonpost .com/wp-dyn/content/article/2006/02/11/AR2006021101409.html (accessed February 12, 2006); and Ivor van Heerden, *Assessment and Remediation of Public Health Impacts Due to Hurricanes and Major Flooding Events,* Annual Interim Progress Report from the Center for the Study of Public Health Impacts of Hurricanes at LSU to the Louisiana Board of Regents, December 21, 2004. See also van Heerden reports from 2003 and 2002.
149 A report by the 9/11 Commission concluded: Phil Hirschkorn, "9/11 Panel Focuses on Rescue Efforts," *CNN,* May 18, 2004, http://www.cnn .com/2004/US/05/18/911.commission (accessed January 12, 2006).
149 All are required by law: "Louisiana code requires nursing homes to submit an evacuation plan each year to the parish government, which is to

review the viability of the plan. As part of its annual inspections, the state Department of Health & Hospitals checks only to ensure a plan has been submitted. But the two do not exchange information or work together. Although local officials said they had told dozens of homes they had inadequate evacuation plans, the Louisiana Department of Health & Hospitals, which regulates and licenses nursing homes, has cited only one home in the past year for having an inadequate plan." From Roma Khanna, Lise Olsen, and Anita Hassan, "Elderly Were Left with Weak Safety Net," *Houston Chronicle,* December 10, 2005, http://www.chron.com/disp/story.mpl/metropolitan/3516805.html (accessed December 10, 2005).

149 That's why only 21 percent: Eric Lipton, "Committee Focuses on Failure to Aid New Orleans's Infirm," *New York Times,* February 1, 2006, http://select.nytimes.com/search/restricted/article?res=F20912FF345B0 C728CDDAB0894DE404482 (accessed February 1, 2006).

9 • Missing and Misplaced Leadership: Who's in Charge?

155 Representative Christopher Shays: "Congress Grills Michael Brown," CBS/*Associated Press,* September 28, 2005, http://www.cbsnews.com/stories/2005/09/27/ katrina/main886469.shtml (accessed January 26, 2006); "FEMA Chief Relieved of Katrina Duties," NBC News and News Services, September 12, 2005, http://www.msnbc.msn.com/id/9266986 (accessed January 26, 2006).

156 Witt aimed—and in large measure: U.S., House Committee on Government Reform, testimony of James Lee Witt, March 24, 2004, 96th Congress (Washington, D.C.: GPO, 2004).

158 In a March 21, 2006: Dana Milbank, "A 'Unified Command Structure' in Search of a Leader," *Washington Post,* March 21, 2006, p. A2.

159 In early April 2006: Eric Lipton, "FEMA Calls, but Top Job Is Tough Sell," *New York Times,* April 2, 2006, p. 1.

160 As Vice Admiral Richard Carmona: U.S. Surgeon General Richard Carmona, personal interview, March 2006.

162 The Robert T. Stafford Disaster Relief: Under the framework of the Stafford Act and in line with the Posse Comitatus Act, Defense Support to Civil Authorities (DSCA) (formally titled the Military Assistance to Civil Authorities, 2005) is the process used by the Department of Defense to respond to a request for military assistance from state emergency response agencies (typically through a request from the governor) or by a lead federal agency (typically FEMA) following a megadisaster. Likewise, DSCA is the process by which local and state civil authorities request military assets in light of a megadisaster. DSCA has been viewed as a positive element in disaster response (see Hurricane Andrew and

Oklahoma City), but it has also been limited due to intra-agency coordination and personal communications issues (e.g., military versus civilian culture). John Milliman, John Grosskopf, and Ozzie Paez, "An Exploratory Study of Local Emergency Managers' Views of Military Assistance/ Defense Support to Civil Authorities (MACA/DSCA)," *Journal of Homeland Security and Emergency Management* 3, no. 1 (2006). Online at http:// www.bepress.com/cgi/viewcontent.cgi?article=1205&context=jhsem.

168 "More than any other": Garance Franke-Ruta, "Spin Doctors: Tommy Thompson Is Not a Bioterrorism Expert. So Why Does He Play One on TV?" *Washington Monthly,* September 2002.

170 "The person at home": U.S. Surgeon General Richard Carmona, personal interview, March 2006.

10 • The Strange Psychology of Preparedness and Why the Public Isn't Buying

181 My colleagues and I: The National Center for Disaster Preparedness (NCDP) has commissioned surveys of the American public's attitudes and views on terrorism, preparedness, and associated issues annually beginning in the months after September 11, 2001. The 2005 survey was completed in July 2005, just after the London Underground bombings and just before Hurricane Katrina. A follow-up survey was conducted just after the Gulf storms.

Each survey includes trended questions as well as questions specific to the given time period. Trended questions include confidence in government; willingness and ability to evacuate; personal and family preparedness plans; personal sacrifice; community preparedness; and perceptions and engagement of all-hazard preparedness. All questions are cross-tabulated with a variety of demographics including race, age, gender, income, region, size of community, political affiliation, and education. Further, selected questions establishing categories among respondents (e.g., those who have personal and family preparedness plans versus those who do not) are cross-tabulated with other selected questions (e.g., awareness of community preparedness plans) to observe correlations. The surveys are developed by NCDP investigators in conjunction with the Marist College Institute for Public Opinion, which administers the survey, codes the data, and produces the frequency tables.

181 Even an executive order: The White House, *Citizen Preparedness in War on Terrorism Executive Order,* November 9, 2001.

182 "If Katrina didn't spur": In polls conducted on behalf of the Council for Excellence in Government and the American Red Cross before and after Hurricane Katrina, most people reported that they were no more prepared after the Gulf hurricanes than before they watched this terrible

disaster. A plurality (38%) of the American public said that Katrina and Rita gave them absolutely no motivation to prepare and only 12% said they had done a great deal to prepare. Most of the American public said they had not taken the basic steps to assemble emergency supplies or plans to communicate or reunite with family members after a disaster because they don't think that it will happen to them or they are not sure what to do. See *The Aftershock of Katrina and Rita: Public Not Moved to Prepare* (Washington, D.C.: Council for Excellence in Government and the American Red Cross, 2005).

185 "In communicating risk": Peter M. Sandman and Jody Linard, "Fear of Fear: The Role of Fear in Preparedness . . . and Why It Terrifies Officials," September 7, 2003, http://www.psandman.com (accessed April 16, 2006).

187 Gallup surveys showed: Gallup Organization, *The Gallup Poll #255* (Washington, D.C.: Gallup Organization, 1941).

187 Communities were supposed to: For an in-depth look at civil defense, see Laura McEnaney, *Civil Defense Begins at Home: Militarization Meets Everyday Life in the Fifties.* (Princeton, N.J.: Princeton University Press, 2000).

187 Despite aggressive campaigns: Gallup Organization, *The Gallup Poll #262* (Washington, D.C.: Gallup Organization, 1942).

187 In 1943, when asked: Gallup Organization, *The Gallup Poll #301* (Washington, D.C.: Gallup Organization, 1943).

188 In 1954, when asked: Gallup Organization, *The Gallup Poll #531* (Washington, D.C.: Gallup Organization, 1954).

188 In 1960, as the nuclear arms race intensified: Gallup Organization, *The Gallup Poll #627* (Washington, D.C.: Gallup Organization, 1960).

188 A year later, in 1961: Gallup Organization, *The Gallup Poll #651* (Washington, D.C.: Gallup Organization, 1961).

188 When Gallup asked: Ibid.; Gallup Organization, *The Gallup Poll #652* (Washington, D.C.: Gallup Organization, 1961).

189 Not even the Cuban Missile Crisis of 1962: Tom W. Smith, *The Impact of the Cuban Missile Crisis on American Public Opinion* (Chicago: National Opinion Research Center, 2002).

189 Amazingly, 41 percent: Ibid.

190 "During the intensity": H. Jack Geiger, personal Interview, April, 2006.

191 One of the most helpful theoretical: For more information on the Stages of Change model, see D. Grimley, J. O. Prochaska, et al. (1994), "The Transtheoretical Model of Change" in *Changing the Self: Philosophies, Techniques, and Experiences,* edited by T. M. Brinthaupt and R. P. Lipka (Albany, N.Y.: State University of New York Press); pp. 201–227; and J. O. Prochaska, J. C. Norcross, et al. *Changing for Good* (New York: William Morrow and Company, Inc., 1994).

11 • Introducing Change

198 They assert that: David Ropeik and George Gray, *Risk: A Practical Guide for Deciding What's Really Safe and What's Really Dangerous in the World Around You* (New York: Houghton Mifflin, 2002).

198 Greg Thomas comments: Greg Thomas, *Freedom from Fear* (New York: Random House Reference, 2005), p. 30.

199 An estimated $3.4 billion was: See comments by Jerry Ellig at the American Enterprise Institute's discussion "Airport Security: Time for a New Model" at the Mercatus Center, George Mason University, Fairfax, Virginia, February 15, 2006.

199 And failures continue: "Airport Insecurity: *Seattle Times* Special Report," *Seattle Times,* July 11, 2004, http://seattletimes.nwsource.com/news/nation-world/airportinsecurity (accessed January 12, 2006).

12 • International Models

202 For the rest: Quotes compiled from international newspapers on www.worldpress.org. The sampling includes media that report from all parts of the political spectrum, from liberal to conservative.

205 All schools, senior-citizen homes: Israeli News Agency, *Emergency War Civil Defense Procedures in Israel,* 2003, www.israelinewsagency.com/israelwarcivildefense.html (accessed April 26, 2004).

206 Further, only about a third of: Ariel Merari, "Israel's Preparedness for High Consequence Terrorism," in Arnold M. Howitt and Robyn L. Pangi (eds.), *Countering Terrorism: Dimensions of Preparedness* (Cambridge, Mass.: MIT Press, 2003), pp. 349–370.

206 As a result : Ibid.

207 And among legislators: Robyn L. Pangi, "Consequence Management of 1995 Sarin Attacks on Japanese Subway System," in Arnold M. Howitt and Robyn L. Pangi (eds.), *Countering Terrorism: Dimensions of Preparedness* (Cambridge, Mass.: MIT Press, 2003), pp. 371–410.

209 Although they were ultimately: The initial version of the Patriot Act in the U.S. was passed in the heady rush of the early "war on terror," and concerns continue to be raised about some of its key premises. After all, among other highly aggressive provisions, the legislation gave the government new authority to pursue and expand wiretapping of citizens and detain "enemy combatants" in potential violation of the Geneva Convention and U.S. principles of due process.

209 The acts remained in place until 1973: Laura K. Donohue, "Civil Liberties, Terrorism, and Liberal Democracy: Lessons from the United Kingdom," in Arnold M. Howitt and Robyn L. Pangi (eds.), *Countering*

Terrorism: Dimensions of Preparedness (Cambridge, Mass.: MIT Press, 2003), pp. 411–446.

212 The earthquake that struck: *Integration of Public Administration and Earthquake Science: The Best Practice Case of Qinglong County,* United National Global Programme for the Integration of Public Administration and the Science of Disasters, October 10, 1999, http://www.global watch.org/ ungp/qinglong.htm (accessed April 12, 2006).

214 Moreover, Swedish Customs: Mattias Wengelin, "The Swedish Port Security Network—An Illusion or a Fact?" *Journal of Homeland Security and Emergency Management* 3, no. 1 (2006), http://bepress.com/jhsem/vol3/iss1/8 (accessed February 21, 2006).

214 In contrast, most U.S. schools: Sam Enriquez, "Huge '85 Earthquake Jolted Mexico into Preparedness," *Los Angeles Times,* September 19, 2005, http://www.latimes.com/news/nationworld/world/la-fg-quake19 sep19,0,6277996.story?coll=la-tot-promo&track=morenews (accessed March 10, 2006).

215 "It appears that the money": Sheila Grissett, "Shifting Federal Budget Erodes Protection from Levees," *New Orleans Times-Picayune,* June 10, 2004, http://nolassf.dev.advance.net/newsstory/leveeo8.html (accessed March 14, 2006).

215 Rotterdam's Maeslant storm: "SEMP Biot #318: How the Netherlands Defends the Largest Port in Europe Against Flooding," Suburban Emergency Management Project, http://www.semp.us/biots/biot_318 .html (accessed May 31, 2006).

215 In countries like the Netherlands: John Schwartz, "Category 5: Levees Are Piece of a $32 Billion Pie," *New York Times,* November 29, 2005, p. A1. http://select.nytimes.com/search/restricted/article?res=F30816F93 F550C7A8EDDA80994DD404482 (accessed May 10, 2006).

13 • Rational Preparedness for an Uncertain Future

226 "If there was anything good": U.S. Surgeon General Richard Carmona, personal interview, March 2006.

226 These self-sufficient: Mimi Hall, "US Lags on Plans for Mobile Hospitals," *USA Today,* April 17, 2006, p. A1.

228 For the LRN to be effective: Stephen S. Morse, PhD, Associate Professor of Clinical Epidemiology, Mailman School of Public Health, Columbia University, personal interview, New York, April 4, 2006.

228 One scenario I did not address earlier: Lesser versions of solar storms occur regularly. Many scientists predict that an upsurge of these events will pose threats to satellite and communication networks by 2012.

229 And in a pandemic: Michael T. Osterholm, "Preparing for the Next Pandemic," *Foreign Affairs,* July/August 2005.

Index

A Note About the Author

Dr. Irwin Redlener is the Director of the National Center for Disaster Preparedness at Columbia University's Mailman School of Public Health and President of the Children's Health Fund, which he cofounded with singer Paul Simon. He has three children and lives with his wife in New York.

A Note on the Type

This book was set in Granjon, a type named in compliment to Robert Granjon, a type cutter and printer active in Antwerp, Lyons, Rome, and Paris from 1523 to 1590. Granjon, the boldest and most original designer of his time, was one of the first to practice the trade of typefounder apart from that of printer.

Linotype Granjon was designed by George W. Jones, who based his drawings on a face used by Claude Garamond (ca. 1480–1561) in his beautiful French books. Granjon more closely resembles Garamond's own type than do any of the various modern faces that bear his name.

Composed by
Stratford Publishing Services, Brattleboro, Vermont
Printed and bound by
Berryville Graphics, Berryville, Virginia
Designed by
Iris Weinstein